Equality Among Unequals in International Environmental Law

Equality Among Unequals in International Environmental Law

Differential Treatment for Developing Countries

Anita Margrethe Halvorssen

Routledge
Taylor & Francis Group
LONDON AND NEW YORK

First published 1999 by Westview Press

Published 2018 by Routledge
52 Vanderbilt Avenue, New York, NY 10017
2 Park Square, Milton Park, Abingdon, Oxon OX14 4RN

Routledge is an imprint of the Taylor & Francis Group, an informa business

A CIP catalog record for this book is available from the Library of Congress.
ISBN 13: 978-0-367-00727-0 (hbk)

Contents

Cases

Free Zones Case, 1930, P.C.I.J. (ser. A) No. 24.
Diversion of Water from the River Meuse Cases, 1937 P.C.I.J. (ser. A/B) No. 70.
Trail Smelter Case, 3 U.N. Rep. Int'l Arbitral Awards, 1911 (1941).
Corfu Channel Case, I.C.J Reports (1949), 1.
Asylum Case (Colom. v. Peru), 1950 I.C.J. 266.
Lake Lanoux Case, 12 U.N. Rep. Int'l Arbitral Awards, 281 (1957).
North Sea Continental Shelf Cases, I.C.J. Reports (1969), 44.
Nicaragua v. United States (Merits), I.C.J. Reports (1986), 14.

Major Treaties and Other International Instruments

1997 Kyoto Protocol to the United Nations Framework Convention on Climate Change, U.N. Doc. FCCC/CP/1997/7/Add.1 (1997).

1995 *Berlin Mandate: Reviewing of the Adequacy of Article 4, Paragraph 2(a) and (b), of the Convention, Including Proposals Related to a Protocol and Decisions on Follow-up*, Conference of the Parties, 1st Sess., Dec. 1/C P1, Apr. 7, 1995.

1995 Agreement for the Implementation of the Provisions of the United Nations Convention on the Law of the Sea of Dec. 10, 1982 Relating to the Conservation and Management of Straddling Fish Stocks and Highly Migratory Fish Stocks, U.N. Doc. A/CONF.164/22/Rev.1 (1995).

1994 Protocol to the Convention on Long-Range Transboundary Air Pollution on Further Reduction of Sulphur Emissions, Oslo, June 14, 1994, annex II, 33 I.L.M. 1540.

1994 Convention to Combat Desertification in Those Countries Experiencing Serious Drought and/or Desertification, Particularly in Africa, June 17, 1994, 33 I.L.M. 1332.

1992 UNCED, Agenda Item 21, U.N. Doc. A/Conf.151/PC/100/Add.1 (1992).

1992 Treaty on European Union and Final Act, Feb. 7, 1992, 31 I.L.M. 247.

1992 *Rio Declaration on Environment and Development*, U.N. Conference on Environment and Development, U.N. Doc. A/Conf.151/26/Rev.1 (Vol. 1) (1992).

1992 *Report of the Conference on Environment and Development (UNCED), Agenda 21*, U.N. Conference on Environment and Development, U.N. Doc. A/CONF.151/26/Rev.I (Vol.2) (1992).

1992 Non-Legally Binding Authoritative Statement of Principles for a Global Consensus on the Management, Conservation and Sustainable Development of All Types of Forests, June 13, 1992, 31 I.L.M. 881.

1992 *Institutional Arrangements to Follow Up the United Nations Conference on Environment and Development*, G.A. Res. 47/191 (Dec. 22, 1992).

1992 Framework Convention on Climate Change, May 29, 1992, 31 I.L.M. 849.

1992 Convention on Biological Diversity, June 5, 1992, 31 I.L.M. 822.

1991 Bamako Convention on the Ban of the Import into Africa and the Control of Transboundary Movement and Management of Hazardous Wastes Within Africa, Jan. 29, 1991, 30 I.L.M. 773.

1991 Adjustments to the Montreal Protocol on Substances that Deplete the Ozone Layer, June 29, 1990, 30 I.L.M. 537.

1990 *Bergen Ministerial Declaration on Sustainable Development in the ECE Region*, U.N. Doc. A/Conf.151/PC/10 (1990).

1989 Basel Convention on the Control of Transboundary Movements of Hazardous Wastes, concluded at Basel, Mar. 22, 1989, 28 I.L.M. 649.

1987 Montreal Protocol on Substances that Deplete the Ozone Layer, Sept. 16, 1987, 26 I.L.M. 1541.

1986 IAEA Convention on Early Notification of a Nuclear Accident, Sept. 26, 1986, 25 I.L.M. 1369.

1986 IAEA Convention on Assistance in Case of a Nuclear Accident or Radiological Emergency, Sept. 26, 1986, 25 I.L.M 1377.

1985 Vienna Convention for the Protection of the Ozone Layer, Mar. 22, 1985, 26 I.L.M. 1529.

1985 ASEAN Agreement on the Conservation of Nature and Natural Resources, July 9, 1985, *reprinted in* BASIC DOCUMENTS OF INTERNATIONAL ENVIRONMENTAL LAW, 1550 treaty no. 70 (Harald Hohmann ed., 1992).

1982 World Charter for Nature, Oct. 28, 1982, G.A.Res. 37/7, 23 I.L.M. 455.

1982 United Nations Convention on the Law of the Sea, concluded at Montego Bay, Dec. 10, 1982, 21 I.L.M. 1261 (1982).

1979 Convention on Long-Range Transboundary Air Pollution, Nov. 13, 1979, 18 I.L.M. 1442.

1976 Barcelona Convention for the Protection of the Mediterranean Sea Against Pollution, Feb. 16, 1976, 15 I.L.M. 290.

1974 Nordic Environmental Protection Convention, Feb. 19, 1974, 13 I.L.M. 591 (1974).

1973 International Convention for the Prevention of Pollution by Ships, Nov. 2, 1973, 12 I.L.M. 1319 (1973).

1973 Convention on International Trade in Endangered Species of Wild Fauna and Flora, Mar. 3, 1973, 993 U.N.T.S. 243.

1972 Resolution on the Institutional and Financial Arrangement for International Environmental Cooperation, U.N. GAOR, adopted Dec. 15, 1972, 13 I.L.M. 234 (1974).

1972 Declaration of the United Nations Conference on the Human Environment, adopted June 16, 1972, U.N. Doc. A/CONF.48/14 and Corr.1, *available in* 11 I.L.M. 1416.

1972 Convention on the Prevention of Marine Pollution by Dumping of Wastes and Other Matter, Dec. 29, 1972, 1046 U.N.T.S. 120.

1972 Convention for the Protection of World Cultural and Natural Heritage, Nov. 23, 1972, 1037 U.N.T.S. 151.

1971 Convention on Wetlands of International Importance Especially as Waterfowl Habitat (Ramsar), Feb. 2, 1971, 996 U.N.T.S. 245.
1969 Vienna Convention on the Law of Treaties, May 23, 1969, 1155 U.N.T.S. 331.
1969 Convention Relating to Intervention on the High Seas in Cases of Oil Pollution Casualties, Nov.29, 1969, 970 U.N.T.S. 211, *available in* 9 I.L.M. 25.
1969 Convention on Civil Liability for Oil Pollution Damage, Nov. 29, 1969, 12 U.S.T. 2989.
1969 Agreement for Cooperation in Dealing with Pollution of the North Sea by Oil, June 9, 1969, 704 U.N.T.S. 3.
1968 Declaration on Air Pollution Control, Mar. 8, 1968, in Res. 68(4) of the Committee of Ministers, Council of Europe, Doc. 19, *reprinted in* BASIC DOCUMENTS OF INTERNATIONAL ENVIRONMENTAL LAW (Harald Hohmann ed., 1992).
1968 African Convention on the Conservation of Nature and Natural Resources, Sept. 15, 1968, 1001 U.N.T.S. 3.
1957 Treaty Establishing the European Economic Community, Mar. 25, 1957, 298 U.N.T.S. 11.
1954 International Convention for the Prevention of Pollution of the Sea by Oil, May 12, 1954, 327 U.N.T.S. 3.
1947 General Agreement on Tariffs and Trade, Oct. 30, 1947, 55 U.N.T.S. 187.
1945 U.N. CHARTER, June 26, 1945, 1 U.N.T.S. xvi.
1940 Convention on Nature Protection and Wildlife Preservation in the Western Hemisphere, Oct. 12, 1940, 161 U.N.T.S. 194.
1933 Convention Relative to the Preservation of Fauna and Flora in their Natural State, Nov. 8, 1933, 172 U.N.T.S. 241.
1911 Treaty for the Preservation and Protection of Fur Seals, Feb. 7, 1911, U.S.-Gr. Brit. 37 U.S.T. 1538, 104 B.F.S.P. 175.
1909 Treaty Relating to Boundary Waters Between the United States and Canada, Jan. 11, 1909, U.S.-Gr. Brit., 36 U.S.T. 2448.
1902 International Convention for the Protection of Birds Useful to Agriculture, Mar. 19, 1902, 102 B.F.S.P. 969.

Preface

To deal effectively with global environmental problems, such as climate change, global cooperation is called for, yet all too many developing countries lack the economies, infrastructures, or technical capacity to tackle these problems. In order to promote the participation of developing countries in international environmental agreements adopted to prevent or mitigate the problems, the special situation of the developing countries needs to be taken into account. However, in international law all nations traditionally have been treated equally and their treaty obligations have generally been the same. Yet, the new trend of using incentives to promote developing country participation in international environmental agreements, in effect giving them differential treatment, results in asymmetrical treaty obligations. This trend of using differential treatment for developing countries, I contend, must continue and become part of the framework of international environmental law. This is a prerequisite for sustainable development in our interdependent planet. This book, therefore, concentrates on analyzing what has been done on the international plane to promote the participation of developing countries in international environmental agreements and suggests some of the things that remain to be done.*

---

* This book was written in partial fulfillment of the requirements for the degree of Doctor of the Science of Law, Columbia University, New York.

Acknowledgments

I am indebted to my advisor, Professor Frank P. Grad, whose advice and encouragement were invaluable. He made my task all the more bearable, with wide-ranging discussions on legal and other matters, while nudging me to completion. Particular thanks should also be given to Professors Oscar Schachter, Bradley Karkkainen, Michael Young, and George Pring whose comments were most helpful. I have also benefitted from discussions of various aspects of the work with Professors Daniel Magraw and Gunther Handl, Ambassador Bjoernar Utheim and Carole Lindsay, attorney-at-law.

As most of the research was done while living in Boulder, Colorado, a special thank you goes to the faculty, staff, and students of the University of Colorado, School of Law. Being an adjunct instructor at the Law School and a Fellow at the Natural Resources Law Center enabled me to make many good contacts leading to more useful materials for research. The assistance of Jane Thompson, Leanne Walther, Michael Fontenot, Georgia Briscoe, and Diana Garry was very helpful. My gratitude also goes to Diana Stahl for getting the manuscript in camera-ready form. The assistance of William Shapiro and Stephen Fauver was also most helpful.

A special thank you also goes to my parents Stein and Louise Halvorssen, my sister Christine Cohen, and Rafael and Betty Castillo, for always being supportive and supplying me with articles for research. Maria Isabel Fleury and Andres Halvorssen also provided invaluable assistance. My children, Anita Louise and Rafael Michael, also deserve a thank you for being patient while Mamy was working late. Above all, I am grateful to my husband, Rafael E. Castillo, for his good ideas and for keeping me going. This book is dedicated to him.

1

Introduction

The interdependence of the elements of the natural environment is a global phenomenon, yet most of our past actions to protect the environment have focussed on "local" problems.[1] Contemporary environmental problems, such as depletion of the stratospheric ozone layer, climate change,[2] and loss of biodiversity can have global ramifications or at the very least, consequences extending beyond national borders. Global environmental problems can only be solved by involving the whole international community.

International environmental law, a branch of public international law, is a growing field of law that is setting the legal standards to deal with such global environmental issues. It encompasses a separate body of law for the protection of the environment,[3] which will serve as the underlying basis of this book. International environmental law is usually divided into two categories: (1) environmental protection and pollution control, and (2) conservation and management of natural resources and ecosystems. However, some scholars have added a third category: sustainable development.[4] International environmental law is used herein in its broadest sense, that is, including considerations of socio-economic issues. Another approach to categorizing international environmental law is described by Schachter. He uses trans-boundary environmental harm to decide what kind of environmental damage should be included in international law.[5] He divides the areas of harmful situations that should be included in international environmental law into the following three categories: (1) situations in which human life support systems are degraded by substances due to human conduct, such as air pollution, (2) the depletion of natural resources and artifacts of value to human beings, and (3) environmental harm to other species, to physical features of the earth and to outer space, whether or not such harm affects human beings.[6]

A new overarching field of international law—international law for sustainable development—has recently been introduced within the context of the work of the United Nations Commission on Sustainable Development and other fora.[7] It seeks to address global environmental issues, economic development issues, and a host of other issues included in Agenda 21,[8] without replacing the separate fields of law, such as international environmental law and international economic law.[9] The principles introduced in the process of defining a body of international law for sustainable development will be used to the extent they are relevant to the present study.[10]

The United Nations Conference on the Human Environment,[11] held in Stockholm in 1972, gave legitimacy to approaching environmental policy as a universal concern among nations.[12] Later, in the 1980s, several groups in the international community realized the need to strengthen the cooperation between developing and industrialized countries[13] to find solutions to these global environmental problems without halting economic development.[14] This led to the introduction of a new approach: sustainable development—development that "meets the needs of the present [generation] without compromising the ability of future generations to meet their own needs"[15] or phrased in a different manner, a development path that "sustain[s] human progress not just in a few places for a few years, but for the entire planet into the distant future."[16] This approach was meant to replace economic development with no restraints, given the realization that there are limits to the capacity of the global environment to accommodate ever-increasing resource use. In addition, the approach was meant to address the special situation of developing countries, trying to improve their lot, but having to deal with poverty and debt problems, in addition to environmental degradation. In some instances, developing countries face additional demands on their environment through the use of their resources by developed countries, as well as their own attempts to industrialize. In these circumstances, requiring the developing countries to implement similar environmental measures as the developed countries could be unrealistic; they should have some alternatives.

What sustainable development means as a concept is still much debated. Some scholars posit there will always be a conflict between developmental and environmental interests.[17] The implications of sustainable development have become somewhat less ambiguous and more operational since the Rio Conference[18] in 1992, which provided further guidance on the concept's meaning.[19] Therefore, in the context of this book, I will use sustainable development as the goal of integrating environmental and developmental issues in accordance with the Brundtland definition given above, and the instruments that resulted from the Rîo Conference.

At the Rio Conference, sustainable development became the official policy of the international community when the conference participants adopted the Rio Declaration.[20] In addition, poverty and international debt were officially recognized as additional sources of environmental degradation, adding to the problems that emerged with industrialization, social changes, and advances in technology.[21]

Although developing countries at present use less than half as much of the world's natural resources as the developed countries,[22] the developing countries are projected to become the major polluters in the decades to come.[23] Because the effect of global emissions and other environmental threats often transcend political boundaries, it is apparent that universal participation in international environmental agreements is one of the major factors necessary in order for the agreements to be effective in addressing these problems. As Weiss aptly notes, "[n]o one country or even group of countries has the capability to protect the environment over time by its own isolated efforts."[24] This became very clear with regard to the ozone agreements. Without the participation of essential developing countries – especially the ones that would use increasingly larger amounts of CFCs – the Parties to the Montreal Protocol[25] would not be able to fulfill their goal of bringing down and eventually eliminating the use of chlorofluorocarbons (CFCs).[26] With regard to climate change, the International Energy Agency states that ". . . any international initiative to reduce CO_2 emissions that is not adopted by non-OECD[27] regions would be unlikely to have any major effect on global emissions and even less on atmospheric concentrations."[28] To take it one step further, universal participation is also important in order to avoid pollution havens and free-riders[29] in the international community.

To encourage universal participation in the international environmental agreements and their implementation, the agreements need to provide incentives and disincentives for developing countries. The methodology of creating and implementing incentives or disincentives (where appropriate) in international environmental agreements specifically for developing countries, in effect giving them differential treatment or differential responsibilities, is key to achieving this goal. Incentives have not traditionally been used in treaties to get states to agree to becoming parties to the instruments.[30] Yet, in the more recent international environmental agreements, entered into after the Stockholm Conference, states have increasingly included incentives in the agreements.[31]

Principle 7 of the Rio Declaration recognizes this development as it stipulates that states have "common but differentiated responsibilities" with regard to addressing global environmental problems.[32] This principle emanated from the application of the broader principle of equity in international law, and from the acknowledgment that the differing situations of the developing countries need to be considered if they are to be encouraged to take part in international environmental agreements.[33] The application of this principle likely requires all states to participate in addressing environmental problems by adopting environmental standards, yet there should be different obligations for specific states, taking into account their contributions to a particular environmental problem, and ability to respond, prevent, reduce, or control the identified threat.[34] This method allows for greater flexibility in how different categories of states with different situations can address specific global environmental threats, thereby increasing the likelihood of their participation in the treaties.

Recent treaty texts have different categories of contracting parties, which have differentiated obligations.[35] Such categories can include the developing countries, the developed countries, and the countries in economic transition.[36] Alternately, as examined in Chapter 4, one could use uniform norms, yet then one would risk the least-common-denominator problem and/or the loss of some important signatories.[37] The use of differential treatment or differential norms for developing countries makes it more appealing for them to become parties to the treaty at an earlier stage, usually because they find it would not interfere as much with their development interests.[38] These differential norms or incentives for developing countries include delayed compliance schedules, and technical and financial assistance, which in effect subsidize developing country compliance.[39]

The thesis of this study is that the developing trend of using delayed compliance schedules and other incentives, such as technical and financial assistance in international environmental agreements directed specifically at developing countries, in effect, giving developing countries differential treatment or responsibilities, is the most effective way to have these countries "buy" into the idea of environmental responsibility and to move them forward more quickly on the pathway to sustainable development. Examining existing international environmental agreements, reveals a change in approach over time, from the universal applicability of norms to a recognized system of asymmetrical norms – "common but differentiated responsibilities," such as delayed compliance schedules and other incentives, which take into account the situation of developing countries.

This mechanism of using asymmetrical norms – differential norms – for the benefit of developing countries as reflected in Principle 7 of the Rio Declaration should become firmly entrenched as part of the framework of international environmental law. The Montreal Protocol demonstrates that this mechanism can indeed promote universal participation, in view of the fact that most developing countries, in addition to the developed countries have joined the protocol.

Yet, I posit that the use of incentives, on the whole, should only be for an initial period, allowing the developing countries to "catch up" with the developed countries while simultaneously addressing environmental problems. Furthermore, the resulting programs or projects need to be closely monitored, and transparency, public participation, and accountability should be the guiding principles in accordance with the sustainable development objectives of the Rio Conference.

The differential obligations which result from the use of such incentives for developing countries impose new obligations on the developed countries as they are the ones who have to "fund" or subsidize the incentives, through such mechanisms as technology transfers and special funding mechanisms. The developing countries, on the other hand, may be viewed as receiving a promised assistance, yet the assistance is only to be used in pursuing sustainable development. They have the reciprocal obligation to cooperate by participating in the international environmental agreements, which will benefit everyone, once they are effectively implemented.

Examining the relevant international institutions and NGOs, one becomes aware that their roles have also evolved over time, and new entities have been established, to promote the participation of developing countries in the international environmental agreements. The Global Environment Facility is a prime example. This new entity, which was designated as the temporary fund for the Framework Convention on Climate Change and the Convention on Biodiversity, has the United Nations Environment Programme (UNEP), the World Bank, and the United Nations Development Programme (UNDP) as its implementing agencies.

The debt burden, poverty, and growing populations of developing countries may have resulted in many of them being unable to participate in the treaty-making process because of lack of resources, or if they have become parties, they have had a hard time fulfilling their treaty obligations. In many cases and for various reasons, they may lack the regulatory and technical capabilities or enforcement mechanisms, and, compared to developed countries, they may have fewer resources to direct toward environmental protection[40] The political will to participate may also be lacking for various reasons, such as a lack of popular support due to the public's lack of knowledge concerning the effects of environmental degradation. To get effective, long-term results, developing countries need support throughout the process of international environmental law-making, implementation, and compliance. This includes, to name a few mechanisms of support: financial support to participate in the negotiations that result in new treaties, assistance in developing their own national laws to implement the treaties, and technical support for the work required to monitor the environmental programs and report back to the appropriate international organization on their progress in implementing the agreements.

These types of support, many of which are specified in the provisions of the international environmental agreements, as examined in Chapter 5, will provide the necessary incentive for many developing countries to participate in international environmental law-making and implementation. A good example of the effect of such incentives arose in connection with the ozone agreements. India and China refused to become parties to the Montreal Protocol when it was adopted in 1987, but then, with the adoption of the London Amendments to the Protocol in 1990,[41] which provided financial assistance to developing countries, they vowed to become parties to the agreement.[42]

In the context of this study, I shall use incentives in the sense of selective incentives, the selected parties being developing countries. In addition, the term incentive is used interchangeably with differential treatment (differential norms), as selective incentives by definition lead to special treatment for the selected parties, in this case, developing countries.[43]

With respect to disincentives, trade sanctions are having a positive effect, as far as getting non-parties to becoming parties to the treaties, be they developing or developed countries. In addition, the non-compliance procedure of the Montreal Protocol looks promising as far as getting parties to comply with their treaty obligations.[44]

When examining incentives in the context of developing countries, one becomes aware of three important caveats. First, no two developing countries are alike.[45] It would be difficult to equate, for instance, the need for the development of environmental laws for Kenya, which has highly trained lawyers, with Namibia, where until recently, access to even primary education was strictly limited.[46] In the perfect application of incentives for developing countries, in the form of technical and financial assistance, every component of external assistance should be thoroughly adapted to the local conditions and experience of the recipient country.[47] In addition, the relative size of the developing countries – in terms of population and geography – and the impact of their human activities on the global environment also differs between them, and this has a bearing on the effectiveness of the international environmental agreements. For instance, India and China are essential parties to these agreements because of their enormous size and ever-increasing impact on the global environment.

Second, one must be candid about the extent of the knowledge and abilities of developed countries.[48] Many developing countries are much better at recycling than many developed countries. Recycling takes place on a different level, for instance, turning old tires into sandals. In this sense, they lack the problems of supermarket over-packaging[49] that is a major source of waste in many industrialized countries.

Third, there is the caveat concerning poverty. As Magraw aptly notes, "[t]he moral imperative to alleviate absolute poverty has profound implications for international environmental law."[50] On the one hand, improving the standard of living of the absolute poor will mean a greater exploitation of natural resources in these countries,[51] at least temporarily. In my judgment, this can be done in a sustainable manner with the use of incentives. On the other hand, environmental norms must be structured so as not to hamper the efforts made to lift people out from absolute poverty.[52] There needs to be some leeway built into the system.

Therefore, this study argues that the trend of using differential treatment and responsibilities for developing countries in the form of incentives, such as delayed compliance schedules and technical and financial assistance, in environmental treaties, needs to continue and become part of the framework of international environmental law in order to promote universal participation in the creation and implementation of treaties, ultimately making them more effective. This, in turn, will contribute to the practical implementation of the goal of sustainable development.

Chapter 2 introduces the sources of international environmental law in this context, reviews the development of this new branch of international law, and explains how it has evolved to take into account the situation of developing countries. In addition, Chapter 2 analyses the principle of equity or fairness in international law in relation to the use of differential treatment for developing countries in international environmental agreements. Chapter 3 discusses the concept of sustainable development and its legal implications. Chapter 4 analyses the main sources of conflict with regard to the treatment of developing countries in the international regulatory process and examines the use of uniform versus differential norms. Chapter 5 examines the incentives specifically addressed to developing countries and disincentives, as they appear in the provisions of some of the international environmental agreements and assesses the merits of the different types of differential norms. Chapter 6 addresses how international institutional structures can facilitate the participation of developing countries in international environmental agreements. Chapter 7 analyses various special funding mechanisms that have emerged, which have created more incentives for developing countries to participate in international environmental agreements. Chapter 8 examines the role of non-governmental organizations in promoting universal participation. In conclusion, Chapter 9, summarizes the goals, strategies, and effective mechanisms that enable developing countries to begin to effectively participate and move toward more equal participation in the regulatory process to address global environmental problems.

Notes

1. *See* James Barnes, *The Growing International Dimension to Environmental Issues,* 13 COLUM. J. ENVTL. L. 389 (1988).

2. *But see* Fred Singer, *A Treaty Built on Hot Air, Not Scientific Consensus,* WALL ST. J., July 25, 1997, at A2 (referring to the Framework Convention on Climate Change, and arguing that global warming is mostly a "phantom" problem).

3. *See* PATRICIA W. BIRNIE & ALAN E. BOYLE, INTERNATIONAL LAW AND THE ENVIRONMENT 1 (1990).

4. *See* Daniel Bodansky, Professor of Law, University of Washington School of Law, LAW A545: International Environmental Law (Autumn 1996) (visited March 1997) <http://www2.law.washington.edu/Bodansky/iel96f.htm> (also listing Trade and the Environment as a separate section). (current information available as of Mar. 5, 1999 at <http://www2.law.washington.edu/bodansky/uw/teaching/iel/a545frame.htm >).

5. *See* OSCAR SCHACHTER, INTERNATIONAL LAW IN THEORY AND PRACTICE 366 (1991).

6. *See id.*

7. *See* Mary Pat Williams Silveira &, with Barbara Ruis, *International Law for Sustainable Development: An Attempt at Definition,* 2 NAFTA, LAW AND BUSINESS REVIEW OF THE AMERICAS 13 (1996). (The term was used in Agenda 21, but it referred

to "international law in the field of sustainable development." *See infra* text following Chapter 3 note 32).

8. Agenda 21 is a non-binding blueprint for action for a "global partnership for sustainable development." *Report of the Conference on Environment and Development (UNCED), Agenda 21*, U.N. Conference on Environment and Development ¶ I.I, at 9, U.N. Doc. A/CONF.151/26/Rev.I (Vol.2). *See infra* text accompanying and following Chapter 2 note 172.

9. *See* Silveira, *supra* note 7, at 3. *See infra* text accompanying and following Chapter 3 note 29 (discussing international law for sustainable development).

10. *See Report of the Expert Group Meeting on Identification of Principles of International Law for Sustainable Development, Background Paper No.3*, U.N. Commission on Sustainable Development, 4th Sess. (1996), [hereinafter Report of the Expert Group—Sustainable Development]. *See infra* text accompanying Chapter 3 note 97.

11. *Report on the United Nations Conference on the Human Environment at Stockholm*, 11 I.L.M. 1416 (1972) [hereinafter Report on the Stockholm Conference].

12. *See* LYNTON CALDWELL, INTERNATIONAL ENVIRONMENTAL POLICY 19 (1990) *See also* Oscar Schachter, *The Emergence of International Environmental Law*, 44 J. INT'L AFF. 457 (1991) (stating that the Stockholm Conference recognized the environment as a "holistic entity, the 'biosphere,' to be protected in its entirety by international law and organizations." *Id.*).

13. In the context of this book, I will use the classification system used by the U.N. to distinguish between developing and industrialized countries. *See* U.N. DEVELOPMENT PROGRAMME, HUMAN DEVELOPMENT REPORT 1997 at 244 (1997). Countries with economies in transition will be included among the industrialized countries unless otherwise specified.

14. Among them, the World Commission on Environment and Development (WCED or Brundtland Commission) whose work resulted in the report OUR COMMON FUTURE. *See infra* note 15.

15. WORLD COMMISSION ON ENVIRONMENT AND DEVELOPMENT, OUR COMMON FUTURE 8 (1987). Also referred to as the Brundtland Commission's Report [hereinafter Brundtland Commission's Report] *See infra* Chapter 2 note 162 and accompanying text.

16. *Id.* at 4.

17. Meeting with Oscar Schachter, Professor of Law, Columbia University School of Law (Oct. 22, 1997).

18. *Report on the United Nations Conference on Environment and Development* (UNCED), U.N. Doc. A/CONF/151 (also referred to as the Rio Conference) [hereinafter Rio Conference].

19. For a closer examination of the concept, see *infra* Chapter 3.

20. *See* LAKSHMAN GURUSWAMY ET AL., INTERNATIONAL ENVIRONMENTAL LAW AND WORLD ORDER 220 (1994); *Rio Declaration on Environment and Development*, U.N. Conference on Environment and Development, U.N. Doc. A/Conf.151/26/Rev.1 (Vol.1). *See infra* text accompanying Chapter 2 note 177.

21. *See* Phillipe Sands, *Introduction* to GREENING INTERNATIONAL LAW at xv (Phillipe Sands ed., 1994).

22. *See* UNEP/WMO Information Unit on Climate Change (Dec. 1994) (the developed countries have 20% of the world's people, but use 80% of the world's

resources).

23. *See* INTERNATIONAL ENERGY AGENCY (IEA), WORLD ENERGY OUTLOOK 49 (1995).

24. Edith Brown Weiss, *International Environmental Law: Contemporary Issues and the Emergence of a New World Order*, 81 GEO. L.J. 706 (1993).

25. *See* Montreal Protocol on Substances that Deplete the Ozone Layer, Sept. 16, 1987 (entered into force Jan.1,1989), 26 I.L.M. 1541 [hereinafter Montreal Protocol].

26. For more on CFCs, see *infra* Chapter 2 note 134.

27. "OECD" is the Organization for Economic Co-operation and Development. The member states of OECD are Australia, Austria, Belgium, Canada, Czech Republic, Denmark, Finland, France, Germany, Greece, Hungary, Iceland, Ireland, Italy, Japan, Korea, Luxembourg, Mexico, the Netherlands, New Zealand, Norway, Poland, Portugal, Spain, Sweden, Switzerland, Turkey, the United Kingdom, and the United States of America. *See* OECD (Last updated May 5, 1999) <http://www.oecd.org/about/member-countries.html>.

28. WORLD ENERGY OUTLOOK, *supra* note 23, at 53.

29. Free-riders in this context, are nations that do not participate in environmental treaties, but benefit from the results of the treaties without having had any of the burdens the treaty might impose. *See* Brown Weiss, *supra* note 24, at 693. For instance, the Montreal Protocol has reduced the depletion of the ozone layer, thereby reducing some of the destructive effects of a thinner ozone layer, such as ultraviolet rays which can cause skin cancer. All countries get these same benefits whether they are parties to the Montreal Protocol or not. The nations not participating in the treaties make it more difficult for the parties to the treaties by creating an uneven playing field with regard to production costs and so on.

30. Weiss, *supra* note 24, at 691.

31. *See id.*

32. *See infra* text accompanying Chapter 4 note 47, for the full text of Principle 7.

33. *See* Sands, *supra* note 21, at xxxiv. *See infra* text accompanying Chapter 2 note 201.

34. *See id.* at xxxiv. For further discussion on this, see *infra* text following Chapter 4 note 47.

35. *See* Marc Pallemaerts, *The Future of Environmental Regulation: International Environmental Law in the Age of Sustainable Development: A Critical Assessment of the UNCED Process*, 15 J.L. & COM. 652 (1996).

36. *See infra* text accompanying Chapter 5 note 1.

37. *See* PETER H. SAND, LESSONS LEARNED IN GLOBAL ENVIRONMENTAL GOVERNANCE 6 (1990).

38. *See* Daniel Magraw, *Legal Treatment of Developing Countries: Differential, Contextual, and Absolute Norms*, 1 COLO. J. INT'L ENVTL. L. & POL'Y 74 (1990).

39. *See infra* Chapter 5, for an analysis of the merits of the different types of differential norms.

40. *See* Magraw, *supra* note 38, at 70.

41. *See* Adjustments to the Montreal Protocol on Substances that Deplete the Ozone Layer, June 29, 1990, 30 I.L.M. 537 [hereinafter Montreal Protocol—London Amendments].

42. China ratified the Montreal Protocol on June 14, 1991 and India ratified it on

June 19, 1992. *See* 16 INT'L ENV'T REP. (BNA) 699 (1993).

43. *See* SAND, *supra* note 37, at 8.

44. *See* Montreal Protocol—London Amendments, *supra* note 40, annex IV.

45. *See* William Wilson, *Environmental Law as Development Assistance*, 22 ENVTL. L. 954 (1992).

46. *See id.* at 954.

47. *See id.*

48. *See id.*

49. *See id.*

50. Magraw, *supra* note 38, at 71.

51. *See id.*

52. *See id.*

2

Background

Sources of International Environmental Law

In order to examine differential treatment for developing countries in international environmental law it is helpful to understand the sources from which that law is derived. The sources also enable us to tell whether a particular doctrine, principle, or rule actually has the force and effect of law,[1] though as this section will illustrate, this can be quite controversial with regard to what qualifies as customary international law.

International environmental law has the same sources as international law, as it is a specialized branch of that general law.[2] The traditional and generally accepted sources of international law are laid down in Article 38(1) of the Statute of the International Court of Justice.[3] This article is a provision of a legal instrument that is meant to govern the International Court of Justice (ICJ), but has come to apply generally, defining legal authority upon which decision-makers decide cases and advocate policies.[4] Article 38(1) denotes the sources of international law as follows: (a) international conventions, whether general or particular; (b) international custom, as evidence of a general practice accepted as law; (c) general principles of law, recognized by civilized nations; and (d) judicial decisions and teachings of the most highly qualified publicists, as subsidiary means for the determination of rules of law.[5]

Treaties

Treaties are the most frequently used method for creating binding international environmental law. Treaties are defined in the Vienna Convention on the Law of Treaties, as "an international agreement concluded between States in written form and governed by international law, whether embodied in a single instrument or in two or more related instruments and whatever its particular designation."[6] Article 11 of this treaty states that "[t]he consent of a State to be bound by a treaty may be expressed by signature, . . . ratification, . . . or by any other means if so agreed."[7] This emphasizes the point that treaties are only binding between the parties to the agreement. Mutual consent between sovereign nations to be bound to the agreements they make follows from the customary law principle of *pacta sunt servanda* (agreements are binding and should be implemented in good faith).[8]

In international law there is no common legislature, court, or enforcement power because the existing lawmaking bodies, courts, and sanctions are all based on treaties that are only binding between the parties. However, all nations are bound by customary international law, which can also originate from international agreements that have become a reflection of state practice and are perceived as binding customary law (*opinio juris*), as discussed below. On the other hand, treaties can also represent a codification of customary international law.

International environmental law, just as trade law, is one of the most invasive laws, as its agreements interfere with what has traditionally been considered part of state sovereignty. For instance, the Basel Convention[9] requires states to monitor waste disposal, and the Montreal Protocol[10] requires states to reduce or eliminate their consumption of CFCs.

The treaty-making process, which includes negotiations, adoption, ratification, and entry into force (becoming effective law), often takes a long time. This was the case of the United Nations Convention on the Law of the Sea (UNCLOS),[11] which was adopted at Montego Bay on 10 December 1982, after more than a decade of negotiations, and entered into force on 16 November 1994. First a treaty is adopted, after being negotiated by the participating states. Then it has to be ratified, unless the parties agree to be bound by signature. Ratification usually requires that the states formally deposit their instrument of ratification after having been approved by their national legislative body. The treaty then has to be ratified by a certain number of states or certain named states, specified in the treaty, at which point it enters into force.[12]

Many treaties, however, do not receive the specified number of ratifications for them to become effective law, or do not include states whose involvement is essential to the achievement of their purpose.[13] The Montreal Protocol almost suffered the fate of not having some essential states as parties, such as India and China, until the Multilateral Fund was introduced in 1990 with the London Amendments and Adjustments that enticed these states to join.

The more recent international environmental agreements, in contrast to the traditional comprehensive treaties such as UNCLOS, often include a framework treaty creating general rights and obligations, such as the Vienna Convention for Protection of the Ozone Layer, to be followed by one or more specific protocols, such as the Montreal Protocol on Substances that Deplete the Ozone Layer. At the time of their adoption, these two agreements represented exceptions to the time-consuming ratification process; the Vienna Convention entered into force three years after it was adopted, while the Montreal Protocol only took sixteen months from the time it was concluded until it entered into force.

However, with regard to international environmental treaties, there is a tendency to hasten the process, especially if there are important interests at stake. In the case of the Chernobyl accident, the International Atomic Energy Agency moved quickly to negotiate a notification convention and an assistance convention,[14] which only took a month and a year, respectively, from the time of adoption until they became effective.[15]

Once a framework treaty and its Protocol(s) are in force, one can get around lengthy negotiation and ratification procedures with regard to amending them, if they have provisions that allow for changes by majority voting of the parties to strengthen the regulations taking into account new scientific data. Article 6 of the Montreal Protocol, represented a novel characteristic at the time, requiring that an assessment be done by the parties at least every four years, allowing for periodic review of the control measures compared to evolving scientific knowledge. At the first Meeting of the Parties in Helsinki in 1989 it was apparent that major changes in the Protocol were necessary.[16] Then at the second Meeting of the Parties, in London in 1990, commitments made in Helsinki became a reality.[17] These included the tightening of the control measures, leading to a total phase-out of the original five CFCs and three halons[18] and the addition of new chemicals to the list of controlled substances.

Customary International Law

Customary law, unlike conventional law, is universally binding. The creation of customary international law calls for the fulfillment of two requirements. The first requirement, the objective element, is that the custom must be evidenced in state practice.[19] According to the *Asylum* case[20] which provides the leading pronouncements by the ICJ on this issue, the state practice must be "constant and uniform."[21] Bodansky expresses this requirement as "empirical claims about the ways that states (and other international actors) regularly behave."[22] The other requirement is the subjective element, that the state practice must be supported by *opinio juris* as expressed in the *North Sea Continental Shelf* cases and reiterated in the *Case of Nicaragua v. United States.*[23] *Opinio juris* is defined as "the conviction that conduct is motivated by a sense of legal obligation, not merely comity."[24] Whether these two requirements have been fulfilled has become more and more difficult to ascertain because of the increasing number of states that are part of the international community.[25] At present, 180-plus states are members of the United Nations. Identifying universal practice among so many states of diverse legal systems, cultures, policies, and interests is becoming an increasingly difficult task.[26] In addition, given the different types of manifestations of state conduct from which *opinio juris* may be inferred, identifying such a legal conviction remains a problem.[27]

Schachter states that environmental treaties, on the whole, are not accepted as expressions of customary law and are regarded as binding only for the parties.[28] Whether "soft law" or non-binding resolutions qualify as customary international law, will be discussed below.

General Principles Of Law

The category in the Statute of the International Court of Justice, Article 38(1)(c), called "General principles of law recognized by civilized nations," traditionally refers to common legal maxims applied in all municipal legal systems, particularly rules of procedure, evidence, and jurisdiction,[29] but has no well-accepted meaning.[30] International tribunals have also used elements of legal reasoning and private law analogies to make international law a practical system for application in a judicial process.[31] General references to abuse of rights and good faith have also on occasion been relied upon by the Court.[32] Brownlie asserts that the principle of equity is encompassed by Article 38(1)(c).[33] He states that, strictly, it cannot be a source of law, and yet it may be an important element in the process of deciding a case.[34] Equity is defined by Brownlie as "considerations of fairness, reasonableness, and policy often necessary for the sensible application of the more settled rules of law."[35] In the *Diversion of Water from the River Meuse* cases, Judge Hudson in an individual concurring opinion stated that "Article 38 of the Statute expressly directs the application of "general principles of law recognized by civilized nations," and in more than one nation principles of equity have an established place in the legal system,"[36] indicating that equity could be included in Article 38(1)(c).

Subsidiary Sources

Judicial decisions do not have the status they do in many national legal systems, since there is no doctrine of precedent or principle of *stare decisis* in the international courts. Article 38(1)(d) of the ICJ Statute is made subject to Article 59 of the Statute that dictates that "the decisions of the Court have no binding force except between the parties and in respect of that particular case."[37] However, international lawyers regard the decisions as "highly persuasive authority of existing international law," despite these qualifications.[38] The Court cites its earlier decisions, but it is not treated as conclusive evidence of the law.[39] Its authority depends on the subsequent recognition by states as being acceptable.[40]

On another note, as Birnie and Boyle state, "the body of jurisprudence accumulates, particularly in the case of ICJ, and contributes to the progressive development of international law,"[41] despite the function of the Court-which is to declare and clarify the law, not create it. This is due to the fragmentary nature of much of international law and the generality of its concepts and principles, giving plenty of room for "creative" judicial application.[42] In international environmental law this is particularly the case, yet there are few decisions on contentious issues which directly raise environmental issues, the most notable one being the *Trail Smelter* case.[43]

Schachter states that the subsidiary source called "the teachings of the most highly qualified publicists of the various nations" has always been more important in international law than municipal law, especially since the basic systematization of international law was done largely by the writers.[44] Some writers are referred to in the ICJ, mostly in the pleadings and the separate and dissenting opinions.[45] However, the ICJ is reluctant to identify publicists in the judgments themselves, partly due to national bias and also because the availability of treaties and official records of state practice has to a large extent reduced the necessity of turning to their writings as evidence of custom, unless the writers are unanimous in their interpretation, which is rarely the case.[46]

"Soft Law"

"Soft law" is a new and highly debated term, yet it represents an old issue in the field of international law, namely the legal status of "resolutions" and "declaration of principles" by intergovernmental bodies. Traditionally, most international law scholars discuss the status of U.N. General Assembly resolutions and declarations and the possibility of resorting to them as evidence of opinio juris of states, especially if they are adopted unanimously. These resolutions *per se* are not binding, but may become binding customary law as a consequence of subsequent state practice.[47]

"Soft law" covers a broader area, including resolutions made by international conferences and many different international commissions and organizations, such as the United Nations Environment Programme (UNEP), not just those made by the U.N. General Assembly. It is defined as "norms that are not strictly binding but are still generally likely to be observed."[48] "Soft law" includes codes of practice, recommendations, guidelines, standards, and declarations of principles, usually adopted in the form of resolutions.[49] Principle 7 "common but differential responsibilities" of the Rio Declaration falls within the "soft law" category. It recognizes that states have common but differentiated responsibilities in regard to the different contributions to global environmental degradation.

As "soft" law is not considered binding, it is increasingly being used in international environmental law as a way to make the international community more likely to participate in the law-making process. Increased use of "half-way stages" in law-making through the use of "soft law" are needed in the face of difficulties in securing widespread consent to treaties or customary law, in order to create universal standards for environmental protection to deal with urgent problems.[50]

With the increased number of "resolutions" or "declaration of principles," one has to ask whether these "soft law" instruments fall within one of the categories of the ICJ Statute mentioned above, bringing them under the rubric of one of the accepted sources of international law. Bodansky argues that most international environmental law "principles" do not fall within any of the proposed theories of "general principles of law" under Article 38(1)(c). He states that they do not seem to represent principles common to most national legal systems, nor are they principles of logic or natural law.[51]

Few "principles" of international environmental law (or "soft law" as they are often referred to) qualify as customary according to the traditional version of customary international law.[52] Most of the claims that norms of international environmental law are part of customary law are based on collating texts, for instance treaties and resolutions, produced by states to see whether a critical mass of authority exists in support of the custom. This methodology of focusing on verbal rather than physical practice by states, Bodansky argues, appears to be a misguided method for discovering behavior regularities because in the environmental field verbal claims and physical behavior often do not coincide.

This argument seems to support Schachter's view of state practice, illustrated when he discusses the status of Principle 21 of the Declaration on the Human Environment, adopted at the Stockholm Conference.[53] Principle 21 reads as follows:

> States have, in accordance with the Charter of the United Nations and the principles of international law, the sovereign right to exploit their own resources pursuant to their own environmental policies, and the responsibility to ensure that activities within their jurisdiction or control do not cause damage to the environment of other States or of areas beyond the limits of national jurisdiction.[54]

In the typical United Nations style of formulation it affirms the competing principles of international responsibility and national authority within a general setting of international rights and obligations.[55]

Principle 21 is generally recognized as expressing a rule of customary international law.[56] However, Schachter disagrees, stating that Principle 21 and similar texts are still *de lege ferenda* (what the law should be) because there is only fragmentary evidence of State practice and opinio juris, Principle 21, being at best, a starting point.[57] Schachter argues that Principle 21 has not yet become State practice because "States generally do not 'ensure that the activities within their jurisdiction do not cause damage' to the environments of others." In addition, he states that governments have not given any meaningful evidence that they consider this principle as binding customary law. I agree with Schachter as far as the second statement of the Principle is concerned – regarding responsibility of states, but I think the first statement regarding sovereignty over natural resources would fulfill the requirements to qualify as customary international law.[58]

Several of the principles in international environmental law are an expression of the ideals of the international community, but of course, the hope is that some of these ideals will in turn become treaties. Bodansky agrees with this, when he states that international environmental norms, no matter whether they are considered legal or nonlegal, will set the terms of international discussions and serve as the framework for negotiations.[59] Rather than debating their legal status, he feels they should be translated into concrete treaties and actions.[60]

Bodansky's theory is that there is no point in arguing the legal status of international environmental law "principles" as long as there is virtually no third-party control in the implementation and enforcement of environmental norms.[61] By this he means that courts and arbitral tribunals play a minor role in addressing international environmental issues. If third-party control had been the norm, then the distinction between legal and nonlegal norms would matter, since only legal norms are enforceable.[62] In the same manner, Schachter states that the categorization "binding" or "hortatory" (i.e., without legal force) are less appropriate and he prefers to characterize the resolutions as "evidentiary," meaning they are evidence for the asserted proposition of law.[63] Characterizing them in this manner reflects the fact that they are not binding, yet are "relevant and entitled to be given weight in determinations of the law in question."[64]

In their book on international law and the environment, Birnie and Boyle categorically state that "soft law," including declarations of principles, recommendations, and resolutions clearly are not law in the sense used by Article 38(1).[65] However, they do consider them to have some authority, even if they are not binding. Weiss classifies them as non-binding legal instruments, which I think reflects their true nature.[66]

Due to their vagueness and generality, "soft law" norms allow a large amount of discretion in their application.[67] This results in allowing states to assume certain obligations that they might not otherwise have accepted. The term "soft law" does convey the element of strong expectation that states will gradually conform their behavior to its requirements.[68] However, this vagueness also has its disadvantages, as Bodansky argues, "states may basically do what they like and argue that their actions are consistent witl customary international law."[69] On the other hand, being non-bindin entails less transaction costs and the ability to respond to rapid changes ii line with new scientific understanding of environment issues,[70] in contras to the normally long lag time for the adoption of treaties.

The trend toward hardening the international legal order is encourage by the very existence of the "soft law" instruments, and some have becom "hard law."[71] UNEP's Cairo Guidelines and Principles for the Environmen tally Sound Management of Hazardous Waste serves as an example in tha it was the basis for the 1989 Basel Convention on the Control of Trans boundary Movements of Hazardous Wastes.[72] The "soft law" Principle 7 o the Rio Declaration stipulating "common but differential responsibility," has also been translated into binding law in the Framework Convention or Climate Change providing different commitments for developed anc developing countries.[73]

Development of International Environmental Law

Although it is a new field, international environmental law has beer foreshadowed in earlier international agreements and cases. These treaties and cases, some of which are mentioned below, have served as importan precedents for the subsequent development of international environmenta law. The treaties in particular, show a pattern of constantly increasing thei scope. Some of the first treaties concerned specific species, then later, the treaties made a whole ecosystem their priority. The more recent treaties address global issues like climate change and depletion of the stratospheric ozone layer, while simultaneously taking socio-economic conditions into account. Some of them include specific incentives for developing countries, in effect giving them differential treatment.

Before 1900 the treaties had another perspective than the present agreements. With few exceptions, they did not focus on pollution or other ecological issues. Instead, they were based on unrestricted national sovereignty over natural resources, addressing boundary waters, navigation, and fishing rights in shared waterways.[74] The 1909 agreement[75] between the United States and the United Kingdom (which was then in charge of Canada's foreign affairs) proved a turning point, in that it prohibited water pollution from one state injuring the other state.[76]

In practice, the exclusive sovereignty over natural resources became increasingly modified as states began to relinquish some of their sovereignty in order to protect birds, fish, and marine mammals.[77] The first treaty relating to particular species of wildlife was the 1902 Convention for the Protection of Birds Useful to Agriculture.[78] The 1911 United States-Great

Britain Treaty for the Preservation and Protection of Fur Seals[79] took the same approach, emphasizing the utility of the species.[80]

By the 1930s and 1940s states began to emphasize natural resources, entering into agreements to protect fauna and flora generally.[81] Among the agreements are the 1933 London Convention on Preservation of Fauna and Flora in Their Natural State[82], (applying to Africa) and the 1940 Convention on Nature Protection and Wildlife Preservation in the Western Hemisphere.[83] These treaties also express the obligation to cooperate, a commitment included in almost all international environmental treaties.[84]

In the context of transboundary pollution, the first customary international norm applicable to environmental issues appeared in 1941.[85] The *Trail Smelter* case,[86] a tort case between the U.S. and Canada, confirmed that a state is responsible for environmental damage to other countries caused by activities within its own territory.[87]

The Arbitral Tribunal concluded that:

> [U]nder the principles of international law, . . . no State has the right to use or permit the use of its territory in such a manner as to cause injury by fumes in or to the territory of another or the properties or persons therein, when the case is of serious consequence and the injury is established by clear and convincing evidence.[88]

This case is significant because it clearly limited state sovereignty in a more general manner than had resulted from treaties or cases that had been negotiated or decided earlier. The principle of international responsibility, reflected in this case, was also the basis for the Stockholm Principle 21.[89]

The United Nations Scientific Conference on the Conservation and Utilization of Resource was convened in 1949.[90] The conference considered the problems involved in the resource field, addressing six different categories of resources: minerals, fuel and energy, water, forests, land, and wildlife and fish. However, it did not adopt any recommendations or action plan.[91] Although characterized by some scholars as the United Nations' first environmental conference, others feel it did not take a holistic view of the relationship between population, resources, and environment.[92] The latter viewpoint seems to reflect what in the literature is sometimes referred to as the modern resource—economical and ecological—approach. This approach aims at protecting the environment for its intrinsic value while also combining it with the goal of sustainable use and optimal resource management.[93]

During the 1950s, efforts were made to deal with marine pollution.[94] The first treaty in this area was the 1954 Convention for the Prevention of Pollution of the Sea by Oil.[95] This convention was replaced by a more meticulous one in 1973.[96]

As will become clear from this study, international environmental law, more than any other branch of international law, has developed very quickly, due to threats to the environment affecting all human beings. Rachel Carson's book, Silent Spring,[97] and similar European books promoted the awareness of environmental issues within nations in the 1960s.[98] Silent Spring played a decisive roll in the development of the pesticide legislation in the United States[99] Also, concerned citizen groups, communicating with one another across national borders, pressured their governments for legislative and administrative action to protect and restore the quality of the environment.[100] At the same time, enlightened public environmental awareness quickly expanded from local to national and from national to international levels.[101] Meanwhile, ecological catastrophes such as the oil spill caused by the oil tanker Torrey Canyon instigated governments to act rapidly to counter marine pollution.[102] Treaties were signed concerning interventions in case of oil pollution casualties,[103] civil liability for oil pollution damage,[104] and regulating oil pollution in the North Sea.[105]

International organizations also began to realize the emergence of a new problem, and in 1968 the Council of Europe adopted the first general environmental document approved by an international organization, the Declaration on Air Pollution Control.[106] The second major step in international environmental law was taken by Africa in the signing of the 1968 African Convention on the Conservation of Nature and Natural Resources,[107] replacing the 1933 London Convention.[108] The African Convention is a comprehensive treaty dealing with conservation and utilization of plant, animal, soil and water resources. This convention demonstrates how some developing countries were involved in efforts to protect the environment as early as the sixties. In 1968 UNESCO and a number of other international agencies sponsored the Biosphere Conference,[109] which introduced the biosphere concept as the focus of international consideration.[110] One of the most important initiatives taken by an international organization was in December 3, 1968, when the U.N. General Assembly adopted Draft Resolution 2398 (XXIII) setting in motion the Preparations for the Stockholm Conference held in June 1972.[111]

The Stockholm Conference

The Stockholm Conference, which produced major developments in international environmental law, had as its objective:

> to provide a framework for comprehensive consideration within the United Nations of the problems of the human environment in order to focus the attention of Governments and public opinion on the importance and urgency of this question and also to identify those aspects of it that can only, or at best be solved through international cooperation and agreement.[112]

At the Stockholm Conference, the developing countries resisted highlighting environmental issues because they were afraid that would slow down their economic development and limit their sovereignty. They feared that ecological values would take priority at the expense of development.[113] The following remark by the Sri Lankan ambassador to the U.N. in 1970 illustrates the outlook of most developing countries at the time:

> Developing countries have of late been warned of the price that has to be paid in the form of environmental pollution for industrial development. All developing countries are aware of the risks, but they would be quite prepared to accept from the developed countries even 100 percent of their gross national pollution if thereby they could diversify their economies through industrialization.[114]

However, the attitude among developing countries has been changing as the international community has realized it is faced with a common threat: the degradation of the global environment. In China, for instance, the government encourages people to develop an agricultural system that takes into account environmental factors.[115] Cheng Zheng-Kang states that "[b]oth developed and developing nations need to fulfill their respective responsibilities in helping to solve the problems associated with global change."[116] As Caldwell aptly notes, "Nations cooperate when convinced that their interests will be served by cooperation."[117]

The Stockholm Conference proved to be different from many other United Nations conferences because it initiated positive measures that translated its resolutions into actual accomplishments. One of these accomplishments was the establishment of the United Nations Environment Programme (UNEP).[118] In addition, it adopted the Declaration on the Human Environment (Stockholm Declaration), consisting of 26 principles, and an Action Plan for the Human Environment consisting of 109 recommendations.[119]

Six of the principles included in the Stockholm Declaration specifically address the special circumstances of developing countries. Principle 9 emphasizes how the transfer of technical and financial assistance to developing countries is necessary to solve the environmental problems caused by underdevelopment. Principle 10 focuses on the importance of the stability of prices and adequate earnings for primary commodities and raw material for environmental management.

Principles 11, 12, and 23 address the issue of the environmental policies of all States having an impact on development in third world countries. These standards should not adversely affect the development potential of developing countries and should consider the systems and values of each country. In addition, technical and financial assistance should be made available to developing countries for incorporating such measures into their own development planning. Principle 20 addresses the issue of technology transfer to developing countries.

Principles 21 and 22 of the Declaration have an important significance to the development of international environmental law. As mentioned above, the much-debated Principle 21, giving sovereign nations the right to develop their natural resources, according to their own environmental policies, and at the same time making them responsible for preventing their activities from harming other states or the global commons, is generally accepted as customary international law, even though state practice to that effect is negligible.[120]

To give effect to Principle 21, the governments recognized the need to develop a specific body of law.[121] Principle 22 states: "States shall cooperate to develop further the international law regarding liability and compensation for victims of pollution and other environmental damage caused by activities within the jurisdiction or control of such States to areas beyond their jurisdiction."

On the whole, the Stockholm principles have not had a significant effect on the environment; environmental degradation on a global scale is steadily becoming worse. However, the Stockholm Conference did emphasize how humanity could irreversibly harm the environment and therefore staked out the course: that the human environment needed to be protected and enhanced through common efforts at the local, national, and international levels.[122]

Post Stockholm

The Stockholm conference accelerated the negotiations of other treaties adopted under the UN's auspices,[123] including the World Heritage Convention,[124] the Convention on International Trade in Endangered Species (CITES),[125] the London Ocean Dumping Convention,[126] and the International Convention for the Prevention of Pollution by Ships (MARPOL).[127] The first convention of the Regional Seas Programme, initiated by UNEP, was also adopted at this time.[128]

Since the Stockholm Conference took place, marking the beginning of the modern era of international environmental law,[129] hundreds of international environmental agreements have been adopted. International environmental law has evolved from bilateral to multilateral approaches to address global environmental issues.[130] In addition, there has been a move from remedial action to more preventive measures.[131]

At the global level, the 1982 United Nations Convention on the Law of the Sea[132] created an unprecedented, comprehensive framework for the establishment of global regulations for the protection of the marine environment, including provisions on environmental impact assessment, technology transfer, and liability, and meticulous institutional structures.[133] Though it didn't come into force until November 16, 1994, its provisions have already had an influence on other international environmental agreements.

Due to the apparently imminent threat of depletion of the ozone layer caused by man-made chemicals, the Vienna Convention for the Protection of the Ozone Layer was negotiated in 1985.[134] The Vienna Convention represents the first time an international agreement required preventive action before actual harm had been proven.[135] And in 1987, in quick response to a threatening hole in the ozone layer believed to be caused by chlorofluorocarbons (CFCs) and other commercially produced chemicals, the international community adopted a protocol to the Vienna Convention, the Montreal Protocol on Substances that Deplete the Ozone Layer.[136] The Montreal Protocol has had a great significance on the development of international environmental law in that it introduced new methods of lawmaking in this field. These innovations include the delayed compliance schedule for developing countries, the non-compliance procedure (established to deal with conflicts with regard to implementation, among the parties to the Protocol), and the Protocol's funding mechanism. The Protocol has been used as a model for several more recent treaties, such as the Framework Convention on Climate Change.[137]

Equally important advances have been made at the regional level. The Convention on Long-Range Transboundary Air Pollution of 1979,[138] applicable to the members of the United Nations Economic Commission for Europe, established a framework for cooperation to deal with long-range air pollution and its effects on forests and lakes. One of the protocols to the Convention, the 1985 Protocol on the Reduction of Sulphur Emissions, has resulted in a 50 percent reduction in sulfur emissions by the twenty-one Parties to the Protocol.[139] In Africa, a ban on the importation of hazardous wastes and strict regulations for moving it within Africa was created with the Bamako Convention on Hazardous Wastes.[140] And in Asia, the Convention on the Conservation of Nature,[141] adopted by the members of the Association of Southeast Asian Nations (ASEAN), provides for ecosystem protection and regulates trade in endangered species.[142]

Other regional institutions have also been essential in the development of international environmental law. The Nordic Environmental Protection Convention,[143] adopted by the Nordic Council serves as a model for environmental cooperation between neighboring states. It entails a principle of non-discrimination for citizens of the Nordic countries, parties to the treaty, in bringing suits in other Nordic countries than their own for environmental damage caused by activities in those other countries.

The European Union (EU) began its action programs in environmental law as early as 1973, even though its founding document, the Treaty of Rome, did not mention environmental issues as part of its domain.[144] Then, through the Single European Act,[145] amending the Treaty of Rome in 1986, the EEC received clear authority to act on environmental issues. More recently, the Treaty on European Union[146] in its Article 3, expressly mentions environmental policy as one of its activities. There is no doubt that the EU has taken important international action in the environmental field, though the extent of implementation of its legislation within its member states has had varying degrees of success depending on the state.[147]

In regard to economic and financial institutions, the General Agreement on Tariffs and Trade,[148] (now the World Trade Organization (WTO)) created a Group on Environmental Measures and International Trade in 1971 (convening for the first time in 1991), to consider environmental measures which could affect trade.[149] More recently WTO has established a permanent committee, the Committee on Trade and Environment (CTE), to deal with trade and environmental issues.

The role of the World Bank in the environmental context has been growing steadily, and presently it is the largest provider of funds for environmental projects. In 1987 the World Bank established an Environment Department, and in 1989 it promulgated its Environmental Impact Assessment Operational Directive, all in an effort to integrate environmental considerations into development projects.[150] In addition, there has been an increase in targeted funds, made available by donor nations for specific aspects of environmental work.[151] These are either managed exclusively by the World Bank or operated jointly with other agencies. Two such jointly operated funding mechanisms are the Multilateral Fund of the Montreal Protocol and the Global Environmental Facility.[152]

Considered a breakthrough in international environmental law, the Parties of the Montreal Protocol—through the London Amendments and Adjustments[153]—created the Multilateral Fund in 1990.[154] This Fund was established in order to help developing countries meet certain incremental costs associated with the implementation of the Montreal Protocol.[155] And, in an agreement with the Montreal Protocol's Executive Committee in 1991, the World Bank was given the authority to manage investment projects with money transferred from the Fund to the Bank's Ozone Projects Trust Fund. Furthermore, in 1991, the Global Environmental Facility was established by the World Bank, UNEP and the United Nations Development Programme (UNDP). Its main purpose is to help finance projects which benefit the global commons.[156]

After the Stockholm Conference, in addition to treaties, non-binding legal instruments, often categorized as "soft-law" have multiplied.[157] The

1978 UNEP Draft Principles on Shared Natural Resources[158] is an example of a soft-law text.[159] Another example is the World Charter for Nature approved by the General Assembly in 1982.[160] Some of these instruments have been incorporated into binding treaties, others have been accepted as customary international law, and the rest, while remaining as soft-law instruments, are evidence of predominant concepts and the direction of international environmental law.[161]

The Brundtland Commission, The Rio Conference, and Post Rio

In 1987 the United Nations General Assembly adopted Our Common Future,[162] a report issued by the Brundtland Commission or the World Commission on Environment and Development (WCED), an independent group established by the General Assembly in 1984 and chaired by the former Prime Minister of Norway, Gro Harlem Brundtland. This Commission's Expert Group on Environmental Law adopted 22 legal principles for environmental protection and sustainable development. Many of the instruments adopted at UNCED incorporated some of these principles. The Brundtland Commission synthesized the earlier aims enunciated in instruments such as the World Charter for Nature, by demonstrating the need to achieve the goal of 'sustainable development.'[163] Since 1987, 'sustainable development' has become a household concept in international environmental law-making.

Following up on the Brundtland Commission's suggestion, the United Nations General Assembly proposed the United Nations Conference on Environment and Development (UNCED) in 1989 by passing Resolution 44/228. UNCED, also called the Earth Summit or Rio Conference,[164] took place in Rio de Janeiro in June of 1992, twenty years after the Stockholm conference. The Rio Conference represents a watershed in the efforts to integrate environment and development issues. It represents a process to resolve these issues. However, as will be seen throughout this study, the question of how successful these efforts have been as far as paying real attention to, and showing strong commitment to solving the important issues, such as loss of biodiversity, rather than merely producing very vague and general instruments, still remains to be answered.[165] The Kyoto Protocol, adopted December 11, 1997,[166] is a step in the right direction as it includes binding limitations on greenhouse gas emissions by developed countries, but much work still remains to be done.

At Rio, five new legal instruments were adopted, two of them binding and three of them non-binding. The Framework Convention on Climate Change[167] and the Convention on Biological Diversity,[168] have since come into force.[169] The non-binding legal instruments include the Rio Declaration,[170] a set of 15 Forest Principles,[171] and Agenda 21.[172]

Agenda 21 is a comprehensive, but non-binding, action program for governments, development agencies, U.N. organizations, and independent sectors in all major areas affecting the relationship between the environment and the economy, designed to merge the goals of continued economic development and environmental protection. Agenda 21 represents a road map of actions needed to be implemented in order for states to achieve sustainable development.[173] It has been described as the most important outcome of the Rio Conference, the ultimate success or failure of the conference resting on Agenda 21.[174] It has some 500 pages, arranged into four sections: I) social and economic dimensions, II) conservation and management of resources for development, III) strengthening of major groups,[175] and IV) means of implementation.[176]

The Rio Declaration is partly a renewed version of the Stockholm Principles, yet it also includes new principles which have not been universally accepted before, such as the right to development.[177] It represents a careful balance of the principles considered important to the developed and the developing countries.[178] In the context of this study, I will focus mostly on Principle 7, as it is most relevant to the discussion of differential norms.

The Forest Principles were adopted at Rio after two years of debates, plans for a binding treaty having been abandoned early on. The guiding objective of the principles is "to contribute to the management, conservation and sustainable development of forests and to provide for their multiple and complementary functions and uses."[179] In 1995, an Intergovernmental Panel on Forests (IPF) was established as a subsidiary body of the United Nation Commission on Sustainable Development (CSD). This Panel agreed on proposals for action, which were endorsed by CSD.[180] This makes the outlook for agreement on a treaty seem quite promising.

Since the Rio Conference, the United Nations Commission on Sustainable Development (CSD), called for in Agenda 21, was established in January of 1993, with the responsibility of monitoring the implementation of Agenda 21 and other agreements negotiated at Rio.[181] In addition, conferences have been held on many issues relevant to international environmental law, including high seas fisheries,[182] sustainable development of small island developing states,[183] population and development,[184] women,[185] and social issues.[186] Furthermore, the Convention to Combat Desertification,[187] called for at the Rio conference and concluded in 1994, entered into force on December 26, 1996.[188] Agenda 21 also called on the U.N. General Assembly to organize a regular review of its implementation, suggesting that an overall review and appraisal of Agenda 21 take place no later than 1997. The Special Session of the U.N. General Assembly (UNGASS) took place on June 23-27, 1997.[189] UNGASS, reviewing what had been done since the Rio Conference, acknowledged that some positive results had been achieved, among them the entering into force of several of the conventions adopted or suggested at UNCED. However, it concluded in a document called "Programme for the Further Implementation of Agenda 21" that those actions were insufficient, "the overall trends for sustainable development are worse today than they were in 1992."[190] A new review of Agenda 21 was scheduled for 2002.[191] With the adoption of the Kyoto Protocol in December 1997,[192] some progress has already been made since the UNGASS meeting. Hopefully this is only the beginning.

Principles of Sovereignty, Equality, and Equity in International Law

Under international law, nations function under the principles of sovereignty and equality of states, giving them uniform legal personality to act under international law and making them legally independent of other states, though they must recognize these as their equals.[193] In our context, this state of affairs in international law has several consequences. One is that developed and developing countries alike, maintain their sovereign right to internal self-governance. This is expressed specifically regarding the exploitation of the natural resources under their jurisdiction, according to their own policies.[194] This, in turn, makes it more difficult to negotiate and then implement treaties on, for instance, biological diversity and climate change, where universal participation is called for in order for the treaties to be effective. In addition, sovereignty has been used by developing countries as grounds for refusing to accept environmental conditions on loans requested to help them develop in a sustainable manner.[195] In the same vane, developing countries have used sovereignty as grounds for withholding information on aid projects from the public.[196]

One of the greatest problems concerning the principle of sovereignty, is that states are not bound by treaty law unless they consent to be bound by becoming a party to the treaty.[197] However, all nations are bound by customary international law, which can also originate from international agreements that have become a reflection of state practice and are perceived as binding customary law (opinio juris). In practice, states for the most part act in accordance with international law, notwithstanding the lack of enforcement powers, especially if it is in their own self-interests.[198]

Referring to the principle of equality of states, one could argue that developing countries should have the same obligations in environmental treaties as the industrialized nations have—from the outset—with no leeway built into the system. This viewpoint would be in line with the traditional principle of egalitarian reciprocity among all parties in treaty law.[199] In addition, some scholars argue that giving developing countries special considerations or "differential treatment" to promote their participation in international environmental agreements, creates ". . . new problems in defining general state obligations in international environmental law, and in implementing and enforcing these obligations equally."[200]

However, the principle of equity also plays a role in the international legal order, allowing for exceptions in the name of fairness or reasonableness.[201] Schachter sets forth the relationship between equality and equity as follows:

> As one moves from the level of the ideal to practical social policy, equality is in itself too general a concept to support concrete policy choices. Choices must be made among the different kinds of equality: equality of rights, of opportunities, of conditions, and of outcome. And, these different kinds of equality may be incompatible in practice: indeed, this is likely to be the case when there are disparities in resources and capabilities. That is why, since the time of Plato it has been suggested that "equality among unequals" may be inequitable and that *differential treatment* may be essential for "real equality.[202]

The definition of equity was at the core of the debates concerning the situation of developing countries at the Rio Conference.[203] The UNCED conference has been described as a conference concerning equity: "how to allocate future responsibilities for environmental protection among states that are at different levels of economic development, have contributed in different degrees to particular problems, and have different environmental and developmental needs and priorities."[204]

As Grad so aptly notes, one could classify the concept of "differential treatment" of developing countries as a kind of "international affirmative action" notion.[205] Affirmative action in this context, points to a kind of historic, causal-related injustice because developing countries have not had the same socio-economic benefits as the developed countries that over-exploited the global environment, yet they are expected to share the burden of controls on economic development that may have a negative impact on the environment.[206] Since industrialized countries have done most of the polluting, it could be argued that it is only fair that developing countries be given leeway in the environmental control measures. Making exceptions in environmental treaties enables developing countries to adjust to the new agreements: getting the alternative technology needed to replace, for instance, CFC-using technology, and arranging technical assistance and training directed at national capacity-building. Eventually, all nations have to phase out completely the use of certain ozone depleting substances. In the meantime, less exceptions or "differential treatment" would be necessary if more technical and financial assistance were made available to developing countries to enable them to implement the stricter treaty measures sooner. This is in fact the case with 24 developing countries in regard to the Montreal Protocol.[207] Due to funding and programs provided by the Multilateral Fund these countries have been able to start complying with the control measures before their ten-year grace period has come to an end.

The newer international environmental law agreements often make common or general principles and then qualify the more substantive norms with regard to developing countries – as in the Climate Change Convention and the Kyoto Protocol where they have not been required to reduce their greenhouse gas emissions – thereby imposing different obligations on States, taking into account, among other things, who contributed to the degradation.[208] This is now commonly referred to as 'common, but differentiated responsibility', as expressed in the Rio Declaration, Principle 7, in regard to pollution issues.[209]

The idea of treating developing countries differently is not a new one. In the General Agreements on Tariffs and Trade developing countries have been granted special privileges and exemptions not granted to developed countries, in order to assist their economic development.[210] However, in most instances in the field of international environmental law, the "differential treatment" should be only temporary, so as not to be incompatible with the goals and purposes of the treaties. This is very important because otherwise the advances made by the international agreements, as in the case of the Montreal Protocol, could be diminished, for instance, by new chlorides being put into the atmosphere, due to increasing use of freons in developing countries.

Different global environmental problems, be it CO_2 emissions or other problems, would have to be taken into account when deciding what approach to use. One could, for instance, argue that developing countries should always have lower CO_2 emission reduction obligations.

Weiss states that the traditional concept of equity is one of "national sovereign rights to exploit resources within a country's jurisdiction or control, combined with rights to shared or common resources (whether for natural resources or for pollution emissions) on a first-come, first-served basis".[211] She adds that this traditional equity ethic has degenerated, and that a new standard is appearing.[212]

More and more, equity is referred to as meaning "equitable standards for the allocation and sharing of resources and benefits."[213] In addition to the allocation of resources, Weiss asserts that responsibility and liability for pollution has also defined equity in environmental law and that these two issues in many ways represent different aspects of the allocation issue. Just as one needs norms to distribute resources equitably, one also needs norms to equitably allocate responsibility for preventing pollution. There seems to be a growing consensus that most of the global environmental problems we are struggling with at present were caused by the industrialized countries, and policies that place equal responsibility on developing and developed countries for pollution emissions would be inequitable. The traditionally asserted right to pollute at self-determined levels has been limited by international agreements,[214] even though they are not always upheld in practice. Now the equity issues that pose the most controversy concern responsibility for the prevention of harm to global resources and liability for their damage.[215]

Ecological systems do not take borders into account. Therefore, actions taken by one State within its territory, such as activities producing air pollution, will affect neighboring States, and ultimately may affect the global environment, as in the case of global warming. An awareness of the actual impact of environmental factors makes it clear that the global environment and human activities are interconnected.[216] The acceptance of this global interdependence and the actual impact of environmental factors, Schachter posits, is necessary in order to link equity to a redistributive concept based on actual human needs at the present time.[217] "Equity" as a redistributive principle forms the basis of another meaning of equity, other than the historic equity,[218] mentioned above. It requires a structure based on interests and facts.

The fulfillment of the needs of the developing countries has been recognized as a normative principle which is central to the idea of equity and distributive justice.[219] Schachter asserts that "need" is widely accepted as a standard of international distribution. He states further, that developing countries and, by and large, industrialized countries have agreed that need is a legitimate and sufficient ground for preferential distribution.[220] Schachter bases this position on their concurrence in international resolutions, their own policy statements, and a continuing series of actions granting assistance and preferences to those countries in need.[221]

The reason the principle of need has been given a certain practical effect in decisions by the international community, Schachter posits, is not due to a sudden spread of altruism, but a widely felt necessity on the part of governments to respond to tensions and grievances which threaten the balance and stability of international relations.[222] However, this preferential treatment must, in my judgment, have environmental conditions attached to it due to the global interdependence we are now aware of. Without environmental conditions linked to the preferential treatment, the stability of international relations would be threatened due to environmental calamities, induced by development activities that degrade the environment. The newer environmental treaties have funding mechanisms that essentially subsidize national compliance with international environmental agreements by compensating states for certain activities in the global interest by picking up the "incremental costs" of developing countries to fulfill their treaty commitments, as in the Montreal Protocol and the Climate Change Convention.[223] Although the impact of these subsidies on the North-South transfers is still relatively small, they amount to "asymmetrical" obligations, differentiated and balanced on grounds of equity.[224]

Notes

1. *See* GURUSWAMY ET AL., *supra* Chapter 1 note 20, at 44.

2. *See* BIRNIE & BOYLE, *supra* Chapter 1 note 3, at 9. For a complete coverage of the sources of international law, see IAN BROWNLIE, PRINCIPLES OF PUBLIC INTERNATIONAL LAW 1-30 (1990).

3. Statute of the International Court of Justice, June 26, 1945, 1976 Y.B.U.N. 1052, 59.Stat. 1031, U.N.T.S. No. 993 (entered into force Oct. 24, 1945). [hereinafter ICJ Statute].

4. *See* GURUSWAMY ET AL., *supra* Chapter 1 note 20, at 45.

5. ICJ Statute, *supra* note 3, art. 38.

6. Vienna Convention on the Law of Treaties, art. 1(1)(a) concluded at Vienna, May 23, 1969, 1155 U.N.T.S. 331 (entered into force Jan. 27, 1980). Although the Vienna Convention has not entered into force for the United States, it is, however, considered to represent generally accepted principles, which the United States has also appeared to accept. *See* Restatement (Third) of Foreign Relations Law of the United States § 325 (1987). This convention also states that it does not apply to and does not affect the legal force of treaties that are not in written form or treaties made between states and other subjects of international law. *See id.* art. 3(a).

7. *Id.* art. 11.

8. *See id.* art. 26. *See* Brownlie, *supra* note 2, at xlviii.

9. Basel Convention on the Control of Transboundary Movements of Hazardous Wastes, concluded at Basel, 22 March 1989, 28 I.L.M. 649 [hereinafter Basel Convention].

10. Montreal Protocol, *supra* Chapter 1 note 25, art. 2.

11. United Nations Convention on the Law of the Sea, concluded at Montego Bay, Dec. 10, 1982, 21 I.L.M. 1261 (1982) [hereinafter UNCLOS].

12. *See* BIRNIE & BOYLE, *supra* Chapter 1 note 3, at 26.

13. *See id.*

14. *See* GURUSWAMY ET AL., *supra* Chapter 1 note 20, at 516.

15. *See* IAEA Convention on Early Notification of a Nuclear Accident, concluded on 26 September 1986, entered into force on October 27, 1986, 25 I.L.M. 1369; IAEA Convention on Assistance in Case of a Nuclear Accident or Radiological Emergency, concluded on September 26 1986, entered into force on Sept. 26, 1987, 25 I.L.M 1377.

16. *See* Patrick Szell, *Ozone Layer and Climate Change, in* ENVIRONMENTAL PROTECTION AND INTERNATIONAL LAW 172 (Wilfried Lang et al. eds., 1991).

17. *See id.*

18. *See* Montreal Protocol—London Amendments, *supra* Chapter 1 note 41, art. 2A, 2B.

19. *See* BIRNIE & BOYLE, *supra* Chapter 1 note 3, at 15-17.

20. Asylum Case (Colom. v. Peru), 1950 I.C.J. 266, 277.

21. BROWNLIE, *supra* note 2, at 6.

22. Daniel Bodansky, *Symposium: Customary (and Not So Customary) International Environmental Law,* 3 IND. J. GLOBAL LEG. STUD. 108 (1995).

23. *North Sea Continental Shelf* cases, I.C.J. Reports, (1969), p.44, ¶ 77. Nicaragua.v. United States (Merits), I.C.J. Reports, (1986), p.14 .

24. Bodansky, *supra* note 22, at 108.

25. *See* BIRNIE & BOYLE, *supra* Chapter 1 note 3, at 16.

26. *See id.*

27. *See id.* at 19.

28. *See* SCHACHTER, *supra* Chapter 1 note 5, at 365.

29. *See* BIRNIE & BOYLE, *supra* Chapter 1 note 3, at 21-24.

30. Bodansky, *supra* note 22, at n.56.

31. Brownlie, *supra* note 2, at 16.

32. *See id.* at 18.

33. *See id.* at 27. This is to be distinguished from *ex aequo et bono* in art. 38(2) of the Statute of the International Court of Justice which refers to a special power conferred on the Court, to be used if the parties to the dispute agree to it. In the *Free Zones* case, the Court described the power as one prescribing "a settlement disregarding rights recognized by it [the Court] and taking into account considerations of pure expediency,. . ." although it expressed doubts whether it had such a power. Free Zones Case (1930), PCIJ, Ser. A, no.24. *See also* BROWNLIE, *supra* note 2, at 27.

34. *See id.* at 26.

35. *Id.*

36. *Diversion of Water from the River Meuse* cases, P.C.I.J., Ser. A/B, No. 70, 76,(1937).

37. ICJ Statute, *supra* note 3, art. 59.

38. LOUIS HENKIN ET AL., INTERNATIONAL LAW 107 (2nd ed. 1987).

39. *See id.* at 108.

40. *See id.*

41. *See* BIRNIE & BOYLE, *supra* Chapter 1 note 3, at 24.

42. *See* HENKIN, *supra* note 38, at 109.

43. *See infra* note 86 and accompanying text. *See also* BIRNIE & BOYLE, *supra* Chapter 1 note 3, at 11.

44. *See* HENKIN, *supra* note 38, at 111.

45. *See id.* at 112.

46. *See id.* at 111-112.

47. *See* BIRNIE & BOYLE, *supra* Chapter 1 note 3, at 19.

48. Paul Szasz, *International Norm Making, in* ENVIRONMENTAL CHANGE AND INTERNATIONAL LAW 43(Edith Brown Weiss ed., 1992).

49. *See* BIRNIE & BOYLE, *supra* Chapter 1 note 3, at 16.

50. *See id.* at 26-27.

51. *See* Bodansky, *supra* note 22, at 111.

52. *See id.* at 112.

53. Declaration of the United Nations Conference on the Human Environment, adopted June 16, 1972, U.N. Doc. A/CONF.48/14 at 2-65 and Corr.1 (1972), 11 I.L.M. 1416, 1420 (1972) [hereinafter Stockholm Declaration]. The Stockholm Declaration was unanimously adopted at the Stockholm Conference and later endorsed by the United Nations General Assembly. For a discussion of the Stockholm Declaration, see *infra* text following note 111.

54. *Id.*, art. 21.

55. *See* SCHACHTER, *supra* Chapter 1 note 5, at 363.

56. *See* ALEXANDRE KISS & DINAH SHELTON, INTERNATIONAL ENVIRONMENTAL LAW 40 (1991).

57. *See* SCHACHTER, *supra* Chapter 1 note 5, at 364. *See also* Hans Christian Bugge, *International Environmental Law-Status and Challenges, in* INTERNATIONAL ENVIRONMENTAL LAW 59 (Erling Selvig & Hans Christian Bugge eds., 1995) (pointing out that there are still large amounts of transboundary pollution in the world, which in practice seems to be accepted or at least against which few sanctionary measures are imposed).

58. *See* Edith Brown Weiss, *Environmental Equity: The Imperative for the Twenty-First Century, in* SUSTAINABLE DEVELOPMENT AND INTERNATIONAL LAW 18 (Winfried Lang ed., 1995).

59. *See* Bodansky, *supra* note 22, at 119.

60. *See id.*

61. *See id.* at 114-15.

62. *See id.* at 115.

63. SCHACHTER, *supra* Chapter 1 note 5, at 60.

64. *Id.*

65. *See* BIRNIE & BOYLE, *supra* Chapter 1 note 3, at 27.

66. *See* Weiss, *supra* Chapter 1 note 24, at 686.

67. *See id.* at 27.

68. *See id.*

69. Bodansky, *supra* note 22, at 118.

70. *See* Weiss, *supra* Chapter 1 note 24, at 708.

71. *See* BIRNIE & BOYLE, *supra* Chapter 1 note 3, at 27-28.

72. *See id* at 27. *See also* UNEP Environmental Law Guidelines and Principles, Dec. 14/30 of the Governing Council of UNEP of June 17, 1987; Basel Convention, *supra* note 9. *See* BIRNIE & BOYLE, *supra* Chapter 1 note 3, at 27.

73. *See* discussion *infra* Chapter 5 (in regards to promoting the participation of developing states-incentives and disincentives in some international environmental agreements).

74. *See* Weiss, *supra* Chapter 1 note 24, at 675.

75. Treaty Relating to Boundary Waters Between the United States and Canada, Jan. 11, 1909, U.S.-Gr. Brit., 36 U.S.T. 2448.

76. *See* Weiss, *supra* Chapter 1 note 24, at 675.

77. *See* CALDWELL, *supra* Chapter 1 note 12, at 22.

78. International Convention for the Protection of Birds Useful to Agriculture, Mar. 19, 1902, 102 B.F.S.P. 969. *See* Kiss & Shelton, *supra* note 56, at 34.

79. Treaty for the Preservation and Protection of Fur Seals, Feb. 7, 1911, U.S.-Gr. Brit. 37 U.S.T. 1538, 104 B.F.S.P. 175.

80. *See* KISS & SHELTON, *supra* note 56, at 33.

81. *See* Weiss *supra* Chapter 1 note 24, at 676.

82. *See* Convention Relative to the Preservation of Fauna and Flora in their Natural State, Nov. 8, 1933, 172 U.N.T.S. 241.

83. *See* Convention on Nature Protection and Wildlife Preservation in the Western Hemisphere, Oct. 12, 1940, 161 U.N.T.S. 194. *See also* Weiss, *supra* note 24 at 676.

84. *See* Philippe Sands, *International Law in the Field of Sustainable Development: Emerging Legal Principles, in* SUSTAINABLE DEVELOPMENT AND INTERNATIONAL LAW 63 (Winfried Lang ed., 1995).

85. *See* Weiss, *supra* Chapter 1 note 24, at 677. This view is not shared by all scholars. *See* discussion *supra* following note 55 (in regards to Principle 21 of the Stockholm Declaration, which is based on the *Trail Smelter* case).

86. Trail Smelter Case, 1941, 3 UN Rep. Int'l Arbitral Awards 1911 (1941). This principle was confirmed in more general terms in the *Corfu Channel* case, I.C.J. Reports (1949) 22, and later, in the *Lake Lanoux* case, 12 U.N. Reports on Int'l Arbitral Awards, v. XII, 281, at 303 (1957).

87. *See* Weiss, *supra* Chapter 1 note 24, at 677.

88. Trail Smelter Case, *supra* note 86, at 1965.

89. *See* Stockholm Declaration, *supra* note 53 and accompanying text.

90. *See Proceedings of the UN Scientific Conference on the Conservation and Utilization of Resources*, U.N. Doc. A/Conf.10.7, 1956.

91. *See* CALDWELL, *supra* Chapter 1 note 12, at 44.

92. *See* Sands, *supra* Chapter 1 note 21, at xxv. *See also* CALDWELL, *id.* at 44.

93. *See* HARALD HOHMANN, PRECAUTIONARY LEGAL DUTIES AND PRINCIPLES OF MODERN INTERNATIONAL ENVIRONMENTAL LAW 3 (1994).

94. *See* KISS & SHELTON, *supra* note 56, at 35.

95. *See* International Convention for the Prevention of Pollution of the Sea by Oil, May 12, 1954, 327 U.N.T.S. 3. *See* KISS & SHELTON, *supra* note 56, at 35 (applied to ships' oil discharge). Superseded by MARPOL, *infra* note 96.

96. *See* International Convention for the Prevention of Pollution by Ships, Nov. 2, 1973, 12 I.L.M. 1319 (1973)[hereinafter MARPOL].

97. *See* RACHEL CARSON, SILENT SPRING (1962) (concerning the new chemical pesticide technology).

98. *See* Weiss, *supra* Chapter 1 note 24, at 677.

99. *See* Federal Insecticide, Fungicide, and Rodenticide Act, 7 U.S.C.A. § 136a-y (1947).

100. *See* CALDWELL, *supra* Chapter 1 note 12, at 29.

101. *See id.*

102. *See* KISS & SHELTON, *supra* note 56, at 38.

103. *See* Convention Relating to Intervention on the High Seas in Cases of Oil Pollution Casualties, Nov.29, 1969, 970 U.N.T.S. 211, 9 I.L.M. 25.

104. *See* Convention on Civil Liability for Oil Pollution Damage, Nov. 29, 1969, 12 U.S.T. 2989.

105. *See* Agreement for Cooperation in Dealing with Pollution of the North Sea by Oil, June 9, 1969, 704 U.N.T.S. 3. *See* Weiss *supra* Chapter 1 note 24, at 678.

106. *See* The Declaration on Air Pollution Control, Mar. 8, 1968, in Res. 68(4) of the Committee of Ministers, Council of Europe, reprinted in BASIC DOCUMENTS OF INTERNATIONAL ENVIRONMENTAL LAW doc. 19 (Harald Hohmann ed., 1992). *See* KISS & SHELTON, *supra* note 56, at 37.

107. *See* African Convention on the Conservation of Nature and Natural Resources, Sept. 15, 1968, 1001 U.N.T.S. 3.

108. *See* KISS & SHELTON, *supra* note 56, at 37.

109. *See* The Intergovernmental Conference of Experts on a Scientific Basis for a Rational Use and Conservation of the Resources of the Biosphere, Sept. 1968, *reprinted in* UNESCO, USE AND CONSERVATION OF THE BIOSPHERE, PROCEEDINGS OF THE INTERGOVERNMENTAL CONFERENCE OF EXPERTS ON A SCIENTIFIC BASIS FOR A RATIONAL USE AND CONSERVATION OF THE RESOURCES OF THE BIOSPHERE (1970).

110. *See* Caldwell, *supra* Chapter 1 note 12, at 45. Biosphere is defined as the "[r]egions of [the] earth's crust and atmosphere occupied by living matter." THE CONCISE OXFORD DICTIONARY 97 (6th ed. 1976).

111. *See* Report on the Stockholm Conference, *supra* Chapter 1 note 11.

112. Draft Resolution 2398 (XXIII).

113. *See* CALDWELL, *supra* Chapter 1 note 12, at 30.

114. Leonard, H. Jeffrey & David Morell, *Emergence of Environmental Concern in Developing Countries: A Political Perspective*, 17 STAN. J. INT'L L. 281 (1981).

115. *See* Cheng Zheng-Kang, *Equity, Special Considerations, and the Third World*, 1 COLO. J. INT'L ENVTL. L. & POL'Y 66 (1990).

116. *Id.* at 63.

117. CALDWELL, *supra* Chapter 1 note 12, at 3.

118. *See id.* at 58. UNEP was established through the General Assembly Resolution 2997 (XXVII) Institutional and Financial Arrangements for International Environmental Cooperation, G.A. Res. 2997, 27 UN GAOR Supp. (No.30), UN Doc. A/8730 (1972).

119. *See* Report of the Stockholm Conference, *supra* Chapter 1 note 11, at 72.

120. *See* discussion *supra* text accompanying and following note 53.

121. *See* SCHACHTER, *supra* Chapter 1 note 5, at 363.

122. *See* CALDWELL, *supra* Chapter 1 note 12, at 30.

123. *See* Weiss, *supra* Chapter 1 note 24, at 678.

124. *See* Convention for the Protection of World Cultural and Natural Heritage, Nov. 23, 1972, 1037 U.N.T.S. 151.

125. *See* Convention on International Trade in Endangered Species of Wild Fauna and Flora, Mar. 3, 1973, 993 U.N.T.S. 243.

126. *See* Convention on the Prevention of Marine Pollution by Dumping of Wastes and Other Matter, Dec. 29, 1972, 1046 U.N.T.S. 120.

127. *See* International Convention for the Prevention of Pollution by Ships, Nov.2, 1973, 12 I.L.M. 1337.

128. *See* Barcelona Convention for the Protection of the Mediterranean Sea Against Pollution, Feb. 16, 1976, 15 I.L.M. 290.

129. *See* Weiss, *supra* Chapter 1 note 24, at 678.

130. *See* KISS & SHELTON, *supra* note 56, at 6.

131. *See id.*

132. UNCLOS, *supra* note 11.

133. *See* Sands, *supra* Chapter 1 note 21, at xxvii.

134. *See* Vienna Convention for the Protection of the Ozone Layer, Mar. 22, 1985, 26 I.L.M. 1529 [hereinafter Vienna Convention]. In the early 1970s scientists began theorizing that CFCs were depleting the stratospheric ozone layer. Later, in the 1980s, this theory was confirmed. When released into the atmosphere, CFCs destroy the ozone molecule, thus depleting the ozone layer. The stratospheric ozone layer shields the earth from harmful ultra violet rays that can cause skin cancer, cataracts, and inhibit plant development. CFCs, invented in 1928, are non-toxic, unusually stable, and non-flammable chemical compounds used in refrigerators and air conditioners, among other things.

135. *See* BIRNIE & BOYLE, *supra* Chapter 1 note 3, at 406.

136. *See* Montreal Protocol, *supra* Chapter 1 note 25.

137. *See* Framework Convention on Climate Change, May 29, 1992, 31 I.L.M. 849 (1992), entered into force March 21, 1994 [hereinafter Climate Change Convention].

138. *See* Convention on Long-Range Transboundary Air Pollution, Nov. 13, 1979, 18 I.L.M. 1442.

139. *See* Yves Berthelot, *International Response to Environmental Challenges*, *in* INTERNATIONAL ENVIRONMENTAL LAW 66 (Erling Selvig & Hans Christian Bugge eds., 1994).

140. *See* Bamako Convention on the Ban of the Import into Africa and the Control of Transboundary Movement and Management of Hazardous Wastes Within Africa, Jan. 29, 1991, 30 I.L.M. 773. *See* Weiss *supra* Chapter 1 note 24, at 683.

141. *See* ASEAN Agreement on the Conservation of Nature and Natural Resources, July 9, 1985, reprinted in BASIC DOCUMENTS OF INTERNATIONAL ENVIRONMENTAL LAW, 1550 treaty no. 70 (Harald Hohmann ed., 1992).

142. *See* Weiss, *supra* Chapter 1 note 24, at 683.

143. *See* Nordic Environmental Protection Convention, Feb. 19, 1974, 13 I.L.M. 591 (1974).

144. *See* Treaty Establishing the European Economic Community, Mar. 25, 1957, 298 U.N.T.S. 11.

145. *See* Single European Act, Feb. 17, 1986, 25 I.L.M. 503.

146. *See* Treaty on European Union and Final Act, Feb. 7, 1992, 31 I.L.M. 247.

147. VED NANDA, INTERNATIONAL ENVIRONMENTAL LAW AND POLICY 205 (1995).

148. *See* General Agreement on Tariffs and Trade, Oct. 30, 1947, 55 U.N.T.S. 187 [hereinafter GATT].

149. *See* Sands, *supra* Chapter 1 note 21, at xxvii.

150. *See* discussion *infra* Chapter 6 (in regards to the world bank).

151. *See* Kenneth Piddington, *The Role of the World Bank*, *in* THE INTERNATIONAL POLITICS OF THE ENVIRONMENT 225 (Andrew Hurrell and Benedict Kingsbury eds., 1992).

152. *See* discussion *infra* Chapter 5 (in regards to treaty provisions).

153. *See* Montreal Protocol—London Amendments, *supra* Chapter 1 note 41.

154. *See* discussion *infra* Chapter 5 (in regards to financial assistance: financing implementation of the agreements).

155. *See* Sands, *supra* Chapter 1 note 21, at xxvii.

156. *See id.* at xxviii. *See* discussion *infra* Chapter 7 (in regards to GEF).

157. *See* discussion *supra* text following note 46 (in regards to "soft law").

158. *See* UNEP 1978 draft Principles of Conduct in the Field of the Environment for the Guidance of States in the Conservation and Utilization of Natural Resources Shared by Two or More States, 17 I.L.M. 1097 (1978).

159. *See* Sands, *supra* Chapter 1 note 21, at xxviii.

160. *See* World Charter for Nature, Oct. 28, 1982, G.A.Res. 37/7, 23 I.L.M. 455.

161. *See* BIRNIE & BOYLE, *supra* Chapter 1 note 3, at 27, 432. *See* Kiss and Shelton, *supra* note 56, at 48.

162. Approved by UNGA Resolution 42/187 adopted in December, 1987 by consensus, without a vote. *See* GURUSWAMY ET AL., *supra Chapter 1,* note 15.

163. *See* BIRNIE & BOYLE, *supra* Chapter 1 note 3, at 4.

164. Rio Conference, *supra* Chapter 1 note 18.

165. Meeting with Frank P. Grad, Professor of Law, Columbia University School of Law (Oct. 22, 1996).

166. Kyoto Protocol to the United Nations Framework Convention on Climate Change, Dec.11, 1997, UN Doc. FCCC/CP/1997/7/Add.1 (1997) [hereinafter Kyoto Protocol]. The Kyoto Protocol has not yet entered into force.

167. Climate Change Convention, *supra* note 137.

168. The Convention on Biological Diversity, June 5, 1992, 31 I.L.M. 822 (1992) (entered into force Dec. 29, 1993).

169. *See* discussion *infra* Chapter 5 (in regards to treaty provisions).

170. *See* Rio Declaration, *supra* Chapter 1 note 20.

171. *See* Non-Legally Binding Authoritative Statement of Principles for a Global Consensus on the Management, Conservation and Sustainable Development of All Types of Forests, June 13, 1992, 31 I.L.M. 881 [hereinafter Forest Principles].

172. *See* Agenda 21, *supra* Chapter 1 note 8.

173. *See* John Dernbach, *U.S. Adherence to Its Agenda 21 Commitments: A Five-Year Review*, 27 ELR 10505 (1997).

174. *See id.*

175. *See* discussion *infra* Chapter 8 (in regards to the role of non-governmental organizations and other major groups in promoting universal participation).

176. *See* discussion *infra* Chapter 6 (in regards to international institutional structures).

177. *See* Rio Declaration, *supra* Chapter 1 note 20, art. 3.

178. *See* THE EARTH SUMMIT: THE UNITED NATIONS CONFERENCE ON ENVIRONMENT AND DEVELOPMENT (UNCED) 117 (Stanley Johnson ed., 1993).

179. Forest Principles, *supra* note 171, preamble, ¶ b.

180. *See* Report of the Ad Hoc Intergovernmental Panel on Forests, E/CN.17/1997/12, Feb. 12, 1997.

181. *See* discussion *infra* Chapter 6 (in regards to CSD).

182. *See* Agreement for the Implementation of the Provisions of the United Nations Convention on the Law of the Sea of Dec. 10, 1982 Relating to the Conserva-

tion and Management of Straddling Fish Stocks and Highly Migratory Fish Stocks (New York, Dec. 4, 1995), Doc. A/CONF.164/22/Rev.1.

183. *See* UN Global Conference on the Sustainable Development of Small Island Developing States, Barbados, Apr. 25-May 6, 1994, U.N. Doc. A/CONF.167/9.

184. *See* Report of the International Conference on Population and Development, Cairo, U.N. Doc. A/CONF.171/13/Add.1 (1994).

185. *See* Fourth World Conference of Women, Beijing, U.N. Doc. A/CONF.177/20 (1995).

186. *See* Report of the World Summit for Social Development, Copenhagen, U.N. Doc. A/CONF.166/9, Copenhagen (1995).

187. *See* Convention to Combat Desertification in Those Countries Experiencing Serious Drought and/or Desertification, Particularly in Africa, June 17, 1994, 33 I.L.M. 1332 [hereinafter Desertification Convention].

188. *See* discussion *infra* Chapter 5 (in regards to treaty provisions).

189. *See* United Nations, *United Nations General Assembly Special Session* (visited Aug. 15, 1997) <http://www.un.org> [hereinafter UNGASS]. Also referred to as Earth Summit +5.

190. U.N.GAOR, Programme for the Further Implementation of Agenda 21, (unedited edition July 1, 1997), ¶ 4.

191. *See id.* ¶ 6.

192. *See* discussion *infra* Chapter 5 (in regards to treaty provisions).

193. *See* U.N. CHARTER, art. 2, 1 U.N.T.S. xvi ¶ 1 ("The Organization is based on the principle of the sovereign equality of all its Members."). *See also* Brownlie, *supra* note 2, at 287; ALF ROSS, A TEXTBOOK OF INTERNATIONAL LAW 35 (1980).

194. *See* discussion *supra* text accompanying and following note 53 (in regards to Stockholm Principle 21).

195. *See* discussion *infra* Chapter 6 (in regards to 'Conditionality').

196. *See* Jacob D. Werksman, *Greening Bretton Woods, in* GREENING INTERNATIONAL LAW 76 (Philippe Sands ed., 1994).

197. *See* discussion *supra* text accompanying and following note 6.

198. *See* CARL AUGUST FLEISCHER, FOLKERETT [INTERNATIONAL LAW] 17,18 (1984). *See also* LOUIS HENKIN, HOW NATIONS BEHAVE 45 (1970).

199. *See* Peter H. Sand, *Trusts for the Earth: New International Financial Mechanisms for Sustainable Development, in* SUSTAINABLE DEVELOPMENT AND INTERNATIONAL LAW 183 (Winfried Lang ed., 1995).

200. Bugge, *supra* note 57, at 57.

201. *See* discussion *supra* text accompanying and following note 33 (in regards to sources of international environmental law).

202. OSCAR SCHACHTER, SHARING THE WORLD'S RESOURCES 7 (1977) (emphasis added).

203. *See* Weiss, *supra* Chapter 1 note 24, at 702.

204. Sands, *supra* note 84, at 60.

205. *See* Letter from Frank P. Grad, Professor of Law, Columbia University School of Law (June 24, 1996).

206. *See* Gunther Handl, *Environmental Security and Global Change: The Challenge to International Law,* 1 YB INT'L. ENV. L. 29 (1990).

207. *See* discussion *infra* Chapter 5 (in regards to treaty provisions).

208. *See* discussion *infra* Chapter 5 (in regards to Climate Change Convention and Kyoto Protocol).

209. Rio Declaration, *supra* Chapter 1 note 20, Principle 7; *see also* discussion *infra* chs. IV and V.

210. *See* GATT, *supra* note 148, at 187, 252.

211. *See* Weiss, *supra* Chapter 1 note 24, at 702.

212. *See id.*

213. This type of equity is one of five uses distinguished by Schachter. *See* HENKIN ET AL., *supra* note 38, at 102.

214. *See* Weiss, *supra* Chapter 1 note 24, at 704.

215. *See id.* at 705.

216. *See* Letter from Oscar Schachter, Professor of Law, Columbia University School of Law (Feb. 12, 1997).

217. *See id.*

218. *See id.*

219. SCHACHTER, *supra* note 202, at 16.

220. *See id.* at 8.

221. *See id. See also* U.N. Doc. A/46/138, E/1991/52 ¶ 26 (which refers to a widespread commitment, in bilateral and multilateral development assistance, by way of enunciation of policy, which in turn has been followed by procedures and institutional arrangements to put the policy into effect).

222. SCHACHTER, *supra* note 202, at 16.

223. *See* Sand, *supra* note 199, at 183. *See* also discussion *infra* Chapters. IV and V.

224. *See id.*, at 183.

3

Sustainable Development

Integrating Environment and Development

Definition

Sustainable development is a highly debated concept that came into common usage in international agreements after the Brundtland Commission published its report in 1987.[1] Its predecessor was 'ecodevelopment', a concept developed by Maurice Strong at the time he was Secretary-General of the Stockholm Conference.[2] It symbolized a synthesis of development and environmental protection, describing an ideal strategy.[3] However, because of obstacles in its attainment, such as lack of integrated planning and management, the concept lost some of its popularity.[4] Believed to emphasize ecological considerations more than development, the term did not take hold among governments.[5] A new term for a new approach became the concept known as "sustainable development," without losing an environmental content.[6]

In its report, the Brundtland Commission defined sustainable development as "development that meets the needs of the present without compromising the ability of future generations to meet their own needs."[7] The report stated that the major objective of development is the satisfaction of human needs and aspirations.[8] The term sustainable development was described as containing two key concepts:

- the concept of 'needs', in particular the essential needs of the world's poor, to which overriding priority should be given; and
- the idea of limitations imposed by the state of technology and social organizations on the environment's ability to meet present and future needs.[9]

The Brundtland Commission emphasized human needs and the use of economic growth as a means of meeting these needs, but it did impose a limit to such growth: "At a minimum, sustainable development must not endanger the natural systems that support life on Earth: the atmosphere, the waters, the soils, and the living beings."[10] The report states that "the strategy for sustainable development aims to promote harmony among human beings and between humanity and nature." Sustainable development necessitates respect for the environmental life-support system of the planet and the unimpairment of its renewable capabilities,[11] living off of nature's "income," rather than dissipating its "capital."[12] Solow explains sustainability in terms of conserving the generalized capacity to produce economic well-being for the very long term.[13]

In addition, the Brundtland Commission pointed out that sustainable development must take place in all countries—developed and developing.[14] For industrialized and developing countries alike, a change in values, attitudes, and policies is required in order to expand and sustain the ecological basis of development. The Commission's report noted that integration of environmental considerations into all policy-making and planning is crucial if sustainable growth is to be achieved. The report also emphasized the importance of sustainable development especially in developing countries where poverty is the main source of environmental degradation. Development would provide the funding to protect and restore the environment.

Development by itself, however, is not enough.[15] Poverty and development can coexist, and can jeopardize the environment.[16] As Cairncross aptly notes, "Economic growth that relies on destroying the environment may enrich the most powerful, but impoverish the weak."[17] Therefore, sustainable development prescribes that societies meet human needs by increasing growth potential—while sustaining the ecosystem's overall integrity—and by ensuring equitable opportunities for all.[18]

Sustainable development could be described as representing a compromise between economic interests and environmental interests. "Business as usual," meaning economic growth with no restraints, can no longer continue, given the limits to the capacity of the global environment to accommodate ever-increasing resource use. Environmental protection is needed to uphold economic development in the long term. On the other hand, environmental protection measures now have to take socio-economic considerations into account, which in many cases means a lowering of the standards for developing countries for an initial period, giving them a chance to "catch up" with regard to environmental regulations and administration.

Sustainable development has become a popular concept mainly because it is so ambiguous that it has come to mean different things to different ideological groups. One scholar states that some groups grasp the concept of sustainable development in the sense that the environment can be traded off for other assets of value that can be of use for future generations, such as money, factories, and schools, instead of recognizing the environment as the basis for development in the future.[19] Such ideological groups interpret the environment as a minor chess piece that can be exchanged, whereas the environment could be characterized as the chessboard that is being played on.[20] A good example of the former type of interpretation of the concept, was the plan proposed by a former Venezuelan President called "Plan for Sustainable Development in Southern Bolivar State." This plan included the relaxation of environmental regulations to promote large-scale mining in areas that include a national park and a forest reserve—regions that are supposed to be under government protection.[21]

With the international environmental agreements and other instruments adopted at UNCED, emphasizing the integration of environment and development, some of the ambiguity concerning sustainable development has been removed. Agenda 21 and the Rio Declaration provide some guidance on the concepts meaning.

Furthermore, now that the Kyoto Protocol[22] to the Climate Change Convention has been adopted, assuming it comes into force, requiring emission reductions of greenhouse gases (GHGs), the concept of sustainable development has become much more clear and operational. The Kyoto Protocol will provide the specific parameters giving the concept of sustainable development meaning and enabling it to be concretely implemented.[23] The Kyoto Protocol as examined below, places limits on emissions of carbon dioxide and five other greenhouse gases, to be achieved in part by market-based mechanisms such as joint implementation[24] and emissions trading.[25] These mechanisms will lead to energy efficiency and by implementing their commitments the developed countries will begin to internalize the environmental costs of greenhouse gas emissions. The Protocol will fill the gap produced by the market's failure to internalize the environmental cost of the use of the natural resources.[26] Now local economic development decisions will begin to reflect adverse global effects.[27]

Through joint implementation projects to be carried out between industrialized and developing countries, in accordance with the Clean Development Mechanism (CDM) of the Kyoto Protocol,[28] energy efficient technology will be transferred to developing countries. Hopefully in the near future, other developing countries will be joining Argentina in making voluntary commitments to reduce their GHG emissions, possibly through a phased-in period.[29]

What Is International Law for Sustainable Development?

Elizabeth Dowdeswell, the former head of UNEP, has stated that one might equate international law for sustainable development with international environmental law, describing how emerging international environmental instruments routinely consider socio-economic or developmental dimensions with environmental issues, which, she asserted, is what sustainable development is all about.[30]

However, several authorities disagree with Dowdeswell's statement. Williams Silveira asserts that: "the concept of sustainable development represents not the evolution of environmental law but a paradigmatic shift. . . . In fact, while the two are certainly interrelated, there is a paradigmatic shift between "environment" and "sustainable development". To miss this point is largely to ignore the concerns of developing countries."[31] I do, however, think there has been an evolution of international environmental law as shown above,[32] precisely in the direction of considering the concerns of the developing countries, as is the case in the Montreal Protocol where developing countries were given a delayed compliance schedule. On the other hand, I would agree that sustainable development encompasses more than "environment." Sustainable development is a new goal for the international community, broadening the perspective and considering issues such as poverty alleviation, and the right to development. Sustainable development, after all, is the integration of environment and development.

The United Nations Resolution 44/228, adopted by the General Assembly, set out the framework for the UNCED conference and stated that the Conference should, in addressing environmental issues in the development context, have as one of its objectives "To further development of international environmental law. . . . " There is no reference in the whole resolution to "the further development of international law in the field of sustainable development," a phrase later used in the Rio Declaration and Agenda 21, which were adopted at the UNCED Conference. Why the word "further" was used in the second instance is an enigma, since this is potentially an entirely new field of law.[33]

Williams Silveira, among others, considers the international law of sustainable development to be a new branch of international law. This new field of law, Ruis asserts, does not supersede international environmental law, but is considered an overarching branch, which includes international environmental law, international development law, labor law, and all the other areas mentioned in Agenda 21.[34] Neither the Rio Declaration, nor Agenda 21 define this new area of law.[35] However, Agenda 21 is described as addressing problems in "virtually all of the sectoral and cross-sectoral areas of human activity."[36] It is considered—just like the Rio Declaration—to be a comprehensive document in that it attempts to "address the full range of legal principles and political objectives, at international, regional, and national levels to reach sustainable development."[37] From this, one could deduce that international law for sustainable development is a field of law that regulates all areas of human activity in pursuit of sustainable development.

Traditionally, international law is defined as the body of legal rules binding upon states in their relations with one another.[38] However, international law of sustainable development would be broader than that because it also covers non-state actors—such as local authorities—which encompass the national level, in addition to the international level. Developing a new branch of international law that is so broad that it goes beyond even international law, seems like an unwieldy proposition.

Furthermore, in order for there to be an international law of sustainable development, some legal scholars consider the need for a body of law to have its own sources and methods of lawmaking deriving from principles characteristic or exclusive to sustainable development issues.[39] So far, only 'principles' have emanated from the work of the United Nations Division for Sustainable Development.[40] Yet the majority of these principles are not new; they are derived from international environmental law, such as the polluter-pays principle, or international development law, such as the right to development.

On the other hand, Grey argues that legal heuristic concepts once separated or grouped together, organize a practical field and that such groupings of legal rules affect their substance over time.[41] In addition, he states that we tend to underrate the long-term effect of our categorizations and conceptualizations on the way lawyers think about the materials.[42] Even if one considered international law of sustainable development as merely a relabeling of existing fields of law, this could be done for a special purpose, such as increasing the awareness of the interdependence of environmental, social, and economic issues. Yet if it is such a broad, all-encompassing field, there is the likelihood that its own unwieldiness would overcome any positive effects it might have contributed to jurisprudence.

Rather than developing a new branch of international law—international law of sustainable development—I agree with Howard Mann who suggests sustainable development could be the key principle: "In this sense, the contribution to achieving sustainable development could become the key test for assessing the continued legitimacy of existing law, and for evaluating new law regardless of its source."[43] Instead of defining a new overarching branch of law, international law would be looked upon as being pro sustainable development, ensuring that all existing branches of international law would continue to progress, each making its own contribution towards the goal of sustainable development.[44]

Sustainable Development as a Basic Standard of Appraisal

Sustainable development is rapidly becoming the basic standard against which international environmental activities are being appraised politically.[45] Handl states that the concept suffers from internal strain because 'sustainable development' as an international policy or legal concept implies some measure of international accountability, while at the same time it is coupled by an express disclaimer of any intended interference upon state sovereignty.[46] Especially Principle 21 of the Stockholm Declaration (and likewise Principle 2 of the Rio Declaration) reflect this internal contradictory aspect of the concept: the sovereign right of nations to use their natural resources according to their environmental (and developmental) policies, and the obligation to prevent damage that such use may do to other nations or the global commons. However, the internal strain Handl is referring to, is dissipating as there is an apparent trend to impose duties on States with respect to the management of their natural resources to ensure sustainable production and consumption.[47]

Clearly, state sovereignty has waned as more and more nations are becoming parties to international environmental agreements, such as conservation of biological diversity, as set forth in the Convention on Biological Diversity.[48] Earlier such regulations would have been considered an intervention in domestic affairs. In addition, by asserting a general or customary international environmental law obligation to prevent and minimize harm and appreciable risk, as for instance through Principle 21 of the Stockholm Declaration, it is clear that states also recognize that trans-boundary environmental injury is no longer exclusively within the sovereign authority of States.[49] Perhaps with time, the state sovereignty issue in this context will become moot as more and more nations develop their environmental (and developmental) policies in accordance with international agreements and standards. I have stated the ideal situation, but as Schachter points out [in the real world of state practice] market forces prevail. [50] One has yet to see strong evidence that we are going in the direction of sustainable development, other than on paper.

Sustainable Development Indicators

Handl states that one has yet to reach a clear international perception of pathways to sustainable development and agreement on the specific markers that lead to that objective.[51] Following what was envisaged by Agenda 21, several efforts have been made to develop such an internationally accepted system of markers. These indicators provide parameters needed to clarify the operational side of sustainable development, providing a picture of human well-being, national wealth and development.

In the fall of 1995, the World Bank presented its report: "Monitoring Environmental Progress"[52] which describes indicators that can measure whether environmental conditions are getting better or worse. Then in 1996, a more comprehensive set of indicators, the "Framework and Methodologies" was completed for CSD and was tested by 16 states.[53] It has 134 indicators, including economic, social, environmental, and institutional aspects.[54] Programs have also been established in 30 countries, some of them using the CSD indicators. CSD's work program on indicators of sustainable development should result in a practical set of indicators by the year 2000.[55]

Definition of Equity for Environmentally Sustainable Development

The Rio Conference once again placed the focus on the need for a more equitable distribution of resources among States.[56] In this context, Weiss states that four issues need to be addressed in developing a new definition of equity for environmentally sustainable development: 1) that the global environment knows no political boundaries, meaning there is an incentive for all states to reach agreement on an "equitable and efficient basis for allocating responsibility for maintaining the planet"; 2) developing and developed countries each have control over resources that are needed by the others, giving developing countries bargaining power; 3) developing countries probably will suffer most from environmental degradation because poverty is a primary cause of that degradation and they have the least capacity to adapt when global environmental change occurs; 4) future generations, whose interests have not been identified and sufficiently represented in negotiations, are becoming parties to debates about equity.[57]

Regarding bargaining power, the developing countries are now using some of their natural resources as "bargaining chips" because they have become of increasing international importance, such as the tropical rainforests in terms of biodiversity.[58] The use of such a "bargaining chip" took place during the negotiations of the Convention on Biological Diversity.[59] The developing countries perceived that the foremost areas of biological diversity were located within their boundaries, giving them bargaining power in the negotiations.[60] This bargaining power lead the developing countries to negotiate for the inclusion of several articles in the Convention on Biological Diversity for the benefit of developing countries, such as, the sharing of profits from the commercial use of genetic resources[61] and the transfer of technology[62]—in return for the use of genetic resources by the industrialized countries.[63]

Schachter's concept of equity as a redistributive principle based on human needs, as discussed above, also comes into play here. Justifying preferential treatment as determined by actual human needs at the present time presents a balancing act. For instance, should the "actual" needs of a billion Chinese for energy available in coal be given preference over the adverse effects of the resulting green-house gases on small island states which are likely to disappear as a result of rising sea levels due to climate change?[64] Based on Schachter's concept of equity as a redistributive principle, the answer is not a given. The Chinese "energy need" should be dealt with, but not based on the use of coal. They should receive technical and financial assistance in order to use alternative forms of energy, such as natural gas or solar energy. If the coal were to be used because no alternatives were made available or alternative solutions would result in mass starvation, it would have to be a temporary solution with built-in mechanisms to reduce its negative effects.

The Debate Concerning Environment and Development

The Rio Conference also helped reduce the gap, though not eliminate it, between the concepts of environment and development.[65] Economic development must go hand in hand with protection of the environment in order to stay at a sustainable level, where the environment has the capacity to renew itself.[66] Essentially, industrialized countries have as one of their main priorities the need to find solutions to global environmental threats, while most developing countries, struggling with poverty and debt, have given priority to development, rather than being concerned with the environment. There are several issues involved in the debate concerning environment and development, two of which are more relevant in the context of this study.

First, industrialized countries, having already become developed, are recognizing the environmental cost of that development, and realizing that there is a need for change in their production and consumption patterns. The World Bank has coined a phrase I think is most fitting in our context: "The key is not to produce less, but to produce differently."[67] More and more evidence is showing that unwise environmental policies can carry true economic costs, resulting in lost production, wasted investment, or less productivity of labor.[68] The reduction in the productivity of labor can be directly connected to the health effects of pollution, such as chronic respiratory illnesses due to air pollution or diseases due to lack of clean water.[69]

Although it does not mention industrialized countries specifically, the first part of Principle 8 of the Rio Declaration addresses itself to developed countries when it requires that "States should reduce and eliminate unsustainable patterns of production and consumption. . . . "[70] in order to attain the goal of sustainable development. This is a new principle not stated in the 1972 Stockholm Declaration. Agenda 21, the blueprint for action, states: "the major cause of continued deterioration of the global environment is the unsustainable patterns of consumption and production, particularly in the industrialized countries."

Two important factors are essential: One is to move from non-renewable to renewable resources.[71] The other is to use resources efficiently in order to minimize the total use of resources.[72] Getting the prices right, to include ecological cost, is one of the major challenges.[73] The know-how needed to reduce for instance, energy consumption is already available.[74] Sharing knowledge and providing financial assistance to developing countries ensnared with dangerous and outdated technology should take priority.[75]

The underlying elements of Principle 8 are essentially not new, to some extent the principle "codifies" what has been taking place in industrialized countries for some time now. Enterprises and governments alike, are increasingly utilizing environmental impact assessments and environmental audits in their activities, and devising environmentally sound technologies for use in their production processes. Many enterprises which earlier would merely consume environmental assets and consider them "free goods" now recognize the environment as "an indispensable asset for creating a sustainable world."[76] Consumers are also demanding products that do not degrade the environment. In addition, national accounts are beginning to reflect new priorities by including natural resource accounting. As Porras notes, "the Rio Declaration provides a reminder that the intra-generational equity goal of sustainable development can only be achieved if industrialized countries cease to benefit, to the detriment of developing countries, from their ongoing unsustainable practices."[77]

In addition, industrialized nations have acknowledged that developing countries must adopt development models that are sustainable because their own survival depends on it.[78] Were all nations to developed at the rate and the manner in which the developed countries became industrialized, the global environment would have been much worse off than it is today. For instance, if all households in developing nations had refrigerators using CFCs, and CFCs and other ozone-depleting chemicals were used in manufacturing in these countries, then the stratospheric ozone layer would be much more depleted than it is today. Scientists have predicted that without international cooperation, such as the cooperation that produced the Montreal Protocol, the ozone layer—that thin life-protecting layer that absorbs harmful ultraviolet radiation—would be seriously depleted for decades to come.[79] Such depletion would lead to intense radiation that could produce 60 million additional skin cancer cases worldwide by 2075, and major damage to agriculture and aquatic life.[80] As Weiss has aptly noted "no one country or even group of countries has the capability to protect the environment over time by its own efforts alone."[81] All nations must participate in the efforts toward reaching the goal of sustainable development.

Another issue in the debate concerning environment and development, is that developing countries demand technical and financial assistance in order to make their development policies sustainable. However, emphasizing their sovereign right to exploit their natural resources according to their own policies, developing countries are reluctant to accept conditions placed on such assistance. Principle 4 of the Rio Declaration addresses this issue, stating that "[i]n order to achieve sustainable development, environmental protection shall constitute an integral part of the development process and cannot be considered in isolation from it." This principle can be interpreted as requiring that all aspects of economic and other development take environmental considerations into account, and that States and multilateral development Banks are permitted or even required to attach environmental conditionalities on their development loans.[82]

Placing conditions on aid or assistance is common practice in the international arena, just as it is on the domestic plane.[83] The main difference is that the new conditions refer to taking environmental considerations into account, which in the context of international environmental agreements are being required of all nations that are parties to the treaties. Furthermore, it seems reasonable for developing countries to accept environmental conditions if that is the reason for the assistance in the first place: to make the development policies sustainable. If these conditions are in the form of requirements based on universally agreed upon international environmental and development standards, including widespread participation in an open and accountable decision-making process, then they would perhaps be more politically acceptable to the borrower and more likely to be complied with.[84] A good example of such a condition would be the environmental impact assessment which is required for certain projects.

The Brundtland Commission did not elaborate on what kind of development, 'sustainable development' was supposed to be. It only indicated which approach should be used in development planning.[85] This was to integrate environment and development policies. The main virtue of sustainable development is that it restrains the earlier unqualified development concept.[86] Handl notes that the concept has begun to act as a de facto restraint on environmental decision-makers, such as the Valdez Principles, an environmental code of conduct committing U.S. corporations to follow sustainable development policies in their business activities.[87]

Bias toward Development over Environmental Objectives

Using sustainable development as the new goal, the principles in the non-binding Rio Declaration stipulate general rights and obligations with respect to the protection of the global environment. The Rio Declaration has been described as an updated version of the Stockholm Declaration, adding new concepts and concerns and giving more significance to development interests.[88] In the same manner, Handl notes, there is a bias toward development over "environmental/preservationist" objectives.[89]

Principle 2 of the Rio Declaration stating the basic entitlement and the international responsibility of states regarding use of natural resources is a replica of the Stockholm Principle 21, except that it adds 'and developmental' to the policies which States are to follow in regard to the use of their own natural resources.

> States have . . . the sovereign right to exploit their own resources pursuant to their own environmental *and developmental* policies [emphasis added]. . . .[90]

Some authorities use this change in the text as evidence to support the view that the delicate balance between environment and development objectives is being tipped in favor of development interests.[91]

Williams Silveira remarks that: "Sustainable development is not a euphemism for environment. The emphasis is on 'development'—development that proceeds sustainably but proceeds nonetheless."[92] Schachter also notes that the use of the word "sustainable" instead of a specific reference to environment is itself indicative of support for development rather than limitations on development.[93] These kinds of statements can be seen as reinforcing the misgivings that some scholars have expressed regarding sustainable development, that it does not represent a balance between environment and development, but is a way of making it look like the two concepts are being integrated, yet in reality "it's business as usual" . . . "hardly paying lip-service to sustainability."[94]

Perhaps another way to look at this new 'twist' appearing in Principle 2 is that developing countries are getting more of a say in the international arena. Whereas, during earlier negotiations industrialized countries had the upper hand, so to speak, now developing countries have bargaining chips, as mentioned earlier, which they are taking advantage of. One would hope that the consensus reached at Rio, where international cooperation was recognized for the linchpin it is,[95] can be put into practice, steering the international community away from the North-South polarization which is to everyone's detriment and towards sustainable development in the Brundtland Commission and UNCED's sense of the word.[96]

Industrialized countries are becoming more aware of, and slowly accepting the notion that developing countries need more time and assistance than industrialized countries in order to achieve the same or similar environmental objectives. This is also reflected in the Rio Principle 7 which stipulates "common, but differentiated responsibilities" with regard to global environmental degradation, and in the existing international environmental agreements that are being negotiated, where developing countries are given differentiated standards, such as in the Climate Change Convention.[97]

On another note, Handl states that the Rio Conference failed to balance environmental and development concerns in a suitable manner to ensure that qualitative, rather than quantitative development, would predominate as the international community's main tenet.[98] As defined by the Brundtland Commission, sustainable development indicates an anthropocentric or utilitarian interpretation, imposing restraints on development activities to the extent that these would weaken the environmental basis for further development in the future.[99] This definition seems to entail a good standard, limiting exploitation to the carrying capacity of the environment. However, for some scholars this definition does not address the issue of nature's intrinsic value, which would demand a more qualitative development process.[100] Such an eco-centric viewpoint is perhaps important to consider, but it is not likely to win support in an international community that only recently began to realize that it is important to take the environment into account in the development process.

Legal Aspects of the Concept of Sustainable Development

Sands has described the legal elements of the concept of sustainable development as being comprised of at least four separate but related objectives which in Agenda 21 and the Rio Declaration were translated into proposals and principles to govern human activity: 1) the commitment to preserve natural resources for present and future generations, 2) appropriate standards for the exploitation of natural resources, 3) equitable use of natural resources, taking into account the needs of other States and peoples, and 4) requiring that environmental considerations be integrated into economic and other development plans and that development needs be taken into account in the use of environmental measures.[101] To these objectives perhaps one should add a fifth goal: international account-ability.[102] By this, I refer to the responsibility states have to prevent damage that use of their natural resources may do to other nations or the global commons (Principle 21 of the Stockholm Declaration and Principle 2 of the Rio Declaration).

Perhaps one way to prevent such damage would be mandatory reporting requirements for states, obliging them to record the results of their efforts made toward sustainable development—in accordance with their international environmental obligations. These results would then be reported to, for instance, the U.N. Commission on Sustainable Development (CSD) or another similar body, so these results could be reviewed. If the review revealed poor results, the negligent state would be held accountable, either by demanding that it demonstrate new strategies or by using some sort of sanctions. Naturally, technical and financial assistance for developing countries would be built into this reporting system. At present, states are required by Agenda 21 to report to the Commission on Sustainable Development on their implementation of Agenda 21, but this is only voluntary. There are no sanctions involved, and the Commission has no power to impose sanctions.[103] With regard to environmental treaties, the Montreal Protocol does have a mechanism, the non-compliance procedure, which ultimately allows the Meeting of the Parties to "decide upon and call for steps to bring about full compliance with the Protocol," including using cautions and suspensions.[104]

Sustainable development principles

In 1995, an expert group, established to identify principles of international law for sustainable development, gathered all the principles that relate to sustainable development and came up with a group of nineteen principles categorized into five groups as follows: 1) Principle of interrelationship and integration 2) Principles and concepts relating to environment and development, 3) Principles and concepts of international cooperation, 4) Principles and concepts of participation, decision-making and transparency, and 5) Principles and concepts of dispute avoidance and resolution procedures, monitoring and compliance.[105]

Several of these principles are derived from the Stockholm Declaration Principles, which were reiterated, and some of them amended in the Rio Declaration and Agenda 21. The Rio Declaration also draws upon and mirrors principles that had already been adopted in many international environmental agreements and instruments.[106] In addition, the Rio Declaration also includes new principles which earlier had not been universally accepted, such as the right to development.[107] Whether one labels these principles as "principles of sustainable development" or "principles of international law *for* sustainable development" they can still be useful for the interpretation and application of existing legal obligations on the pathway to sustainable development.

Most of the sustainable development principles included in the abovementioned five groups, are relevant in the context of this study, yet some are worth mentioning specifically such as, equity, common but differentiated responsibilities, public participation, access to information, environmental impact assessment, informed decisions-making, and monitoring and compliance with international commitments. These principles are examined, in turn, throughout this study.

Intra-Generational and Inter-Generational Equity

Sustainable development inherently implies intergenerational equity, as do the international environmental agreements that are negotiated.[108] It is development that should benefit present, as well as future generations, in other words sustainable development dictates equity between the generations. Intergenerational equity is considered to be the conceptual or philosophical underpinning of sustainable development.[109]

The Brundtland Commission's Report expanded on the concept of intergenerational equity when it stated that "the narrow notion of physical sustainability implies a concern for social equity between generations, a concern that must logically be extended to equity within each generation."[110] Intra- and intergenerational equity are indeed difficult issues to address, yet this account of using differential treatment for developing countries in order to promote universal participation in international environmental law would not be comprehensive without some discussion of these important matters.

Equity between generations and within generations is often referred to as inter-generational and intra-generational equity, respectively. Intergenerational equity and especially intra-generational equity, were at the core of the Rio Conference in 1992 and formed the basis of many of the instruments adopted there. Before the concept of "intergenerational equity" was introduced, the interests of future generations were referred to in early environmental treaties by terminology such as "safeguarding for future generations," in the International Convention for the Regulation of Whaling.[111] The more recent treaties refer to protecting the resource or ecological systems "for the benefit of present and future generations of humankind," as for instance the Climate Change Convention.[112] Principle 7 of the Rio Declaration, on the other hand, referring to "common, but differential treatment" can be interpreted as requiring intra-generational equity.

One of the most recognized theories on intergenerational equity was introduced by Edith Brown Weiss.[113] Weiss states that the assumption that our descendants would inherit better conditions than we have, has now been brought into question because of our power to alter the planet irreversibly. This, Weiss explains, is the reason we must now concern ourselves with the condition of the natural and cultural heritage that we will pass on to future generations, including our own rights of access to and the benefits of the legacy we have received from past generations.[114] The question of the legacy for future generations was brought into focus already in 1972 with the "Project on the Predicament of Mankind," initiated by the Club of Rome, which resulted in the report called "Limits to Growth."[115]

The authors demonstrated through a computer model called "World3," that the limits to growth would be reached within the year 2072.[116] This was done under the assumption that the growth trends in population, industrial production, pollution, and resource depletion would continue unchanged. The report also stated that humanity had a choice, and could choose an alternative model that would result in global equilibrium, establishing a condition of economic and ecological stability. This alternative model could be designed to ensure a human economy that meets the basic material needs of each person on Earth and gives each person an equal opportunity to realize his individual potential within the physical limits of the Earth.[117]

Limits to Growth was strongly criticized by many scientists.[118] Professor Paul A. Samuelson perhaps captured the essence of the complaints when he stated that the Forrester-Meadows studies were "superficial on the factual side."[119] The problem with Limits to Growth, Kaysen stated, "is that it does not take the measurements of resources in economic terms into account."[120] The models gave too little weight to the effect of scarcity on price and use.[121] Samuelson explained that under new circumstances of scarcity, numerous new substances would become cheapest and safest.[122]

It was the methodology rather than the subject of Limits to Growth that was criticized, Nordhaus asserted[123]: the models were not based on empirical studies.[124] Nordhaus pointed out that most empirical studies have shown that with affluence, population growth declines leading to completely different results for the Forrester and Meadows models.[125] He also stated that the models do not use prices or political systems, which would allow the system to respond to scarcities by substituting scarce resources with plentiful materials and resources.[126] Evidence at this point in time, seems to favor the critics of Limits to Growth. It is very unlikely that growth will come to a standstill in 2072. Exponential growth need not continue unabated resulting in collapse. Growth can eventually slow down and then taper off.[127]

Schachter states that even if the "Limits to Growth" school's doomsday predictions are highly debatable, there is little doubt that the expected growth of population and industry will have serious consequences for future generations.[128] Even if we act now, it takes a lot of time and effort to mitigate the existing problems and trying to prevent future degradation of the environment. Schachter adds that an increased recognition of these effects implies that the question of the appropriate rate of growth will become a societal decision, rather than one being left to market forces or individual decisions. In this manner the decision will focus more on the issue of equity between generations and the extent of the sacrifice that should be borne for the sake of posterity.[129]

Weiss states that each generation has an inherent relationship to other generations, past and future, in using the common heritage of natural and cultural resources of our planet.[130] Problems of equity between generations arise from the exhaustion of natural resources for future generations, degradation in quality of resources for future generations, and access to use and benefits of the resources received from past generations. Because future generations have no representative in the decision-making processes today, potential trade-offs between the preferences of present and future generations are usually ignored.[131]

One would think most members of the present generation have enough environmental problems to cope with, without having the additional concern for people that are still not in existence. However, Weiss' theory can perhaps also be used as a conceptual approach to implementing long-term planning regarding the use of natural resources and protection of the environment. Most companies and government institutions, for instance, think in terms of a one-year budget, or maybe even a five-year plan. But with the long-term effects on the environment by our present activities, such short-term planning, in my judgment, is not sufficient.

The main thrust of Weiss' theory is that each generation is both a custodian and a user of our common natural and cultural heritage.[132] Each generation receives a natural and cultural legacy in trust from previous generations and holds it in trust for future generations. This relationship implies that each generation has moral obligations, such as, to conserve the natural and cultural resource base for future generations, duties which are transformed into legally enforceable norms that Weiss calls "planetary obligations." In addition, the relationship gives each generation certain global rights as beneficiaries of the trust of their ancestors ("planetary rights"). Weiss' doctrine of intergenerational equity, or justice between generations, consists of these intergenerational or planetary rights and obligations. As they are made more specific and codified into international law, these rights and obligations become enforceable. They can be codified into international agreements, national and local laws, transformed into customary international law, or adopted as general principles of law.[133]

Kant considered it disturbing that earlier generations had to bear the burdens only for the sake of later generations.[134] Recognizing that we can do something for posterity but it can do nothing for us, Rawls, however, disagrees with Kant stating that it is an unalterable situation and therefore "the question of justice does not arise."[135] Furthermore, Rawls asserts that "persons in different generations have duties and obligations to one another just as contemporaries do."[136]

In describing her theory, Weiss draws analogies with domestic legal systems, specifically the fiduciary relationship of a trust. The beneficiaries of one type of charitable trust in common law have the right to enjoy the benefits of the trust, and at the same time have an obligation not to dissipate the corpus of the trust for future beneficiaries.[137] The trustees have a duty to act for the benefit of beneficiaries. A global trust to ensure the welfare of future generations would satisfy the requirement of a charitable trust, since it promotes the community interests in its broadest sense. However, Weiss points out, it does not postulate a set of values to be pursued in the use of the trust resources, but rather preserves the corpus of the trust for eventual valuation by future generations according to their own values.

Weiss posits that our fiduciary obligation as trustees of the planetary trust can be inferred from the nearly universal recognition and acceptance among peoples of an obligation to protect the natural and cultural heritage for future generations. This obligation, she maintains, is deeply entrenched in many different legal traditions of the international community, as expressed in basic political documents. Weiss quotes Islamic law, " each generation uses and makes the best use of nature, according to its need, without disrupting or upsetting the interests of future generations."[138] The concept of protecting the natural environment for future generations was explicitly incorporated in the language of several treaties as early as 1972, such as the Convention for the Protection of World Cultural and Natural Heritage.[139]

If one acknowledges that intergenerational equity is already part of the fabric of international law, then one could perhaps argue that what Weiss has done is develop a more comprehensive theory to support the emerging concern for the interests of future generations. Yet, as Schachter states, "the allocation of resources between present and future generations is mainly a function of investment determined by market and political factors."[140] As Birnie and Boyle state, future generations will benefit to the extent that the international agreements are successful, however, actual state practice casts doubts on the level of commitment.[141] One can readily agree with Birnie and Boyle, in that the core of Weiss' theory—humanity having a responsibility for future generations—is indisputable, yet the issue is one of implementation.[142]

Weiss states that the purpose of human society must be "to realize and protect the welfare and well-being of every generation".[143] This, she states, requires sustaining the life-support systems of the planet, the ecological processes, environmental conditions, and cultural resources important for survival and well-being of the human species, and a healthy and decent human environment. The Rio Declaration expresses the same kind of philosophy, stating in Principle 1 that human beings are "entitled to a healthy and productive life in harmony with nature."[144]

The three principles of intergenerational equity Weiss sets forth are as follows:

> First, each generation should be required to conserve the diversity of the natural and cultural resource base, so that it does not unduly restrict the options available to future generations in solving their problems and satisfying their own values, and should be entitled to diversity comparable to that of previous generations (conservation of options). Second, each generation should be required to maintain the quality of the planet so that it is passed

on in no worse condition than the present generation received it, and should be entitled to a quality of the planet comparable to the one enjoyed by previous generations (conservation of quality). Third, each generation should provide its members with equitable rights of access to the legacy from past generations and should conserve this access for future generations (conservation of access). [145]

These principles, Weiss states, are a way of implementing "sustainable development" as defined by the Brandthand Commission.[146] A case in point concerning all three principles would be the exploitation of oil.[147] Oil extraction depends on the price of oil. If oil prices were predicted to drop in the future or new sources of energy were to eliminate the need for oil, many oil producers would most likely extract all the oil now, rather than lose that income in the future. (However, in practice this would probably flood the market, leading to lower oil prices.) But how would future generations interpret such actions? Some would say that future generations would prefer money in the bank, available for investments, instead of inheriting a natural resource in the ground that would probably be worthless. However, the equation is not that simple. If you follow Weiss' principles, extracting all the oil, assuming it were possible,[148] in my opinion, would eliminate an option for future generations because oil is a non-renewable resource, thereby constituting a breach of principle 1, by unduly restricting the options for future generations.[149] In addition, it would also constitute a breach of principle 2, by reducing the quality of the planet due to all the pollution caused by the increased use of fossil fuels. Furthermore, it would also constitute a breach of principle 3, conservation of access for future generations.[150]

Principle 3 (conservation of access), is the most relevant principle in the context of this study. Weiss describes Principle 3 as offering a principle of justice between generations and among members of the same generation. She mentions three problems of equity regarding access and use of natural and cultural resources. The first problem of equitable access concerns the needs of future generations, if viewed as resulting in the present generation having no right to exploit and use the natural and cultural resources. In the extreme (preservationist) view, Weiss argues, it would deprive the present generation of its legitimate claim to use the earth's natural resources, especially access for the poor, and would be untenable.[151]

The second problem, an intra-generational one, concerns the relationship of members of the present generation. Weiss notes that because of economic disparities in the world community, many members of the present generation are unable to realize their right of access to and use of the natural and cultural resources. Weiss posits the principle of conservation of access "gives to all members of the present generation a claim to the benefits of the planetary legacy, and imposes upon them the obligation to ensure that all members realize this claim."[152] Thus, to the extent that some members of the international community are too impoverished to have access, the others must assist them to gain such access.[153]

The third problem arises when the activities of some members of the present generation prevent other members of their generation from benefiting from the natural and cultural resources by causing environmental or other damage to the resources. Weiss states that parties externalize the cost of their own activities by inflicting them upon other parties, who must then bear the burden without the benefit. She posits that from the right of access there is a corresponding duty to avoid adverse impacts. Thus, Weiss states we cannot use our planetary resources in a way that prevents other members of the present generation from having reasonable access to these resources.

The intergenerational rights and obligations are collective in that they are defined by the position of each generation as part of human society extending through time.[154] Weiss states that planetary obligations are binding upon each person as a member of the international community. Nations, being entities which represent people in the international community, and exercising sovereignty over their own citizens, serve as guarantors for fulfilling these obligations. Weiss posits that since nations are continuing entities, they represent past, present and future generations. Yet, as nations are political entities they sometimes represent the people they govern, but often they represent only the people who are in power at a given moment, with no regard for anyone else, especially not future generations. To avoid such conflicts, Weiss' idea of appointing ombudsmen or commissioners for future generations seems to be a good solution.[155] Weiss points out that the Brundtland Commission suggested the use of ombudsmen at the national level.[156] These ombudsmen are to represent the interests of present and future generations (which Weiss stipulates as ensuring compliance with planetary obligations and rights as prescribed by law) and act as environmental watchdogs, by alerting governments and citizens of impending threats. Canada and New Zealand both have established such commissioner positions.[157]

Weiss writes that in order to implement justice between generations, intergenerational equity would also have to encompass the intra-generational context, as a means of distribution of rights and obligations within the present generation. She also states that all members of the international community must cooperate in order to implement our obligations to future generations.

Ntambirweki emphasizes that "[i]t is presumptuous to speak of intergenerational equity when there is no intra-generational equity."[158] Furthermore, he states that "[w]ithout righting the wrongs of today, and extinguishing present inequalities, there will remain nothing to bequeath to the future".[159] However, Weiss seems to be aware of this problem when she asserts that a state existing in extreme poverty today, will not be willing to join in efforts to conserve the planet for future generations. She suggests the use of incentives to raise the standard of living in poor countries. According to Weiss, intra-generational justice requires wealthier countries and communities to assist impoverished ones in realizing equitable access to the economic benefits from the natural resources and to help them protect these resources.[160]

Understandably, developing countries struggling with poverty and indebtedness at present, have not made remedying environmental problems for the sake of present generations a priority, let alone future generations. Industrialized countries, on the other hand, have made certain efforts to protect and restore the environment, in addition to contingency planning for the future, though in many cases they are only half-hearted. Perhaps the solution lies in working on both fronts simultaneously. However, this would entail a transfer of funds and technical assistance (using grants, joint ventures etc.) to developing countries to enable them to deal with their present problems,[161] at the same time as they plan for the future. If one examines the more recent international environmental agreements, assuming they are implemented, this seems to be the direction we are headed. For instance, the Climate Change Convention and its Kyoto Protocol have the potential of moving large amounts of public and private investment capital from the industrialized countries to the developing countries.[162]

Notes

1. Brundtland Commission's Report, *supra* Chapter 1 note 15.

2. *See* CALDWELL, *supra* Chapter 1 note 12, at 202. Ecodevelopment is the short term for ecologically sound development. *Id.*

3. *See id.* at 200, 201.

4. *See id.*

5. *See id.*

6. *See id.*

7. *See* Brundtland Commission's Report, *supra* Chapter 1 note 15, at 8, 43-46.

8. *See id.*

9. *Id.* at 43.

10. *Id.* at 44.

11. *See* CALDWELL, *supra* Chapter 1 note 12, at 210.

12. *See* Handl, *supra* Chapter 2 note 206.

13. *See* Robert Solow, *An Invited Lecture on the Occasion of the Fortieth Anniversary of Resources for the Future, October 1992: An Almost Practical Step Toward Sustainability* (visited Mar. 7, 1999) <http://www.rff.org>.

14. *See* Brundtland Commission's Report, *supra* Chapter 1 note 15, at 44.

15. *See id.*

16. *See id.*

17. FRANCES CAIRNCROSS, COSTING THE EARTH 20 (1992). *See also* Partha Dasgupta, *Environmental and Resource Economics in the World of the Poor* (visited Mar. 7, 1997) <http://www.rff.org> (explaining "the persistence of large-scale poverty traps in a growing economy").

18. *See* Brundtland Commission's Report, *supra* Chapter 1 note 15, at 45.

19. *See* John Firor, 'Sustainable Development', speech delivered at the Council on Foreign Relations, Denver Chapter, April 4, 1995.

20. *See id.*

21. *See* Diana Jean Schemo, *Legally, Now, Venezuelans to Mine Fragile Lands*, N.Y. TIMES, Dec. 8, 1996, at A5. *See* discussion *infra* text accompanying and following Chapter 7 note 54.

22. Kyoto Protocol, *supra* Chapter 2 note 166.

23. *See* David Hodas, *The "Rio" Environmental Treaties Colloqium: The Climate Change Convention and Evolving Legal Models of Sustainable Development* 13 PACE ENVTL. L. REV. 96 (1995).

24. *See* discussion *infra* Chapter 5 (in regards to joint implementation).

25. *See* discussion *infra* Chapter 7 (in regards to emissions trading).

26. *See* Hodas, *supra* note 23, at 85.

27. *See id.*

28. Kyoto Protocol, *supra* Chapter 2 note 166, art. 12. *See* discussion of CDM, *infra* Chapter 5. Joint implementation among developed countries is dealt with separately in Article 6. *See Address by the President of the Republic of Argentina, Report of the Conference of the Parties, 4th Sess.*, United Nations Framework Convention on Climate Change, U.N. Doc. FCCC/ CP/1998/16, Annex I, at 35 (1999).

29. Asbjorn Torvanger, Klimaavtalen er Historisk (The Climate Change Agreement is Historic), Cicerone nr. 1, at 9 (1998).

30. *See* Elizabeth Dowdeswell, *Development of International Law, in* INTERNATIONAL ENVIRONMENTAL LAW 19 (Erling Selvig & Hans Christian Bugge eds., 1994).

31. Mary Pat Williams Silveira, *Essay: International Legal Instruments and Sustainable Development: Principles, Requirements, and Restructuring*, 31 WILLIAMETTE L. REV. 239, 241 (1995).

32. *See* discussion *supra* Chapter 2, (in regards to the development of international environmental law).

33. This turn of events during the UNCED preparations could be the subject of a separate paper and will not be addressed here.

34. Interview with Barbara Ruis, Associate Expert (Legal), Division for Sustainable Development, United Nations, New York (Feb. 3, 1997). [This is her personal opinion.] However, the Report of the Expert Group Meeting on Identification of Principles of International law for Sustainable Development states that "Interrelationship and integration reflect the interdependence of social, economic, environmental and human rights aspects of life that define sustainable development, and

could lead to the development of general rules of international law in which these separate fields retain their distinct characters but are subject to an interconnected approach. However, it is understood that this approach does not *subsume* the distinct fields of international law into international law for sustainable development." Report of the Expert Group, *supra* Chapter 1 note 10, at 7(emphasis added).

35. *See* Agenda 21, *supra* Chapter 1 note 8, ch. 39.1.

36. Silveira, *supra* note 31, at 240.

37. *Id.* at 241.

38. *See* ROSS, *supra* Chapter 2 note 193, at 11.

39. Derived from Birnie & Boyle, *supra* Chapter 1 note 3, at 1 (referring to Brownlie's criteria for the existence of a body of law).

40. *See* Report of the Expert Group—Sustainable Development, *supra* Chapter 1 note 10. *See also* discussion *infra* text accompanying note 105 (in regards to Sustainable development principles).

41. *See* Thomas Grey, discussion paper, *quoted in* materials from Seminar in Legal Education, Liebman & Strauss 2-3, Columbia University (Fall, 1990).

42. *See id.* at 3.

43. Howard Mann, *Comment on the Paper by Philippe Sands, in* SUSTAINABLE DEVELOPMENT AND INTERNATIONAL LAW 72 (Winfried Lang ed., 1995).

44. *See id.*

45. *See* Handl, *supra* Chapter 2 note 206, at 24.

46. *See id.* at 25.

47. *Report of the Secretary General, Rio Declaration on Environment and Development: Application and Implementation*, U.N. CSD, 5th Sess., U.N. Doc. E/CN.17/1997/8 (1997).

48. *See* Convention on Biological Diversity, *supra* Chapter 2 note 168.

49. *See* SCHACHTER, *supra* Chapter 1 note 5, at 368-369.

50. *See* Schachter, *supra* Chapter 2 note 216.

51. *See* Handl, *supra* Chapter 2 note 206, at 26.

52. WORLD BANK, MONITORING ENVIRONMENTAL PROGRESS (1995).

53. U.N. DEPARTMENT OF INFORMATION, INDICATORS OF SUSTAINABLE DEVELOPMENT: MONITORING HUMAN PROGRESS, (June 1997).

54. *See id.*

55. *See* Programme for the Further Implementation of Agenda 21, *supra* Chapter 2 note 190, ¶ 114.

56. *See* Gunther Handl, *Controlling Implementation of and Compliance with International Environmental Commitments: The Rocky Road from Rio*, 5 COLO. J. INT'L ENVTL. L. & POL'Y 305 (1994).

57. *See* discussion *infra* text following note 108 (in regards to intra-generational and inter-generational equity).

58. Proponents of joint implementation have argued that this mechanism also confers a new "bargaining chip" on developing countries in the sense that they would be in possession of low-cost greenhouse gas abatement potential. *See* David Dudek & Jonathan Wiener, Joint Implementation, Transaction Costs, and Climate Change, 13 OCDE/GD(96)173, 8 (1996). *See* Joint Implementation Chapter 5.

59. *See* Weiss, *supra* Chapter 1 note 24, at 707.

60. *See id.*

61. *See* Biodiversity Convention, *supra* Chapter 2 note 168, at art. 15, ¶ 7.

62. *See id.* at art. 16.

63. One model of how this arrangement can work in practice, is a 1991 agreement between pharmaceutical company, Merck & Co., and Costa Rica's National Institute of Biodiversity (INBio), in which the pharmaceutical company paid $1 million for conservation programs in return for access to Costa Rica's plant, insects, and microbes. In addition, INBio receives a share of the royalties of any commercialized product Merck may develop. *See* Hilary French, *Forging a New Global Partnership*, *in* STATE OF THE WORLD 175 (Lester R. Brown et al., 1995).

64. This scenario is developed from a communication from Professor Schachter. *See* Schachter, *supra* Chapter 2 note 216.

65. *See* Handl, *supra* note 54, at 305.

66. *See* Jorgen Randers, Speech given at the International Forum, Oslo, Norway, March 1, 1993.

67. WORLD BANK, WORLD DEVELOPMENT REPORT 1992, DEVELOPMENT AND ENVIRONMENT 25 (1992).

68. *See* CAIRNCROSS, *supra* note 17, at 19.

69. *See id.*

70. *Rio Declaration, supra* Chapter 1 note 20, Principle 8. *See* Ileana Porras, *The Rio Declaration: A New Basis for International Cooperation, in* GREENING INTERNATIONAL LAW, 27 (Philippe Sands ed., 1994).

71. *See* Thorbjorn Berntsen, *Is There a Need for Changes in Consumption Patterns?*, *in* INTERNATIONAL ENVIRONMENTAL LAW 14 (Erling Selvig & Hans Christian Bugge eds., 1995).

72. *See id.*

73. *See id.*

74. *See id.* at 15.

75. *See id.*

76. JAN OLAF WILLUMS & ULRICH GOLUKE, FROM IDEAS TO ACTION-BUSINESS AND SUSTAINABLE DEVELOPMENT-THE ICC REPORT ON THE GREENING OF ENTERPRISE 92, 13 (1992).

77. Ileana Porras, *supra* note 70, at 27.

78. *See id.* at 22.

79. *See* MICHIO KAKU, VISIONS: HOW SCIENCE WILL REVOLUTIONIZE THE 21ST CENTURY 330 (1997); Hilary French, *Learning from the Ozone Experience, in* STATE OF THE WORLD 151 (Lester Brown et al. eds., 1997).

80. *See id. See also* RICHARD BENEDICK, OZONE DIPLOMACY 21 (1991).

81. Weiss, *supra* Chapter 2 note 58, at 21.

82. *See* Philippe Sands, *International Law in the Field of Sustainable Development*, 1994 BRIT. Y.B. INT'L L. 324.

83. *See also* discussion *infra* Chapter 6, (in regards to conditionality).

84. *See* Werksman, *supra* Chapter 2 note 196, at 76

85. *See* Caldwell, *supra* Chapter 1 note 12, at 207.

86. *See id.*

87. *See* Handl, *supra* Chapter 2 note 206, at 27.

88. *See* Freestone, *The Road from Rio: International Environmental Law after the Earth Summit,* 6 J. ENVTL. L. 200 (1994).

89. *See* Handl, *supra* note 56, at 12.

90. *Rio Declaration, supra* Chapter 1 note 20, Principle 2 (emphasis added).

91. *See* Marc Pallemaerts, *International Environmental Law from Stockholm to Rio: Back to the Future?, in* GREENING INTERNATIONAL LAW 16, 19 (Phillipe Sands ed., 1994). Pallemaerts goes as far as to predict the possible downfall of international environmental law as an independent branch of international law "as it risks becoming a mere appendage of international development law, and subordinated to economic rationality." *Id.* at 19.

92. Williams Silveira, *supra* note 31, at 251.

93. Schachter, *supra* Chapter 2 note 216.

94. Pallemaerts, *supra* note 91, at 15 (referring to economic growth and development).

95. *See* Agenda 21, *supra* Chapter 1 note 8 ("global partnership for sustainable development" *Id.* ¶ 1.1.).

96. Principle 7 of the Rio Declaration stipulates that "[s]tates shall cooperate in a spirit of global partnership to conserve, protect and restore the health and integrity of the Earth's ecosystem." *See* Rio Declaration, *supra* Chapter 1 note 20, art. 7.

97. *See* discussion *infra* Chapter 5 (in regards to norms that differentiate among states with regard to core obligations).

98. *See* Handl, *supra* note 56, at 310.

99. *See id.*

100. *See id.*

101. *See* Sands, *supra* Chapter 1 note 21, at xxxiii.

102. This objective is derived from Handl. *See* discussion *supra* in text accompany note 46.

103. *See also* discussion *infra* Chapter 6 (in regards to CSD).

104. Montreal Protocol—London Amendments, *supra* Chapter 1 note 41, annex IV, § 9 and annex V. *See also* discussion *infra* Chapter 5 (in regards to disincentives).

105. Report of the Expert Group-Sustainable Development, *supra* Chapter 1 note 10, at 2-3.

106. *See Sands, supra* Chapter 2 note 84, at 57.

107. *See* Rio Declaration, *supra* Chapter 1 note 20, art. 3.

108. This notion is derived from Weiss. *See* Weiss, *supra* Chapter 1 note 24, at 707.

109. *See* Handl, *supra* Chapter 2 note 206, at 21.

110. *See* Brundtland Commission's Report, *supra* Chapter 1 note 15.

111. International Convention for the Regulation of Whaling, 161 U.N.T.S. 72 (1946).

112. Climate Change Convention, *supra* Chapter 2 note 137, art. 3(1).

113. *See* EDITH BROWN WEISS, IN FAIRNESS TO FUTURE GENERATIONS: INTERNATIONAL LAW, COMMON PATRIMONY AND INTERGENERATIONAL EQUITY (1989).

114. *See id.* at 1.

115. *See* DONELLA MEADOWS ET AL., LIMITS TO GROWTH (1972).

116. *See id.* at 29.

117. *See id.*

118. Twenty years after "Limits to Growth" some of the original authors made follow-up computer models that confirmed their earlier conclusions, emphasizing even more strongly that there was still time to change, but time was running out, reducing the options. In the new report "Beyond the Limits," the authors realized

that in the context of resource and pollution flows the sustainable limits were already surpassed for many of them, despite efforts made to invent new institutions and technologies, especially energy efficient technology. *See* DONELLA MEADOWS ET AL., BEYOND THE LIMITS xiv (1992). The report urged the transition to a sustainable society through a "careful balance between long-term and short-term goals and an emphasis on sufficiency, equity, and quality of life rather than on quantity of output." *Id.* at xvi.

119. *See* Interview of Paul Samuelson, *in* WILLEM OLTMAN, ON GROWTH 48 (1974) (getting his reactions to the book LIMITS TO GROWTH).

120. *See* Interview of Carl Kaysen, *in id.* at 66.

121. *See id.* at 49.

122. *See* Interview of Paul Samuelson, *supra* note 119, at 50.

123. *See* Interview of William Nordhaus, *in id.* at 120.

124. *See id.* at 123.

125. *See id.* at 121.

126. *See id.* at 123.

127. *See* Interview of Roger Revelle, *in id.* at 184,185.

128. *See* Schachter, *supra* Chapter 2 note 202, at 12.

129. *See id.*

130. *See* Weiss, *supra* note 113, at 17.

131. *See id.* at 5.

132. *See id.* at 17.

133. *See id.* at 47.

134. *See* JOHN RAWLS, A THEORY OF JUSTICE 291 (1971).

135. *Id.*

136. *Id.* at 293.

137. *See* RESTATEMENT (SECOND) OF THE LAW OF TRUSTS § 176, 379 (1959). *See also* Weiss, *supra* note 105, at 18.

138. *See id.* at 18.

139. *See* Convention for the Protection of World Cultural and Natural Heritage, *supra* Chapter 2 note 124. *See also* Weiss, *supra* note 105, at 29.

140. Schachter, *supra* Chapter 2 note 216.

141. *See* BIRNIE & BOYLE, *supra* Chapter 1 note 3, at 212.

142. *See id.*

143. Weiss, *supra* note113, at 23.

144. *Rio Declaration* Principle 1, *supra* Chapter 1 note 20.

145. *See* Weiss, *supra* note 113, at 38.

146. *See id.* at 39. *See* Brundtland Commission's Report, *supra* Chapter 1 note 15.

147. The following scenario was developed from a conversation with Dr. Brian MacBeth, Feb. 20, 1995.

148. Discovery of oil resources has significantly outpaced the depletion of available oil resources.

149. In addition, there could be a use for the oil that was not yet known, which could make it potentially a valuable resource again in the future.

150. Weiss acknowledges that future generations may be able to develop substitutes for the depleted resources using income, capital, and knowledge received through the present generation's exhaustion of certain natural resources. Yet she also states that the principle of conservation of options would act as an important break on those who would exhaust all known quantities of essentially non-renewable resources such as oil and helium, positing that on balance the resource base must be maintained. *See* Weiss, *supra* note 113, at 42-43, 51.

151. *See id.* at 22.

152. *Id.* at 45.

153. *See id.* at 44.

154. *See id.* at 45.

155. *See id.* at 124.

156. *Id.* See Brundtland Commission' Report, *supra* Chapter 1 note 15, at 332.

157. *See* Office of the New Zealand Parliamentary Commissioner for the Environment (visited March 20, 1999) <http://www.pce.govt.nz> and in Canada, the Commissioner of the Environment and Sustainable Development (visited March 17, 1999) <http://www.oag-bvg.ca>.

158. J. Ntambirweki, *The Developing Countries in the Evolution of an International Environmental Law*, 14 HASTINGS INT'L & COMP. L. REV. 924 (1991).

159. *Id.*

160. *See* Weiss, *supra* note 113, at 28.

161. *See* Richard B. Stewart, *Environmental Regulation and International Competitiveness*, 102 YALE L.J. 2099 (1993) (claiming that a relative small infusion of additional funding from developed countries could enable the strengthening of the standards of developing countries, which in turn would gain economic and environmental benefits).

162. *See* Hodas, *supra* note 23, at 87.

4

Facilitating the Participation of Developing Countries—Sources of Conflict Regarding their Treatment in the International Regulatory Process

The Benefits for Developed Countries of Using Incentives (Differential Treatment) for Developing Countries

The recognition of the interdependence of the environment and the fact that it is oblivious to political borders, as indicated above, has lead to the realization of the need for universal participation in tackling global environmental problems. Involvement of developing countries is essential to ensure the success of international agreements for the protection of globally sensitive natural resources. Facilitating the participation of developing countries through the use of incentives, in effect giving them differential treatment, is one of the most contentious issues in this context.[1]

One could ask: Why should industrialized countries help developing countries by using incentives such as the transfer of environmentally sound technology or financial assistance? Altruism on a grand scale was never a strong point in international relations, relations that are mostly based on reciprocity. Quite to the contrary, the industrialized countries have a lot to gain by supporting developing countries, namely benefits such as, reduced aggregate pollution, the creation of markets for exports of environmentally sound technology,[2] and "[t]he proper management of natural resources that are important not only to the collective human security, but also to the success of private enterprises."[3] What is perhaps difficult to conceive, are the long-term benefits which cannot be measured, but are very important nonetheless, such as preserving biodiversity.[4]

An important issue concerns what is at stake for the developed countries if the developing countries do not improve their development models to take environmental considerations into account. Failure to address the interaction between rising poverty and resource degradation will eventually result in global environmental problems whose harmful impacts will adversely affect developed countries.[5] In addition, the consequences of the degradation of the environment in developing countries will also have other direct and spillover effects into the developed countries.

Developing countries would initially have unfair trade advantages by not implementing environmental protection measures, but eventually environmental disasters such as flooding, due to erosion (or global warming), would lead to lack of food and energy, which in turn would lead to conflicts and more refugees which are already growing to staggering figures each year.[6] Many of these refugees live in camps which usually are run by international organizations funded by the international community. Likewise, the international community, using taxpayer moneys, funds the U.N. troops that are sometimes sent to intervene in the conflicts, yet more often sent in as peacekeepers after the conflicts have ended. These conflicts are oftentimes initially based on issues of natural resources. By not giving developing countries incentives in international environmental agreements, such as technical and financial assistance, it is highly likely that the cost will be greater for the developed countries in the long term. Agenda 21 warrants the provision of technical and financial assistance as serving "the common interest of developed and developing countries,"[7] as these provisions are necessary for them to fully implement their commitments under Agenda 21, whose realization has global benefits.[8]

In addition, in view of the fact that trade has now reached global proportions, destabilized societies in developing countries would lead to lost investments for companies from the industrialized countries. All in all, there would be enormous costs to the developed countries which directly or indirectly are caused by environmental problems in developing countries.

It is in the developed countries' best interest to get involved up front by helping developing countries to participate in international environmental agreements with the objective of preventing environmental degradation, rather than waiting until the problems get out of control and then try to solve them.[9] From the ozone depletion issue, we have learned that the longer one waits before acting, the more potential costs and consequences one can expect later on.[10] This is one of the main reasons the precautionary principle or approach was introduced in Principle 15 of the Rio Declaration, requiring the implementation of measures to prevent environmental degradation before there is full scientific certainty.[11] This principle was incorporated in the case of the Climate Change Convention to Article 3, requiring "precautionary measures to anticipate, prevent or minimize the causes of climate change. . . ."[12] The Biodiversity Convention also includes the principle in its preamble.[13] With respect to biodiversity, certain natural resources cannot be replaced, such as plant species for producing vital medicines we all depend on. By acting now, and assisting developing countries implement the Biodiversity Convention, a significant reduction or loss of biological diversity may be avoided.[14]

The industrialized countries alone cannot solve global environmental problems such as global warming and the thinning of the stratospheric ozone layer. Without all or most of the states' involvement, the goal of the treaties to reduce global emissions, be it ozone-depleting substances or greenhouse gases, would be undermined by the emissions from non-parties. We need to have all or most nations "on board," therefore promoting the participation of developing countries in multilateral treaties and their implementation through the use of differential norms seems to be the best solution, rather than setting uniform standards that are unrealistic for developing countries to attain.

Different Types of International Norms

For our purposes, there are three types of international norms which affect the treatment international law provides developing countries.[15] These norms are the differential, contextual, and absolute norms.[16] Contextual and absolute norms, in turn, are also classified as uniform norms. Magraw defines a differential norm as a "norm that on its face provides different, presumably more advantageous, standards for one set of States than for another."[17] Differential norms are also referred to as double standards or asymmetrical norms in that they provide states with different rights and obligations, deviating from an otherwise symmetrical system of reciprocal rights and obligations. In our context, the differential norms of greatest interest are the ones that distinguish between developed and developing countries. Incentives such as delayed compliance schedules and financial assistance for developing countries fall into this category of norms. Sand defines selective incentives as "certain fringe benefits [that] may persuade a party to participate in a program or standard that it would otherwise find unacceptable."[18] The commonly used selective incentives, Sand notes, is access to funding, resources, markets, and technology.[19] The Montreal Protocol provides an example of a differential norm, in that it allowed developing countries a ten-year grace period before they were obligated to reduce their consumption of ozone-depleting substances in accordance with the agreed reduction schedule.[20]

Another way to take into account the developing countries' situation is by using norms that Magraw categorizes as contextual norms.[21] These norms belong to the category of norms called uniform norms. Magraw defines a contextual norm as "a norm that on its face provides identical treatment to all States affected by the norm, but the application of which requires (or at least permits) considerations of characteristics that might vary from country to country." He states that contextual norms are either general, meaning the terms of the norm do not place a limit on the characteristics that may be taken into account, e.g., "reasonable" or "equitable," or limited, meaning the set of relevant characteristics is defined. Limited contextual norms relevant to developing countries, could refer to resource availability and technical and regulatory capability.[22] The World Heritage Convention does just that, when it refers to States' *resources*, with regard to protecting natural and cultural heritage.[23]

A third and last category of norms identified by Magraw, is the one called absolute norms.[24] These would also be classified as uniform norms. Magraw defines an absolute norm as "a norm that provides identical treatment to all countries and does not require or permit consideration of factors that vary between countries."[25] However, applying an absolute norm often requires the investigation of the facts of the specific case, which can lead to differences of opinion as to what are the relevant facts.[26] Magraw notes that there is no fine line between contextual and absolute norms.

In the context of the treatment of developing countries in international environmental law, one could also say there is no fine line between contextual and differential norms. Both of these norms can be used to benefit developing countries. I would venture to say one could even refer to contextual norms as implicit differential norms and what Magraw refers to as differential norms could be called explicit differential norms. Yet, in my judgment, the explicit differential norms are the ones that are the most effective[27] in promoting the participation of developing countries in the international environmental agreements. Implicit differential norms or contextual norms, which do not specifically mention developing countries, require an interpretation to conclude which countries are eligible for special considerations. For the purposes of this study I have, therefore, structured the analysis using Magraw's differential norms versus uniform norms, which include absolute and contextual norms, rather than using explicit or implicit differential norms, as the division between uniform and differential norms seems to be more clearly defined.

The incentives or differential norms that will be examined in the context of this study are as follows: norms that are asymmetrical with regard to core obligations, financial mechanisms for achieving substantive norms, joint implementation as a method of participation, and finally, technical assistance including access to technology and capacity building.[28] These would be considered to be positive incentives. The negative incentives I will discuss or disincentives that apply to all categories of countries, be they developing or industrialized countries, include trade sanctions and non-compliance procedures. I will also examine an incentive that concerns developing countries, but does not amount to differential treatment within the treaties, as it is not part of the treaty provisions. This incentive consists of the assistance that in recent years has become commonly used in conjunction with international conferences to enable developing countries to participate in the treaty negotiations.

Differential Treatment or Uniform Environmental Norms?

The advantages of using differential treatment rather than uniform environmental norms include compensation for lack of reciprocal state interest, avoiding the least-common-denominator problem, promoting participation in the environmental treaties at an earlier stage, and facilitating harmonization of national environmental standards. These will be examined, in turn, below.

Incentives or differential treatment, such as delayed compliance schedules or financial support, may be necessary to compensate the absence of reciprocal state interest in the proposed regime;[29] in this manner, they represent the "carrot." The negotiations leading up to the adoption of the Montreal Protocol are a prime example of this type of situation. Developing countries felt that the depletion of the stratospheric ozone layer, on the whole, was a problem the developed countries had caused and therefore they should be the ones to solve it, instead of curtailing developing countries of their alternatives for development. To compensate for this, the Montreal Protocol included special treatment, such as a delayed compliance schedule for developing countries that had a certain level of annual per capita consumption of ozone-depleting substances.

Sand states that incentives are one way to avoid the least-common-denominator problem regarding international agreements and/or the loss of some important signatories.[30] This is due to the fact that treaties are based on consensus, since sovereign states are not required to enter into agreements. In order to satisfy the most reluctant party in the negotiation of a treaty, compromise is often arrived at by lowering the standards for all parties to the treaty. By using incentives the higher standards would be maintained, yet the developing countries would be given special treatment, differential treatment, in order to facilitate their participation at an earlier stage. In effect, the incentives would create double standards, but the idea is that most often they are only meant to be temporary.

Some scholars criticize incentives and differential norms, for being discriminatory and leading to loopholes in treaties, seriously hampering the success of the agreements. Handl states that if the incentives affect core obligations in the treaty then they will cause problems in the long run, unless there is a special justification for them, such as accounting for variations in state parties' contributions to the problem.[31]

In my judgment, there are special justifications for temporary incentives for developing countries. These include the fact that developing countries have relatively low technical and regulatory capabilities to devote to environmental protection and lack funding for use in that effort. In addition, their contributions to the environmental problems have been smaller than that of the industrialized countries. In the case of the Montreal Protocol, the core obligation remains intact even though developing countries were given a ten-year grace period. They still have to reduce or eliminate the control substances.[32] Yet until the ten-year grace period is over, the developing countries have different obligations compared to the industrialized countries.

Maintaining uniformity with regard to the core obligations, while taking into account states' socio-economic situations, Handl asserts, are wholly commensurate goals for multilateral regulatory regimes.[33] This kind of norm would represent what Magraw categorizes as a contextual norm. Contextual norms are useful in certain situations, but cannot replace differential norms, as these norms have proven more successful in the more recent international environmental agreements. These provisions have made the treaties more palatable for developing countries to enter into at an earlier stage by including incentives such as delayed compliance schedules and funding which pays for the incremental cost of complying with the treaties. The interests of the developing countries to continue their development efforts are not unduly interfered with, at the same time as the interest of protecting the global environment from degradation is satisfied.[34]

The arguments in favor of uniform standards and against differential norms bearing on the intrinsic nature of the regulatory regime, include the following: higher administrative costs since it's a more complex system if there is a double standard; distortions in trade due to lower environmental standards for some states, which in turn give them a competitive advantage; and the fact that such differential norms are counterproductive in terms of long-term environmental benefits.[35] I will address each of these arguments in turn.

In the context of international environmental agreements, it is clear that higher administrative costs are involved when dealing with double standards, for instance, in implementing the Montreal Protocol. However, the more complex arrangements, such as the delayed compliance schedule of the Montreal Protocol, are well worth the cost if the end result is that developing countries ratify the treaty, then implement it by switching to CFC-substitutes, and finally, that the stratospheric ozone layer becomes less depleted.

The trade distortion argument is part of the larger trade and environment debate, which is still not resolved. It is very likely that developing countries with lower environmental standards, even if they are only temporary, have a comparative advantage in the international competition concerning products, and thereby cause distortions in trade. This is mainly due to the fact that industries located in countries with fewer environmental regulations and liability rules have lower compliance costs than the ones with stringent rules.[36] This same argument can be made with regard to treaties using uniform norms because in some instances the developing countries decide not to participate at all, opening up for even more trade distortions.

However, with regard to treaties using differential treatment for developing countries, this problem would only be temporary, as in the case of the Montreal Protocol which requires the developing countries to fulfill the same commitments as the industrialized countries after the ten-year grace period is over. In the long term, the special treatment given developing countries will not distort trade because harmonization should be the ultimate goal, although this is debated in trade circles. Examples of such harmonization of environmental standards are the voluntary standards of the ISO 14000 series.[37] Some countries, such as Indonesia and Canada, are considering making environmental regulations based on these management standards.[38]

Until they get assistance to improve their environmental situation, however, developing countries are opposed to labeling schemes and other attempts at harmonization because they cannot afford to implement such programs. Their lower environmental standards are, in turn, often used as a basis for creating technical and other trade barriers against their exports,[39] which in their indebted situation are their "lifelines" for debt payments. However, unilateral trade measures against specific countries, based on inadequate pollution controls to remove the "pollution advantage" inherent in the products concerned are on the whole considered illegal according to GATT/WTO rules.[40] Yet these rules would not affect the ISO 14000 standards as long as they are only voluntary. The solution to the competitiveness problem is not returning to absolute sovereignty, but a combination of international efforts to reach partial harmonization of national environmental standards and domestic policy changes to eliminate regulatory and liability burdens that are not necessary.[41] By ratifying and implementing the international environmental treaties, developing countries would benefit from provisions giving them special privileges—similar to the GATT/WTO provisions intended to assist in their economic development[42]—enabling them eventually to raise their environmental standards to the level of the industrialized countries.

Handl notes that a reduction of normative requirements for developing countries will hinder their progress toward an adequate level of domestic environmental protection. In my view, this may not necessarily be the case. In the long term, developing countries that are given the opportunity to "catch up" through the use of incentives, will be better players in the world marketplace than they are now, often not participating at all, but instead constituting a dumping ground for other nations' waste products and contributing to the global environmental problems.

An example of how developing countries are becoming better players can be found in the context of the Montreal Protocol. Twenty-four developing countries have reduced their consumption of ozone-depleting substances ahead of the scheduled 1999 deadline when a freeze on production and consumption goes into effect for Article 5 (developing) countries.[43] This is due, in part, to the funding made available through the Multilateral Fund enabling large-scale technology transfer investments.[44]

Principle 7 of the Rio Declaration introduces the concept of "common but differentiated responsibility" attributing different portions of responsibility to different States according to their level of responsibility for causing environmental degradation in the first place, and their capabilities to deal with the environmental damages.[45] Principle 7 is an elaboration of Principle 6 which states that the special situation and needs of developing countries are to be given special priority.[46] Rio Principle 7 reads as follows:

> States shall cooperate in the spirit of global partnership to conserve, protect and restore the health and integrity of the Earth's ecosystem. In view of the different contributions to global environmental degradation States have *common but differentiated responsibilities*. The developed countries acknowledge the responsibility that they bear in the international pursuit of sustainable development in view of the pressures their societies place on the global environment and of the technologies and financial resources they command.[47]

"Common responsibility" was first used in a treaty text in the Framework Convention on Climate Change, to refer to the shared responsibility developing and developed countries alike, had for protecting common resources.[48] "Differentiated responsibilities" refers to different technological and financial capacities of states and takes into account their different contributions to a particular environmental problem.

The practical consequence of Principle 7 can be seen in the Climate Change Convention, where it is translated into specific obligations to reduce greenhouse gas emissions for developed countries only, and reporting requirements that are differentiated for developed, developing, and least developed countries.[49]

Rio Principle 7 also provides a theoretical framework for the validation in Principle 11, of using different national environmental norms mirroring the different environmental and developmental situation of states.[50] Principle 11 reads as follows: "States shall enact effective environmental legislation. Environmental standards, management objectives and priorities should reflect the environmental and developmental context to which they apply. Standards applied by some countries may be inappropriate and have unwarranted economic and social cost to other countries, in particular developing countries."

Principle 7 and 11 together support the idea that identical environmental standards may not be suitable in all situations, illustrating how the Rio Declaration favors developing countries on the issue of whether states should be required to adopt similarly strict environmental norms.[51] According to Bugge "[i]t is simply impossible to impose the same substantial obligations on countries in such differing situations."[52] In regard to developing countries, some increase in pollution and use of natural resources must take place if they are to increase their production and economic growth.[53] Yet, industrialized countries, on the other hand, have already over-exploited the global environment and as a consequence should reduce their polluting emissions.[54] With technical and financial support, many developing countries could do more to protect the environment and eventually reach the same high environmental standards as developed countries.

Magraw sees a trend after the 1972 Stockholm Declaration where environmental treaties are increasingly likely to contain economic-development-based differential norms and contextual norms that refer to a state's ability with regard to technical and regulatory matters and resource availability.[55] He asserts the possibility of a "soft law"[56] principle or a developing customary norm emerging, requiring that international conventional regimes, whether they are environmental or not, should take the developing countries' interest in reaching the goal of sustainable development into account.[57] This he notes, might be reflected in the regimes by reference to the obligation to take those interests into account or by attempting to ensure that the standards are not impossible for developing countries to fulfill. Ideas like this eventually evolved into what is now Rio Principle 7, "common but differentiated responsibilities."

Magraw notes that the three norms, differential, contextual, and absolute norms have different advantages and disadvantages, and therefore are suitably used in different situations.[58] International instruments can consist of both differential and contextual norms.[59] In my judgment, differential norms or incentives for developing countries seem to be the most effective in promoting universal participation in the ratification and implementation of international environmental agreements in order to effectively protect the global environment.

Examining the international environmental agreements since the Stockholm conference, one can also observe a trend of increased use of differential norms versus contextual norms (a type of uniform norm). With regard to developing countries, it seems that the more often differential treatment is offered in the treaty provisions, the more likely they are to adopt them. One can compare, for instance, the number of developing country parties to the Basel Convention,[60] which has little in the way of differential norms,[61] with the Montreal Protocol,[62] and the Biodiversity Convention,[63] which include several differential norms, as shown below.[64] The latter two treaties have more developing countries participating, very likely due, in part, to the differential treatment given developing countries. This trend also includes treaties adopted before the Stockholm Conference that have since added a funding mechanism to assist developing countries in the implementation of the Convention, such as the Convention on Wetlands.[65] The environmental treaties containing provisions with differential treatment seem more palatable for the developing countries because the incentives such as funding, subsidize activities that would otherwise take funding away from their other priorities such as dealing with poverty and debt issues, while trying to develop economically.

Differential treatment is more effective to promote the participation of developing countries because they are specifically mentioned as the beneficiaries, whereas contextual norms, allowing for consideration of characteristics that might vary from country to country, require an interpretation to decide which countries are encompassed by the provisions. Under special circumstances, for instance, with the fall of the communist block, there is a great demand for funding to clean up the degraded environment in countries with economies in transition. Yet, this funding has often come from the same funds that were supposed to assist the developing countries. This has made many developing countries apprehensive regarding whether their needs will be met.[66] By explicitly allocating the funding for developing countries in the treaties, the money would not be re-allocated to projects in other countries.[67] In the case of the Montreal Protocol, several countries with economies in transition, such as Georgia, have been reclassified as Article 5 (developing country) Parties, and are eligible for funding from the Multilateral Fund. On the other hand, countries with economies in transition that don't qualify as Article 5 countries, such as Russia, can be eligible for funding from GEF.

Alternative Approaches to Promote Participation by Developing Countries in International Environmental Agreements

I have previously stated that using differential norms for developing countries in international environmental treaties is the most effective way to promote the participation of developing countries in these treaties. Are there any alternatives? What other mechanisms can be used to promote developing country participation if one were to use uniform norms? Two alternatives come to mind. One mechanism might be to use uniform norms in the treaty provision, but provide developing countries with compensation for lost opportunity costs. Another mechanism might be to use pre-existing institutions outside the environmental treaties to induce or pressure developing countries to participate in and implement the international environmental agreements.

Using Mechanisms Outside of Treaties

One type of institution that might be used is the non-governmental organization (NGO). NGOs, including business and industry groups, operate at the local, national and international levels.[68] Another category of institutions could be economic development agencies. On the international plane, most of these agencies are part of or related to the United Nations system, such as the World Bank.[69] The two above-mentioned institutions can impact upon the behavior of developing countries in various ways, including conditioning their assistance, independent of the treaties, on the developing country participation in the treaties. These two types of institutions and their unique mechanisms will be addressed, in turn, below.

As will be seen in Chapter 8, NGOs have grown to be a very powerful force over the years, especially in the area of international environmental law. NGOs greatly influence the environmental decision-making process of many governments. However, some NGOs representing commercial interests are not necessarily interested in promoting environmental protection. For instance, some industry associations and lobbying groups, such as oil companies, lobbied against the Climate Change Convention in 1992, and again, more recently, ran advertising campaigns on television against what was to become the Kyoto Protocol, because they see these treaties as threatening their interests. NGOs, therefore, can constitute both a positive and negative force in the context of international environmental treaties.

On the other hand, economic development agencies could leverage the assistance they offer to developing countries to pressure them to join the environmental treaties. The World Bank is today considered the largest source of development lending. However, using loans (even conditional loans) as leverage to get developing countries to participate in the environmental treaties, would perhaps be a less efficient way of addressing the problem, as the loans for projects from these agencies usually go to specific development projects, and not all developing countries apply for loans for projects that effect global environmental issues. In addition, some developing countries decide to opt out of a loan, rather than succumb to pressures, such as India did in the Sardar Sarovar Dam Project.[70]

Even if using NGOs and economic development agencies outside the treaties to encourage participation by the developing countries in the treaties has some benefits, these mechanisms are not as effective as using differential norms or incentives in the treaties themselves and including these outside institutions in addition to the treaties, to assist in their operation. Such treaties provide developing countries with flexibility or differential treatment in implementing the treaties if they join, whereas institutions such as NGOs, cannot offer such flexibility. NGOs, as mentioned above, can also veer either way, some encouraging participation, others not. Using differential norms and providing for the participation of outside institutions in the implementation of treaties is arguably more effective. For example, the treaties could absorb the NGOs that promote environmental protection into the agreements, by giving them specific roles to play in the treaty provisions. An example of this can be found in the Convention to Combat Desertification where NGOs are to function as conduits and ensure that local communities obtain the external resources they need to carry out their own programs.[71] The role of these NGOs would be regulated in the context of the treaty to assist from within. In addition, economic development agencies would also be given roles in various treaties as, for instance, becoming implementing agencies for the funding mechanisms, as in the case of the Climate Change Convention, where the World Bank is part of GEF.[72] This inclusive approach would seems to produce more cooperation between agencies and streamlines the work of the agencies in the particular area that the treaty addresses.

This is not to say that such institutions working from outside the treaties should not exist. There is nothing inherently inappropriate in such institutions operating at the local, national and international level. However, they should not be seen as a possible replacement for the use of differential norms in the treaty provisions as a mechanism to promote the participation of developing countries in international environmental agreements.

Using differential norms, in addition to pre-existing institutions to assist with the operation of the incentives within the treaties would seem to be a more effective means to promoting participation by developing countries, than using treaties having uniform norms and institutions on the outside to urge participation. As will be shown below, NGOs and other major groups, in addition to economic development agencies and other inter-national institutional structures, have a large role to play in promoting the participation of developing countries in international environmental agreements, be it from within or together with treaties.[73]

Compensation for Developing Countries for Lost Opportunity of Traditional Development

More and more treaties since 1972 refer to the needs of developing countries and often grant them concessions.[74] Handl remarks that since then, the basic international consensus on support measures for developing countries' environmental efforts has ripened into a strong argument about international burden-sharing concerning the protection of the global environment.[75] This burden-sharing is reflected in the Rio Principle 7, which refers to 'common but differentiated responsibility.'

Some scholars are also inclined to use Principle 7 as the basis for the use of the term 'legal obligation' or 'entitlement' in reference to the developed countries' duty to help the developing countries in their environmental efforts, rather than a mere moral obligation, to give aid or assistance.[76] Schachter states that there has been a shift from meeting the needs of developing countries on a preferential basis as a concept of charity to one of justice.[77] Linking need to the notion of justice, requires that the satisfaction of needs is seen as an entitlement.[78] This entitlement is then embodied in norms and institutions, and it creates rights and obligations as between recipients and donors, rather than a relationship based on inequality as in the case of charity.[79]

Handl notes that incentives are most often justified as a matter of 'fundamental international equity' when used to promote developing country participation in global environmental regimes.[80] This he bases on the fact that developing countries are now being asked to share the burden of controls on economic development which may have a negative impact on the environment when they have not had the opportunity to generate the same socio-economic benefits as the industrialized countries. If such countries sign treaties with uniform norms, they could be constrained from using what Handl posits could have been their 'natural' development options, thereby incurring opportunity costs. Handl states that these costs incurred to protect environmental resources that are of global interest or special interest to other states, should entitle developing countries to compensation.[81]

Following Handl's train of thought, one could argue that international environmental treaties should contain uniform standards with respect to core obligations, but give developing countries compensation for incurred opportunity costs, thereby enabling them to fulfill their treaty obligations.[82] This compensation could be in the form of incentives that do not affect the core obligations of the treaties, such as technical and financial assistance.

However, where applicable, as in the case of emission, using differential norms or incentives[83] that also bear on the essence of the treaties, would perhaps be a more effective mechanism to promote developing country participation in the treaties. A temporary postponement or lowering of the standards for them would make it more feasible for them to participate in the treaties at an earlier stage, rather than have obligations that are near impossible to fulfill. Absent, for instance, the ten-year grace period in the

Montreal Protocol, developing countries may not have joined at all or agreement may only have been reached at the "lowest-common-denominator" to ensure their participation.

For this reason, implementing the model of the Montreal Protocol seems to be a more feasible approach; using delayed compliance schedules (differential treatment) for the developing countries for an initial period and at the same time supplying them with financial support.[84] For example, the grace period would allow the developing countries to recover some of the investment made in capital equipment using substances such as CFCs, and gives them more time to switch to ozone-safe technologies, since the absorption of new technologies is usually slower in a developing country than an industrialized one.[85]

Notes

1. *See* Handl, *supra* Chapter 2 note 206.

2. *See* Stewart, *supra* Chapter 3 note 161, at 2099, 2104.

3. Jennifer Barsky, *World Business Council Issues Biodiversity Report*, EARTH TIMES (June 23, 1997) <http://www.earthtimes.org/earthsummit.htm> (quoting Yolkanda Kakabadse, president of the World Conservation Union (IUCN)).

4. Scientists and economists have come up with a number for the value of nature through "green accounting": $33 trillion a year, which can lend perspective to the discussion of long term benefits of using incentives for promoting developing country participation in international environmental agreements. Those services will not be available to the same extent as they are today if developing countries continue down the "unsustainable" development path. *See* Mark Muro, *Green Accounting: Gimmick or New Way for Environment?*, EARTH TIMES (June 28, 1997) <http://www.earthtimes.org.earthsummit>.

5. *See* Brundtland Commission's Report, *supra* Chapter 1 note 15, at 366; Dernbach, *supra* Chapter 2 note 173, at 10513.

6. *See* Brundtland Commission's Report, *supra* Chapter 1 note 15, at 5 (predicting an increase in environmental pressure causing population movements).

7. Sands, *supra* Chapter 3 note 82, at 375.

8. *See* Agenda 21, *supra* Chapter I note 8, ¶ 33.3.

9. *See* Kamen Sachariev, *Promoting Compliance with International Environmental Legal Standards: Reflections on Monitoring and Reporting Mechanisms*, *in* 3 YEARBOOK OF INTERNATIONAL ENVIRONMENTAL LAW 32 (1992) (referring to how damage to the environment by human activities is often irreversible and is difficult to assess in monetary values).

10. *See* Hilary F. French, *Learning from the Ozone Experience*. *in* STATE OF THE WORLD 1997 at 169 (Lester R. Brown et al. eds., 1997).

11. The precautionary approach or precautionary principle requires that "[w]here there are threats of serious or irreversible damage, lack of full scientific

certainty should not be used as a reason for postponing measures to prevent environmental degradation." *Bergen Ministerial Declaration on Sustainable Development in the ECE Region*, ¶ 7, U.N. Doc. A/Conf.151/PC/10 (1990). *See* Hohmann, *supra* Chapter 2 note 93.

12. Climate Change Convention, *supra* Chapter 2 note 137, art. 3, ¶ 3.

13. *See* Biodiversity Convention, *supra* Chapter 2 note 168, pmbl., ¶ 9.

14. *See id.*

15. *See* Magraw, *supra* Chapter 1 note 38, at 73.

16. *See id.*

17. *Id.*

18. SAND, *supra* Chapter 1 note 37, at 8.

19. *See id.* at 7.

20. *See* Montreal Protocol-London Amendments, *supra* Chapter 1 note 41, art. 5.

21. *See* Magraw, *supra* Chapter 1 note 38, at 74.

22. *See id.* at 76.

23. *See* Convention Concerning the Protection of the World Cultural and Natural Heritage, *supra* Chapter 2 note 124, art. 4. (emphasis added). *See also* Magraw, *supra* Chapter 1 note 38, at 76.

24. *See* Magraw, *supra* Chapter 1 note 38, at 76.

25. *Id.*

26. *See id.*

27. For further explanation, see *supra* text accompanying and following note 29.

28. These are examined in detail in Chapter 5.

29. *See* Handl, *supra* Chapter 2 note 206, at 9.

30. *See* SAND, *supra* Chapter 1 note 37, at 6.

31. *See* Handl, *supra* Chapter 2 note 206, at 9

32. *See* discussion *infra* Chapter 5.

33. *See id.*

34. *See* Magraw, *supra* Chapter 1 note 38, at 74.

35. *See* Handl, *supra* Chapter 2 note 206, at 9.

36. *See* Stewart, *supra* Chapter note 161 at 2084 (Stewart states that studies show that different environmental standards have an important impact with regard to a few "dirty" industries, and in general there has been a shift of heavy industry and chemical facilities to developing countries. Yet Stewart states that the studies do not show that environmental regulations are a dominant factor in overall international competitiveness. *Id.*

37. The International Organization for Standardization published its first five international standards in the ISO 14000 series of environmental management standards in 1996. The standards are meant to assist business and industry to achieve their environmental goals and regulatory compliance through a process-oriented system. *See* International Organization for Standardization, First Environmental Management System Standards Appear <http://www.iso.ch/presse/PRESSE09.html>. *See also* Elizabeth Pinckard, Note, IS014000, 8 COLO. J. INT'L ENVTL. L. & POL'Y 430-431 (1997). Yet many environmentalists argue that these standards are too low resulting in "harmonization down". The other problem with these standards, as long as they are private and voluntary, is that there is no "outside au-

thority," so to speak, to supervise the standards. In the environmental field, the jury is still out as to whether self-policing is an effective mechanism for protecting the environment. Perhaps it is more likely to be effective when combined with command-and-control measures. Grad, *supra* Chapter 2 note 165.

38. Interview with Tarcisio Alvarez-Rivero, U.N. Department of Policy Coordination and Sustainable Development, United Nations, New York (Oct. 23, 1996).

39. *See* Handl, *supra* Chapter 2 note 206, at 9.

40. Such trade restrictions would violate GATT's Article I(1) (most-favored-nation requirement) and Article III(1) (national treatment clause) and would not be justified under the GATT exceptions in Article XX, subsection (b) or (g). *See* GATT, *supra* note 82, at 187. Thomas J. Schoenbaum, *Free International Trade and Protection of the Environment: Irreconcilable Conflict?*, 86 AM. J. INT'L L. 721 (1992).

41. *See* Stewart, *supra* Chapter 3 note 161, at 2041.

42. *See* GATT, *supra* Chapter 2 note 148, Part IV.

43. *See Tenth Anniversary of Montreal Protocol Occasion to Cite Evidence of Success, Renew Call for Further International Cooperation*, 21 (BNA), Sept. 12, 1997, at 695.

44. *See id.*

45. *See* Porras, *supra* Chapter 3 note 77, at 29.

46. *See* Rio Declaration, *supra* Chapter 1 note 20, princ. 6.

47. *Id.* princ. 7 [emphasis added].

48. *See* Porras, *supra* Chapter 3 note 77, at 28.

49. *See* Sands, *supra* Chapter 3 note 82, at 345. *See also* discussion *infra* Chapter 5.

50. *See id.* at 30.

51. *See id.*

52. Bugge, *supra*, Chapter 2 note 57, at 57.

53. *See id.* Gardner also states that developing country obligations must be defined in less stringent terms, at least for an initial period. *See* RICHARD N. GARDNER, NEGOTIATING SURVIVAL, FOUR PRIORITIES AFTER RIO 35 (1992).

54. *See* Bugge, *supra* Chapter 2 note 57, at 57.

55. *See.* Magraw, *supra* Chapter 1 note 38 at 99.

56. Soft law is a much-debated concept. *See* discussion *supra* Chapter 2.

57. *See* Magraw, *supra* Chapter 1 note 38, at 79.

58. *See id.* at 98.

59. *See* UNCLOS, *supra* Chapter 2 note 11, arts. 202, 203, 207(4) (differential norms), arts. 194(1), 194(4), 199 (contextual norms).

60. Basel Convention, *supra* Chapter 2 note 9. Ratification status as of March 1997: 106 Parties, 72 of which are developing countries. IUCN, <http://sedac.ciesin.org>. (current ratification information is available as of Mar. 5, 1999 at Socioeconomic Data and Applications Center, Environmental Treaties and Resource Indicators Service <http://sedac.ciesin.org.entri/>; United Nations Basel Convention Secretariat, Ratifications <http://www.unep.ch/basel/sbc/ratif.htm>).

61. *See, e.g., id.* art. 10, ¶ 3 (parties are required to cooperate in order assist developing countries in the implementation of some of their obligations).

62. Montreal Protocol, *supra* Chapter 1 note 25. Ratification status as of October 1997: 162 Parties, 116 of which are developing countries. UNEP,<http://www.

pie.org/ozat/protocol> (current ratification status information is available as of Mar. 5, 1999 at U.N. Environment Programme, Ozone Secretariat, *Status of Ratification* <http://www.unep.org/unep/secretar/ozone/ratif.htm>).

63. Biodiversity Convention, *supra* Chapter II note 168. Ratification status as of March 1997: 171 Parties, 132 of which are developing countries. IUCN, <http://sedac.ciesin.org>. (current ratification information is available as of Mar. 5, 1999 at Socioeconomic Data and Applications Center, Environmental Treaties and Resource Indicators Service <http://sedac.ciesin.org/entri/>).

64. *See* discussion *infra* Chapter V.

65. Convention on Wetlands of International Importance Especially as Waterfowl Habitat (Ramsar), Feb. 2, 1971, 996 U.N.T.S. 245 [hereinafter Convention on Wetlands].

66. This issue first arose with regard to Official Development Assistance (ODA). Some of that funding for economic development has been redirected to cover projects in countries with economies in transition.

67. Telephone interview with Andrew Reed, Economic Affairs Officer, Multilateral Fund Secretariat (Jan. 23, 1997).

68. For more on NGOs and other major groups, see *infra* Chapter 8.

69. For more on economic development agencies, see *infra* Chapter 6.

70. For more on the Sardar Sarovar Dam Project, see *infra* text following Chapter 6 note 151.

71. *See* Convention to Combat Desertification, *supra* Chapter 2 note 187, annex I, art. 14 (Regional Implementation Annex for Africa).

72. *See* Climate Change Convention, *supra* Chapter 2 note 137, art. 21, ¶ 3.

73. *See* discussion *infra* Chapters 8.

74. The year 1974 also marked a milestone in this context, with the formal call for a New International Economic Order (NIEO) in the efforts to promote economic development. Magraw posits that NIEO is firmly rooted in the concept of differential treatment for developing countries. *See* Magraw, *supra* Chapter 1 note 38, at 77.

75. *See* Handl, *supra* Chapter 2 note 206, at 30.

76. *See* Porras, *supra* Chapter 3 note 77, at 29.

77. *See* Schachter, *supra* Chapter 2 note 202, at 9.

78. *See id.*

79. *See id.*

80. *See* Handl, *supra* Chapter 2 note 206, at 29. *See also* discussion *supra* Chapter II, Part C ("need" as a standard of equity).

81. *See id.*

82. While Handl endorses uniform norms with regard to core obligations, he does acknowledge that variations in state parties' contributions to the problem could qualify as a special justification for using differential standards, but he rejects differentiation on the basis of development status. *See id.* at 9–10.

83. Based on development status, not only variations in states parties' contribution to the problem.

84. *See* Montreal Protocol—London Amendments, *supra* Chapter I note 41, arts. 5, 10.

85. See David Hurlbut, Beyond the Montreal Protocol: Impact on Nonparty States and Lessons for Future Environmental Regimes, 4 COLO. J. INT'L ENVTL. L. & POL'Y 353 (1993).

5

Promoting the Participation of Developing States – Incentives and Disincentives in Some International Environmental Agreements

In this chapter, I will examine some multilateral environmental conventions with respect to the extent to which they provide incentives or differential treatment for developing countries. The incentives to be examined below include norms that differentiate among states with regard to core obligations, provisions that include technical and financial assistance, and joint implementation. The disincentives to be discussed are the use of trade sanctions directed at non-parties to the treaties and non-compliance provisions directed at reluctant parties. In addition, negotiation assistance will also be discussed, although it is not mentioned in the treaties. Finally, I will make an assessment of the different types of incentives.

As mentioned above,[1] several environmental treaties distinguish between different categories of parties which have differentiated obligations. For the most part the dividing line goes between developed and developing countries. However, as in the case of the Climate Change Convention, some treaties differentiate between 1) industrialized countries (that is, OECD countries and countries undergoing the process of transition to a market economy); 2) only OECD countries;[2] and 3) developing countries. In the case of the Climate Change Convention, the first two groups are classified as Annex I and Annex II parties, respectively. Annex I countries are urged to cut emissions, yet Annex II countries (OECD countries) are singled out as the parties that are to provide financial assistance for developing countries to enable them to implement their general obligations.[3]

As discussed below,[4] the Kyoto Protocol introduced differential treatment among *developed* countries including countries with economies in transition.[5] This is an innovation in global environmental agreements, as opposed to regional agreements, some of which do include provisions with differential treatment among developed countries.[6] Perhaps the next step will be to introduce differential treatment among developing countries.[7]

The Climate Change Convention does mention that the parties, when implementing their commitments in Article 4, are to give full consideration to what actions are needed to meet the specific needs of developing country parties arising from the adverse effects of climate change and/or impact of the implementation of response measures, especially on nine different groups of developing countries, such as small island countries and countries with low-lying coastal areas.[8] In addition, the needs of the least developed countries, are mentioned specifically in Article 4(9). However, these subdivisions of developing countries do not pertain to the core obligations.

What criteria should be used in discriminating between developing countries in regard to core obligations? Most likely it would depend on their current emissions and capabilities with regard to being able to respond, prevent, reduce, or control the emissions. Perhaps distinguishing between their GNP[9] would also be helpful, as the developing countries are a very heterogeneous group, ranging from being low-income countries, such as Haiti to high-income countries, such as Singapore. The least developed would be the prime candidates for a substantial increase in emissions, whereas India and China, that emit large amounts of greenhouse gases, would have to reduce their emissions considerably. In addition, perhaps, developing countries that are oil producing nations should also be considered as a special group to be dealt with accordingly, in the context of emission reductions.

Throughout this study, there are references to the Montreal Protocol and this chapter uses it extensively to illustrate treaty provisions containing various types of differential norms. The Montreal Protocol seems to have become more precedent-setting than one could have imagined in 1987, when it was adopted. On the other hand, one has to note its unique objectives and other qualities,[10] if it is to serve as a model for other treaties. For instance, the Montreal Protocol has the role of reducing and eliminating the consumption and production of ozone depleting substances, not emission reductions as such, though, of course, the end result is the same, since there is a reduction of ozone-depleting substances.[11]

Assistance To Enable Developing Countries To Participate in the Treaty Negotiations

Some scholars suggest that pre-negotiation assistance should be offered to countries whose delegations do not have adequate knowledge of the technical and scientific aspects of environmental policy questions.[12] They suggest panels could be assembled, providing seminars on demand, and informal, off-the-record briefings by experts could be made available for any interested countries. This could be arranged perhaps by UNDP, ahead of scheduled conferences.[13] This is perhaps key to developing country involvement in treaty negotiations, in addition to funding. If all the participants in the negotiations of international agreements are well informed on the issues to be addressed, then they are more likely to express their concerns early on, thereby increasing the possibility of the treaties being successfully adopted.

A voluntary fund was established to support the participation of developing countries, especially the least developed, in both the preparatory process and the Rio Conference itself.[14] This has more and more become the trend with regard to global conferences, where legal instruments including treaties, are often adopted.

In regard to the treaty negotiations themselves, some of the assistance may be very simple, such as the cost of travel to get to the site of the negotiations or assistance with translation services if there is a language communication problem. Funding for developing country participation was made available in connection with the negotiations of the Framework Convention for Climate Change.[15] This enabled developing countries to participate in the international legislative process of the treaty and not just sign onto the final draft. Many treaty secretariats are now funding the participation of developing countries in meetings of treaty bodies after the signing and ratification of the treaties.

Assistance to enable developing countries to participate in the treaty negotiations leads them to a greater understanding of the issues and increases the possibility of the negotiations taking into account the developing country interests that are currently not represented or under-represented in the international legal process. This, in turn, increases the likelihood of the Parties reaching agreement and cooperating in the adoption and implementation of the treaties.

Treaty Provisions

Norms that Differentiate among States with regard to Core Obligations

This group of incentives discriminates among states with regard to core obligations, giving developing countries less stringent commitments or postponing their obligations.

***Provisions with Delayed Compliance Schedules**—Montreal Protocol on Substances that Deplete the Ozone Layer.* As mentioned earlier, the Montreal Protocol,[16] is a protocol of the framework treaty entitled the Vienna Convention for the Protection of the Ozone Layer.[17] The latter deals with protection of the stratospheric ozone layer in general, while the former gives particular content to the framework convention, by among other things, regulating particular substances that deplete the ozone layer. Article 2 of the Montreal Protocol sets timetables with dates and amounts of ozone depleting substances—among them various CFCs and bromide compounds (halons)—the production and consumption of which are to be progressively reduced or eliminated.

Article 5.1, representing one of the major innovations of the Montreal Protocol, entitles developing countries whose consumption and production of specified ozone-depleting substances is less than 0.3 kilograms per capita, to delay compliance with the Protocol's control measures by ten years. The grace period is qualified, to be used only "in order to meet its basic domestic needs."[18] Ultimately, the developing countries are obliged to comply with the production and consumption limits. Article 5.1 is used throughout the Protocol to distinguish developing country parties qualifying for special or differential treatment from other developing country parties and industrialized country parties, without actually defining the term 'developing countries'. A clear definition of 'developing countries' would perhaps have been helpful, since the consumption and production of some countries with economies in transition is less than 0.3 kilograms per capita, placing them in the same situation as qualifying developing countries with regard to ozone-depleting substances.[19] One such country, Georgia, has actually been reclassified as an Article 5 Party.[20]

Article 5.1, a differential norm, is a cause-related concession presenting an equitable solution to the ozone depletion problem, taking into account that the developed countries are the major producers and consumers of CFCs. In addition, the application of an equal phase-out period would place a greater social and economic burden on developing countries, especially for the ones that had previously made investments in capital equipment using CFCs, such as cooling systems and refrigerators.[21] The delay in complying with the control measures gives Article 5.1 Parties a chance to get a return on their investments and time to switch to CFC-free technologies.[22]

At the meeting of the Parties in London in 1990, Article 5 was replaced with a new Article 5, keeping the ten-year grace period, and at the same time expanding the article. Article 5.5 now makes development of the capacity of the developing countries to fulfill their obligations to comply with the control measures, dependent on the effective implementation of the financial cooperation as provided by Article 10 and transfer of technology as provided by Article 10A. The text of Article 5.5 reads as follows:

> Developing the capacity to fulfill the obligations of the Parties operating under paragraph 1 or this Article to comply with the control measures set out

in Article 2A to 2E and their implementation by those same Parties will *depend* upon the effective implementation of the financial cooperation as provided by Article 10 and transfer of technology as provided by Article 10A.[23]

One could interpret the obligation of developing countries to comply as only taking effect if developed countries fulfill their part of the bargain by giving technical and financial assistance to developing countries. In this sense, the condition weakens the ultimate obligation that the developing countries have, which is to comply with the control measures. Another interpretation would be that this paragraph only recognizes the fact that how *effectively* the developing countries will comply will depend on the actions taken by the developed countries in accordance with Article 10 and 10A, yet that their obligations remain the same.[24] With regard to the Montreal Protocol this does not seem to have been a problem in the context of financial obligations of the developed countries. In fact the Protocol is one of the most successful environmental agreements in terms of parties living up to their financial commitments. For the years 1991-1995, the contributions deposited corresponded to 88 percent of pledged contributions.[25]

Provisions with Delayed Compliance Schedules *— Framework Convention on Climate Change.* The Framework Convention on Climate Change has as its main objective the "stabilization of greenhouse gas concentrations in the atmosphere at a level that would prevent dangerous anthropogenic interference with the climate system."[26]

The problem with the climate change issue, is that it is more complex than the ozone layer, in view of the greater uncertainties regarding the climate change process and the role of human activities in that process. However, just as with the ozone layer, where binding limitations were adopted before there was clear proof of actual harm, many scientists urge the international community to take action now,[27] using a precautionary approach.[28] On the other hand, other scientists, claiming it is a natural process, dispute the notion of human activities affecting climate change[29] and many economists fear damage to the national economies, if tough measures to limit greenhouse gases are adopted too quickly.[30]

Unlike the Montreal Protocol, the Climate Change Convention does not have any set targets or timetables for the reduction of greenhouse gases. However, it requires all parties to report on their national programs containing measures to mitigate climate change.[31] This obligation was to be complied with within six months after the Convention entered into force for Annex I parties (developed countries), and three years after the Convention entered into force for non-Annex 1 parties (developing countries), while the least developed countries can make the reports at their discretion.[32] Clearly, the developing countries are given less stringent reporting requirements, the equivalent of the delayed compliance schedule of the Montreal Protocol, in this context.

The Convention refers to "common but differentiated responsibilities" in the Preamble, noting that "the largest share of historical and current global emissions of greenhouse gases has originated in developed countries. . . ."[33] The concept "Common but differentiated responsibilities" is also referred to in Article 3 entitled "Principles," stating that developed country parties "should take the lead in combating climate change and adverse effects thereof."[34] To my knowledge, this is the first environmental treaty that includes the concept "common but differentiated responsibilities," in effect stating that the responsibilities of developed and developing countries are to be different. Even if these principles are only meant to *guide* the parties,[35] it would seem that the Convention lay the foundation for asymmetrical norms with regard to core obligations.

Provisions with Targets and Timetables – *Montreal Protocol on Substances that Deplete the Ozone Layer.* The Montreal Protocol provides the developing countries with a ten-year grace period, and when that period has come to an end, they have to comply with the same obligations as the developed countries have. Essentially, this is a postponement of their obligations. On the other hand, once the control measures are applicable for the developing countries, the determination of the base year level is different for them than it is for the developed countries. The base year level (1986 level for the non-Article 5 states) will be either 0.3 kilograms per capita or the average of annual consumption for the 1995-1997 period.[36]

Provisions with Targets and Timetables – *Framework Convention on Climate Change and the Kyoto Protocol.* Another example of an incentive or differential norm that discriminates among states with regard to core obligations, can be found in the Climate Change Convention, regarding emission reduction targets. Developed countries were urged to reduce their greenhouse gas emissions, while the developing countries were not committed to any limitations.

Article 4, paragraph 2 of the Climate Change Convention requires Parties listed in Annex I of the Convention to adopt policies to limit anthropogenic emissions demonstrating that they are "taking the lead" in modifying greenhouse gas emissions with the "aim" of returning by the year 2000 to their 1990 levels. Committing to "aim" to reduce emissions does not mandate achievement, yet it can be interpreted as a political expectation.[37] There are no such "obligations" for developing countries. These are very vague commitments yet, just as the Vienna Convention lacked detailed commitments and was followed by the Montreal Protocol setting binding limitations on the consumption of ozone depleting substances, a protocol to the Climate Change Convention was proposed and finally adopted, introducing clear targets and timetables for the reduction of greenhouse gases by developed countries after the year 2000.[38]

The Berlin Mandate set a deadline, stipulating that by the time of the third session of the Conference of the Parties to the Climate Change Convention in 1997, a Protocol or similar instrument was to be adopted, strengthening the commitments of the developed countries.[39] In that context, the European Union (EU) suggested a reduction of carbon dioxide emissions by 2010 to levels 15 percent below the 1990 emissions by developed countries,[40] Japan suggested a 5 percent reduction in the period between 2008 and 2012,[41] and the United States suggested a reduction to 1990 levels by 2008-2010. Up until the last few days of the negotiations at Kyoto it was doubtful whether there would be any agreement.

The Kyoto negotiations, however, did produce a treaty, the Kyoto Protocol to the United Nations Framework Convention on Climate Change, adopted December 11, 1997.[42] It stipulates an overall emission reduction for Parties included in Annex I of the Climate Change Convention of at least 5 percent below the 1990 levels of greenhouse gas emissions in the commitment period 2008 to 2012.[43] The Protocol distributes the burden among the developed country Parties using different targets for each country, calculated pursuant to their quantified emission limitations and reduction commitments listed in Annex B of the Protocol.[44] The European Union is to reduce its greenhouse gas emissions by 8 percent, the United States by 7 percent, Japan by 6 percent, whereas Australia, New Zealand, Iceland, and Norway can have a small increase in their emissions in the above mentioned commitment period.[45] This is the first time that a global environmental treaty uses differentiated emission targets among industrialized countries.[46] Yet, there are no limitations on the emissions from developing countries.

Hopefully, the Kyoto Protocol will be amended in the near future to include voluntary emission reduction targets for developing countries[47] or at least limits to their emissions *growth*,[48]otherwise they may undermine the treaty, as they are projected to become the major polluters in the decades to come.[49] At the Fourth Conference of the Parties, in 1998, Argentina did agree to establish emission reduction targets at the fifth session of Conference of the Parties to the Climate Change Convention.[50] Other developing countries should seriously consider joining Argentina in committing to emission reductions as developing countries are more vulnerable to climate change damage and have the least ability to adapt to eventual climate change.

At the Kyoto negotiations, the United States demanded that developing countries participate by committing to voluntary emission reductions, before it accepted mandatory controls on greenhouse gas emissions. Without the United States becoming a party to the Kyoto Protocol, it may not enter into force because the Protocol stipulates that to enter into force 55 parties to the Convention must ratify it and the carbon dioxide emissions from the Annex I ratifying parties must represent 55 percent of the greenhouse gas emissions of Annex I parties for the base year 1990.[51] The United States emits 36.1 percent of the total emissions of greenhouse gases from Annex I parties, whereas Europe emits approximately 24 percent.[52] The EU member countries alone would not represent enough GHG emissions to fulfill the treaty requirements regarding entry into force. On the other hand, if the Protocol were to enter into force, notwithstanding the U.S. absence, it would probably not be a very effective agreement, given the amount of U.S. emissions.[53]

Yet, for the agreement to be ratified by the United States, the Executive must first have the advice and consent of two-thirds of the Senate, which is not likely to happen at present.[54] The U.S. Senate, through a unanimous vote on resolution 98, has expressed that it will not approve the treaty unless commitments to limit greenhouse gases for developing countries are included in such a treaty.[55]

If developing countries were to get specific emission reduction targets, an interesting question would be whether they would get differentiated targets, just as the developed countries got in Kyoto. This is an important issue because many developing countries have very differing circumstances, such as China, whose contribution to greenhouse emissions is many times greater than, for instance, Guatemala.[56]

Financial Assistance: Financing Implementation of the Agreements

Financial assistance in the context of multilateral environmental treaties refers to specific allocations to finance the participation of developing countries in the implementation of the treaties, which also serve as incentives to promote non-party developing countries to ratify the agreements. The Multilateral Fund of the Montreal Protocol, the first funding mechanism to be included in an environmental treaty, will be discussed at length in this context as it has become a model for other treaties. The financial assistance provisions of the Climate Change Convention, the Biodiversity Convention, and the Convention to Combat Desertification will also be discussed.

Montreal Protocol on Substances that Deplete the Ozone Layer—Multilateral Fund. Article 10 of the Montreal Protocol—London Provisions of 1990,[57] required the developed countries to establish a financial mechanism to provide funding and technical cooperation, including transfer of CFC-free technology, for developing countries operating under the Article 5.1 category. A Multilateral Fund was established in 1990, representing a milestone in international environmental law. No other environmental treaty at the time had such a fund. These funds are to be new and additional funds to the regular funds made available for development aid. The Multilateral Fund is administered by the World Bank, the United Nations Development Programme (UNDP), the United Nations Environment Programme (UNEP), and the United Nations Industrial Development Organization (UNIDO).

However, this fund is very specific to the objectives of the Protocol, thereby only recognizing the right of a developing country to receive aid in that context, not aid in general.[58] In addition, the Executive Committee, consisting of seven developing and seven industrialized countries, through its criteria for awarding projects, implicitly places conditions on what the aid can be used for. The Montreal Fund only provides funding for costs which are needed to phase out ozone-depleting substances (ODS) including qualified new equipment, retrofits, royalties, licensing fees, patents, technology transfer fees, and operating costs.[59] Furthermore, the aid is limited in that once the objective of replacing technologies that use ozone-depleting substances with ozone-safe technologies is achieved, putting developing countries on a "level playing field" with its trading partners, then the developing country cannot demand any more aid under the Protocol.[60] The issue of accountability in the use of the aid remains ambiguous.[61] This is due to the fact that even though the Executive Committee has the authority to review reports on the implementation of activities supported by the fund, developing countries, according to Article 9 are not explicitly obligated to offer the books of their domestic agencies to independent auditors.[62]

Failure by developed countries to fulfill their commitments of technical and financial assistance in accordance with international environmental agreements often hampers developing countries in their efforts to comply with international agreements.[63] Major efforts are being made to improve compliance by the parties with regard to control measures, such as in the Montreal Protocol where the parties can use an elaborate non-compliance procedure mentioned below,[64] but perhaps the non-compliance procedure should also be used to address the industrialized countries' obligation to assist developing countries both technically and financially, in accordance with their treaty commitments.[65] This is particularly important because developing countries often depend on that assistance in order to comply with the control measures. However, this would only come about if contributions to the Multilateral Fund were made compulsory.[66] On the other hand, there is likely a limit with regard to how much funding the developed countries can contribute. Economic problems in many of them are an important factor contributing to the decline in ODA funding. Perhaps one could call it "assistance fatigue." Yet, the governments could align themselves with private sources of funding and collaborate in many different ways.[67] Article 10 of the Montreal Protocol specifies that the financial mechanism "may also include other means of multilateral, regional, and bilateral cooperation."[68]

The Multilateral Fund of the Montreal Protocol is financed on the basis of the United Nations scale of assessment by contributions from parties not operating under paragraph 1 of Article 5. The contributions deposited in the Fund for the years 1991-95 corresponded to 88 percent of pledged contributions, amounting to $471,000,000.[69] The arrears were due to countries in transition and one developing country not operating under paragraph 1 of Article 5.[70] These statistics are very optimistic. If all financial mechanisms received funding to the extent of 88 percent, there seems little need to use any non-compliance measures in that context. However, this is not the case with regard to many other funding mechanisms, such as the Global Environmental Facility, described below.[71] The discrepancy between pledged funds and actual deposits with regard to GEF is much larger.

Framework Convention Climate Change. Article 4, paragraph 3 maps out the bulk of the financial responsibilities of the Annex II country parties (OECD countries) as follows:

> The developed country Parties and other developed Parties included in annex II will provide new and *additional* financial resources to meet the agreed full cost incurred by developing country Parties in complying with their obligations under Article 12, paragraph 1. They shall also provide such financial resources, including for the transfer of technology, needed by the developing country Parties to meet the *agreed* full *incremental* costs of implementing measures that are covered by paragraph 1 of this Article and that agreed between a developing country Party and the international entity or entities referred to in Article 11, in accordance with that Article. The implementation of these commitments shall take into account the need for adequacy and predictability in the flow of funds and the importance of appropriate burden sharing among the developed country Parties.[72]

The developed country Parties committed themselves to provide *additional* financial resources to meet the cost of implementation for developing countries. The term "additional" implies that money to implement the Convention was not to be diverted from existing development aid, instead there were to be "new and additional resources" to cover the cost resulting from the developing countries joining the conventions. The developed countries agreed to pay the full costs of developing countries complying with their reporting commitments under Article 12(1), as these were seen as being limited.[73]

On the other hand, the cost resulting from addressing climate change through general commitments, such as implementing mitigating measures, preparing for adaptation to the impacts of climate change, in addition to research and information exchange, the developed countries were not willing to pay in full.[74] For implementing these measures, the developed countries agreed to pay the agreed full *incremental* costs incurred by developing country parties in complying with their obligations under Article 4, paragraph 1. As the costs were deemed to be unlimited and potentially great, the obligation was limited to a process wherein the developing countries had to present potential projects to the Convention's financial mechanism.[75] If the financial mechanism approved the project, the developed countries would pay the "agreed full incremental cost." If it were rejected, then no funding by the developed countries would be required.[76]

The parties to the Climate Change Convention defined a mechanism in Article 11, for the provision of financial resources on a grant or concessional basis, including for the transfer of technology.[77] In addition, the Parties entrusted the operation of the funding mechanism to the Global Environment Facility.[78] This entity is run jointly by the World Bank, the U.N. Programme for Environment (UNEP), and the U.N. Development Programme (UNDP).

Biodiversity Convention. The objectives of the Biodiversity Convention are the conservation of biodiversity, the sustainable use of its components, and fair and equitable sharing of the benefits that result from the utilization of genetic resources.[79] In order to reach these objectives, the Convention includes financial mechanisms to assist developing countries implement the treaty, which in turn, also serve as incentives to promote non-party developing countries to ratify the Convention.

The financial obligations of the developed countries are stipulated in Article 20 as follows:

> The developed country parties shall provide new and additional financial resources to enable developing country Parties to meet the agreed full incremental costs to them of implementing measures to fulfil the obligations of this Convention and to benefit from its provisions and which costs are agreed between a developing country Party and the institutional structure referred to in Article 21, in accordance with policy, strategy, programme priorities and eligibility criteria and an indicative list of incremental costs established by the Conference of the Parties.[80]

The parties to the Convention did not fully follow the model established by the Climate Change Convention. In essence, they chose to give the Conference of the Parties (COP) a more dominant role than the entity that was to carry out the financial mechanism.[81] For instance, the financial mechanism in the Climate Change Convention is to serve under the guidance and be accountable to the COP,[82] whereas in the Biodiversity Convention, COP will decide on the arrangements to give effect to Article 21, after consulting with the financial mechanism.[83] However, after much discussion, the Global Environment Facility (GEF) was chosen as the entity entrusted with the operation of the financial mechanism.[84]

The Biodiversity Convention, just like the Montreal Protocol, has a provision linking the efforts made by developing countries to fulfill their obligations to the provision of financial assistance from developed countries. Article 20, paragraph 4 reads as follows: "The *extent* to which developing country Parties will effectively implement their commitments under this Convention will *depend* on the effective implementation by developed country Parties of their commitments under this Convention related to financial resources and transfer of technology. . . . "[85]

Arguably, one could interpret this provision as conditioning the fulfillment of developing country obligations on receiving financial assistance from developed countries. Yet, during the negotiations of the Convention, developing countries suggested such language, but it was rejected by the Intergovernmental Negotiating Committee.[86] Instead it only acknowledges that the extent to which developing countries will effectively implement the Convention, will depend on receipt of financial resources.[87]

Convention to Combat Desertification. The objective of the Desertification Convention is to combat desertification and mitigate the effects of drought in countries experiencing serious drought and/or desertification, particularly in Africa.[88]

The parties to the Convention agreed not to establish a separate fund, only a Global Mechanism through which developed countries are to mobilize funding from *existing* sources for developing countries.[89] Whether this new mechanism will be able to mobilize the necessary funding for developing countries, remains to be seen. It may be less likely to function effectively in times when developed countries are going through economic recession, leading to reductions in their Official Development Assistance (ODA). Yet, the treaty requires that new avenues for mobilizing funding are also to be sought out, such as debt swaps, through such entities as NGOs and other private sector entities.[90] New and additional funding from GEF is also to be solicited for activities to combat desertification that are relevant to GEF's four focal areas.[91]

Joint Implementation

I have classified joint implementation as an incentive (selective incentive)[92] because joint implementation in accordance with the Clean Development Mechanism (CDM) of the Kyoto Protocol[93] makes the developing countries the recipients of environmentally sound technology and technical assistance, in addition to funding from developed countries.[94] Yet, there is no doubt it also serves as an incentive for developed countries because they can receive credits to use toward their emission reduction commitments from the projects they carry out in developing countries.[95]

Joint implementation, just as emissions trading[96] is a market-based mechanism that has the potential of achieving low cost emission reductions while promoting sustainable development. It is introduced in the Convention on Climate Change Art. 4(2)(a) which stipulates that developed countries may implement policies to limit greenhouse gas emissions jointly with other parties and assist other parties in contributing to the achievement of the objective of the Convention.[97] Pilot joint implementation activities in conjunction with the Climate Change Convention are already underway.[98] The Kyoto Protocol developed this further by including the clean development mechanism in a separate provision, as discussed below.[99]

The concept of joint implementation, initially promoted by Norway in 1991, allows a developed country to fulfill its emissions reduction target in the convention by associating with a developing country that produces a limited amount of greenhouse gas emissions.[100] A system of binding quantitative targets is necessary in order for the joint implementation projects to produce credits for such emission reductions.[101] Such a system of emission reduction targets and timetables was realized through the Kyoto Protocol.[102]

By investing, for instance, in programs to protect the developing country's tropical rainforest or establishing industries that use low-emitting energy technologies, the developed country will now be able to offset some of its emission reduction obligations, rather than face high marginal costs of abatement measures in their own countries.[103] GHG emissions are a global phenomenon in terms of biophysics, therefore, it does not matter where the emission reductions take place.[104]

Dudek and Wiener describe one model of joint implementation as a voluntary agreement between an "investor" and a "host."[105] In their model, the host provides greenhouse abatement services which translate into "credits" which are transferred to the investor and can be reported to the investor's national government to be used toward fulfilling the nations emission reduction obligations under the Kyoto Protocol at a lower cost than the investor would have to pay at home. In return, the investor provides the host with something of value, for instance, cash, low-emitting energy technologies, or water treatment systems.[106] Hosts in general, will be from countries with low marginal costs of abatement, while investors will normally be from countries with high marginal abatement costs.[107] Private enterprises will probably play a big part as investors as they have the financial resources and the incentives to make the investments because they have to abate greenhouse gas emissions in accordance with national emission abatement requirements.[108] NGOs, Dudek and Wiener contend, could also play a role as performers of the actual abatement service, by buying greenhouse gas abatement credits and selling or retiring them, or monitoring and certifying greenhouse gas abatement achievements at specific joint implementation projects.[109]

Joint implementation, just as tradeable permits, has been criticized as a license to pollute.[110] On the other hand, joint implementation promotes developing country participation in the Convention on Climate Change and its Protocol because the developing countries stand to receive large sums of money and transfers of technology.[111] At the same time, this incentive would be a positive argument for the developing countries to join future protocols, where they would also have to commit themselves to limit future emissions of greenhouse gases.[112]

An additional advantage of using joint implementation is that it is cost effective.[113] This would be of special interest for developed countries because it is usually cheaper for them to use pollution abatement measures in developing countries than to do it at home. Furthermore, joint implementation has the added attraction of promoting the transfer of technology and financial resources from industrialized to developing countries in carrying out the joint projects conducted in developing countries.[114]

The Clean Development Mechanism (CDM) was defined with the adoption of the Kyoto Protocol.[115] This mechanism consists of emission reduction activities similar to joint implementation projects carried out among Annex I parties (Article 6), however, CDM is carried out between Annex I and non-Annex I parties as stipulated in Article 12 of the Protocol.[116] The CDM projects are meant to assist developing countries in achieving sustainable development, thereby contributing to the goal of the Climate Change Convention. Annex I countries are authorized by Article 12 to use credits accruing from projects in developing countries to contribute to compliance with their emission reduction targets.[117] In addition, the clean development mechanism can also be looked upon as a funding mechanism; developing countries that are "particularly vulnerable to the adverse effects of climate change" will receive a share of the proceeds to assist them in meeting their adaptation costs.[118]

The clean development mechanism will be subject to the authority and guidance of the Conference of the Parties serving as the meeting of the Parties to the Protocol and will be supervised by an executive board of the clean development mechanism. In addition, operational entities will be designated by the Conference of the Parties to certify emission reductions resulting from each project because the developing countries do not as yet have any emission reduction targets. Clearly, a whole new bureaucracy will be developed in the context of this new mechanism. One can only hope it will be run efficiently.

Technical Assistance—Including Access to Technology and Capacity Building

In general developing countries have relatively low regulatory and technical capabilities for use in regard to environmental protection.[119] This can include legislative drafting skills to draft adequate laws and regulatory and administrative skills to implement pollution control laws, in addition to equipment to detect, monitor, and remedy such harm.[120]

In order to address these issues, several of the more recent multilateral treaties include provisions on technical assistance. Some are all encompassing, such as the Law of the Sea Convention (UNCLOS) while others are more specific, such as the Montreal Protocol. With regard to the latter, such assistance is aimed at neutralizing the otherwise negative effect it would have on the stratospheric ozone layer if the developing countries were not to participate in reducing ozone depleting substances.[121] The same goal applies to the Convention on Climate Change, with regard to gases causing global warming. The developed country parties to the Convention to Combat Desertification also undertake to facilitate the transfer of environmentally sound technology specifically relevant to combating desertification.[122] UNCLOS Article 202 specifies that states are obligated to provide scientific, educational, technical, and other assistance for the protection and preservation of the marine environment, especially to developing states.[123]

In the multilateral environmental treaties, technical assistance includes transfer of technology. Technology has long been recognized as a tool for promoting economic development. However, since the interdependence between environment and development has been recognized by the international community and sustainable development has become the new goal, any type of technology will no longer suffice. The goal of sustainable development can only be reached using environmentally sound technology.

With regard to the transfer of technology, Article 10A of the Montreal Protocol—London Amendments reads as follows:

> Each Party shall take every practicable step, consistent with the programmes supported by the financial mechanism, to ensure:
>
> (a) That the best available, environmentally safe substitutes and related technologies are expeditiously transferred to Parties operating under paragraph 1 of Article 5; and
> (b) That the transfers referred to in subparagraph (a) occur under fair and most favorable conditions.

The use of the word "shall" in this article implies an obligation on the part of the developed countries to ensure the transfer of environmentally safe technology. However, in reality it is the financial mechanism or Multilateral Fund which supports certain programs, that will determine just how much technology actually gets transferred. How much funding is available for the programs is, in turn, determined by the extent to which developed countries fulfill their financial commitments.

Environmentally sound technology is characterized as technology that does not harm the environment and technology that improves the environment. A broad characterization of environmentally sound technologies is used in Agenda 21. It reads as follows: Environmentally sound technologies protect the environment, are less polluting, use all resources in a more sustainable manner, recycle more of their wastes and products, and handle residual wastes in a more acceptable manner than the technologies for which they were substitutes.[124] In addition, Agenda 21 identifies the scope of environmentally sound technology as "not just individual technologies, but total systems which include know-how, procedures, goods and services, and equipment as well as organizational and managerial procedures."[125]

Environmentally sound technologies can also be divided into two categories: hardware and software.[126] Hardware consists of the products or industrial plants, while software represents the know-how or skills needed to apply technical ideas.[127]

By transferring environmentally sound technologies to developing countries, these countries would be able to avoid many of the mistakes of the industrialized countries, in the sense that they would have an alternative development model. Using best available, appropriate technology, developing countries would essentially skip over the polluting technology that industrialized countries had to use because environmentally sound technologies had not yet been invented. This process is known as "leapfrogging."[128]

Agenda 21 states that "the human resource development and local capacity-building aspects of technology choices including gender-relevant aspects, should also be addressed."[129] These technologies, Agenda 21 adds "should be compatible with nationally determined socio-economic, cultural and environmental principles."[130] In other words, the choice of technology depends on the economic conditions and the levels of environmental standards. Environmentally sound technology is therefore a relative term. However, in deciding which technology to choose, using the cost-benefit-analysis as the sole determinant has been discredited by some scholars because it tends to portray environmental and economic considerations as conflicting goals.[131]

The Framework Convention on Climate Change sets out to stabilize the greenhouse gas concentrations in the atmosphere to a level "that would prevent dangerous anthropogenic interference with the climate system."[132] In Article 4.5, the Convention states:

> The developed country Parties [to the treaty] . . . shall take all practicable steps to promote, facilitate and finance, as appropriate, the transfer of, or access to, environmentally sound technologies and know-how to other Parties, particularly developing country Parties, to enable them to implement the provisions of the Convention. In this process, the developed country Parties shall support the development and enhancement of endogenous capacities and technologies of developing country Parties. Other Parties and organizations in a position to do so may also assist in facilitating the transfer of such technologies.[133]

An important issue regarding the transfer to environmentally sound technology is the issue of intellectual property rights.[134] Some of the technology "hardware" and some of the "software" required in the context of the multilateral environmental treaties is privately owned or patented.

Many developing countries have argued that intellectual property should be weakened allowing for more access to technology. They argue that the extent of the protection should comply with their economic policies.[135] Other analysts argue that reduced protection is likely to "lower the level of environmental technology available in developing countries."[136]

It is not feasible that companies that have invested in the development of technology would be willing to give it to developing countries free of charge. To my knowledge, no system of incentives for inventors to create new technologies has yet been designed that surpasses the benefits of intellectual property. Until such a time, it seems sensible to use intellectual property laws that effectively create such incentives, such as in the example below regarding the Montreal Protocol.[137] Agenda 21 also stresses the need to protect these rights.[138] However, not all technology is patented and often the patent period has run out, making the information available to the public. If the technology is patented, special funding can be made available to pay the royalties involved, such as has been done within the context of the Montreal Protocol.[139]

The London Amendments to the Montreal Protocol only requires that the transfer of technology take place under "fair and favorable conditions"[140] and the Climate Convention uses the term "facilitate" without any further elaboration.[141] As was suggested by one scholar, the Multilateral Fund of the Montreal Protocol is being used to pay for royalties, making the CFC-free technology available to developing countries, while providing industry with a return on their investment.[142] In this manner, the incentives for developing new technologies are balanced with the public interests and development goals of the developing countries.[143] The Multilateral Fund, however, emphasizes that technology transfer is ensured by the Fund, but it is not an end in and of itself.[144]

Schachter states that on the international scene, companies often own the technology (be it patented or not) and sell it as other commodities, except that it is not freely available in the open market.[145] In addition, there are other limitations on the transfer of technology because of the "disparities between the donor and the recipient."[146] One such restrictive practice is to impose constraints on the recipient's use and production of the technology. Another is to forbid the purchase of competitive technology.[147] Schachter suggests a solution could be found in the strengthening of the negotiating skills of the developing countries and improving their economic position.[148] Such training of negotiating skills could be part of the technical assistance made available to the developing countries.

In addition to access to technology, the capacity of developing countries to receive technology transfers needs to be strengthened. Very often, when problems arise regarding technology, it is the basic infrastructure that is missing. This has to be taken into account when structuring the assistance to developing countries.

Capacity-Building – Environmental Laws. Chapter 8, Section 15 of Agenda 21 mentions how the enactment and enforcement of laws and regulations are paramount for the implementation of most international agreements in the field of environment and development, and is evident from the frequent treaty obligations to report on legislative measures.[149] Knowledge of environmental laws constitutes part of the technical assistance for developing countries.

Increasingly, Wilson argues, developing countries are demanding assistance in the field of environmental law, yet relatively few environmental lawyers, especially from the United States, the country with the most experience in this area, have been involved, preferring to focus on domestic issues.[150] Wilson states that this focus impedes efforts by developing countries to choose the best from the law experience from the developed countries, making it more difficult for the developing countries to avoid basic mistakes.[151] Because environmental problems are only one of their many competing priorities, it is unreasonable to pile expectations on developing countries without some help.[152] Agenda 21 urges intergovernmental and non-governmental organizations to provide governments, upon request, with an integrated program of environment and development law services tailored specifically to the needs of the recipient legal and administrative systems.[153] Past experience has shown the advantages of combining expert legal advice with specialized legal information services.[154]

As Agenda 21 suggests, international and academic institutions can cooperate in providing trainees from developing countries with postgraduate programs and in-service training facilities in environment and development law.[155] This training would include effective application and progressive improvement of applicable laws, related skills of negotiating, drafting, and mediation, and the training of professors. Existing programs run by intergovernmental and non-governmental organizations could pool their efforts with related university programs, harmonizing curriculum planning and offering an optimal range of options to interested governments and potential sponsors.[156]

The most important issues regarding such training programs are, first of all, that they have to be intensive, extending over at least a year, not just a few days of exposure.[157] Secondly, the programs must have adequate provisions for follow-up, also giving the trainees sufficient literary sources.[158] In addition, the programs have to be customized to fit the needs of the specific developing country. Finally, the recipient governments have to be receptive to changing their legal systems, giving the trainees a chance to practice what they learned, even if changes will not occur overnight.

For the programs to be successful, the recipient governments, on their part, would have to do research ahead of time regarding how their legal system functions in this area and how it affects socio-cultural and economic behavior before new laws are introduced.[159] The environmental laws in particular, must be adapted to the local circumstances and experiences of each of the developing countries.[160]

Disincentives

Trade Sanctions – Getting Reluctant States to Become Parties. Trade sanctions are a type of negative incentive, but not a selective incentive as they do not discriminate between states, but apply to non-parties be they developed or developing countries. Yet, I include them in the context of this study for the sake of completeness, as they have promoted the participation of developing countries in some international environmental agreements.

The first time trade sanctions were used in an international environmental treaty was in the Washington Convention on International Trade in Endangered Species (CITES).[161] Recognizing the need to protect certain species against over-exploitation through international trade, it prohibits all commercial trade of some species and regulates trade in a number of other species.

The importance of CITES in our context is that it bans imports from not just parties to the Convention, but also non-parties.[162] At the same time it has a non-discriminatory provision, Article X, which essentially allows non-parties who can produce the same type of documentation which conforms to the requirements of the treaty, to have that accepted by a party to the Convention, in order that the party may export to or import from that non-party. For many non-parties it made more sense to become a party to CITES, since they had to go to the trouble of complying with the treaty requirements anyway, in order to get similar documentation, allowing them to trade with parties to the Convention. There are mixed reviews on how effectively the trade sanctions in CITES have worked.[163]

Article 4 of Montreal Protocol has trade sanctions that mirror the ones mentioned in CITES. Specifically, it prohibits trade in the controlled substances, the chemicals themselves, such as CFCs and halons. In addition, the article contains trade restrictions which will affect products produced with or containing controlled substances. The latter type of trade restriction would be a strong incentive for developing countries to adopt the Protocol, as goods produced with or containing CFCs make up a large share of their exported commodities.[164]

By promoting universal participation, such prohibitions also indirectly address the free-rider problem and "pollution havens". Trade restrictions would ensure that the goal of the Protocol which is to reduce or eliminate ozone-depleting substances, would not be defeated by a few non-party States establishing themselves as havens where obligations accepted by the rest of the international community could be evaded.[165] Furthermore, the trade restrictions would put pressure on reluctant States wishing to benefit without making a contribution: the free-rider.[166] Developing countries not happy with the financial aid offered by a new treaty would not necessarily be able to stay outside the treaty without suffering any disadvantages.[167]

The issue of using trade sanctions in environmental treaties and their relationship to GATT/WTO is a highly debated one. If the connection between trade and environment is through their relationship to development, arguably, the balance between trade and environmental mandates is defined by sustainable development.[168] In the context of this study, I will not enter a lengthy discussion on the subject, as it constitutes a separate topic. However, to date, WTO has made no formal ruling on the legality of the provisions with regard to the Montreal Protocol or any of the other international environmental agreements containing trade sanctions.[169]

Non-Compliance Procedure – Promoting implementation. The Montreal Protocol has a non-compliance procedure that was formulated in accordance with Article 8. This represents a type of disincentive for parties not complying with the Protocol, whether they are developed or developing countries. Not implementing its obligations under the Protocol can have serious consequences for the party involved. For a developing country it could mean having funding applications for its projects rejected.

Any of the Parties to the Protocol can bring complaints – regarding alleged non-compliance by other Parties – to the Implementation Committee by way of the Secretariat.[170] The party that allegedly is in non-compliance is then given a chance to reply. Both submissions are then reviewed by the Implementation Committee which then reports to the Meeting of the Parties. The Meeting of the Parties then will "decide upon and call for steps to bring about full compliance with the Protocol."[171] This includes "appropriate assistance," (such as assistance for data collection and reporting, technology transfer, and financial assistance), the issuing of cautions, and suspension of specific rights and privileges under the Protocol.[172] However, possible examples of non-compliance have not been adopted.[173]

The non-compliance procedure is becoming more commonly used in international environmental agreements. The Climate Change Convention called for the establishment of a multilateral consultative process in its Article 13, and the Kyoto Protocol requires the Conference of the Parties serving as the meeting of the Parties to the Kyoto Protocol to approve at its first session, appropriate procedures and mechanisms to address cases of non-compliance.[174]

Although the non-compliance procedure in the Montreal Protocol applies to all parties to the treaty, developing countries are given special treatment compared to industrialized countries. Article 5, of the London Amendments to the Montreal Protocol stipulates that if Article 5 Parties have notified the Secretariat that they are unable to implement their obligations because of inadequate funding or transfer of technology from the developed countries in accordance with their obligations,[175] then the non-compliance procedure cannot be invoked against them.[176] This relaxation of the rules of the non-compliance procedure emphasizes the link between the developing countries' fulfillment of their treaty obligations and the developed countries' fulfillment of their financial obligations, as discussed above.

Assessment of the Different Types of Incentives—Differential Norms

Above I have examined several different types of incentives or differential norms, some of which discriminate among states with regard to the core obligations of the treaties, such as delayed compliance schedules, and others which do not, such as technical and financial assistance. Below I examine the merits of the different types of incentives.

New Developments—More Flexibility or Leeway for Developing Countries

In the context of incentives discriminating among states with regard to core obligations, there seems to be a gradual change in the way the treaty provisions address the special circumstances of developing countries, veering more and more away from symmetrical norms. In the Montreal Protocol, the developing countries first got a ten-year grace period, after which they were to comply with the control measures.

The Climate Change Convention, on the other hand, did not include developing countries in its vague provisions requiring emission reductions, thereby giving them even more leeway than the Montreal Protocol. The recent Kyoto Protocol did not change the obligations (or lack thereof) of the developing countries in this regard. Yet, it did institute discrimination among developed countries with regard to their reduction targets, providing new possibilities regarding criteria for differentiating among countries and their obligations.[177]

Perhaps one can interpret this change—giving developing countries more leeway—in treaty provisions as a reflection of the perceived need to have developing countries "on board" the treaties that address globally sensitive environmental resources as soon as possible.

Flexibility Versus Undermining the Treaty: A Question of Balance

While flexibility built into treaty provisions promotes participation, there are potential disadvantages of having such differential treatment that discriminates among states with regard to core obligations. When has this flexibility reached its limits? For instance, the treaty itself could be undermined by having too many different obligations causing monitoring problems or postponement of the fulfillment of the treaty commitments.

With regard to the Kyoto Protocol, where the developing countries still do not have any obligations with regard to reducing greenhouse gas emission, postponement or monitoring problems are as yet not an issue. However, the developing countries will most likely be required to, at least, limit their emissions growth and eventually agree to a phased-in reduction of their emissions through a gradual strengthening of their commitments. Otherwise, the objective of the Kyoto Protocol and the Climate Change Convention would be undermined.[178] The developed countries alone cannot fulfill the goal of stabilizing the greenhouse gas concentrations in the atmosphere to a level that would prevent dangerous anthropogenic interference with the climate system.[179]

The issue of undermining the treaty because of postponement of the obligations or monitoring problems, is often used to argue for the use of uniform norms as mentioned above.[180] This has not yet surfaced as a problem, as most of these incentives are of a recent date. With regard to the ten-year-old Montreal Protocol, the funding mechanism which has financed projects and programs in developing countries has enabled twenty-four of them to start the phase-out of control substances before their grace period was over.[181] In this manner, the postponement issue may have been overcome.

On the other hand, in part because of the flexibility or differential treatment given developing countries in the Montreal Protocol, a black market in CFCs has developed. In an attempt to curb such illegal trade, the Conference of the Parties at their Ninth Meeting, in September of 1997, agreed to establish a licensing system to be used in the import and export of many of the CFCs and other ozone depleting substances.[182] The licensing system will be in effect in 2000.[183] Some developing countries can delay implementing the system until 2001 and 2005 for certain substances.[184] In addition, all developing countries will be able to receive assistance from the Multilateral Fund to establish such a licensing system.[185]

Other Issues Concerning Incentives

Delayed compliance schedules and other incentives or differential norms that affect core obligations will only work for tackling certain types of global environmental problems, particularly those dealing with unwanted emissions through the use of targets and timetables. Other incentives such as technical and financial assistance, being more general in nature, can be used in most of the international environmental agreements.

Appearing in several of the environmental treaties adopted in the last twenty to twenty-five years, technical and financial assistance seem to be the most commonly used incentives in the treaty provisions.[186] Doing an assessment of the different environmental treaties, one might observe that provisions containing technical and financial assistance, in many cases have become more effective since the introduction of funds giving such provisions more substance.[187]

Very often, the older of these treaties would not elaborate on the mechanisms to be used for providing this assistance, only urging that technical and financial assistance should be given to developing countries. Whatever projects may have been undertaken on a bilateral level or through international organizations were done purely on an ad hoc basis. Currently, by establishing funding mechanisms, the projects and activities are better coordinated, and cooperation between different institutions is much more likely to take place.

The above-mentioned funds—the Multilateral Fund and GEF[188]—are very important in a practical sense. They provide the incremental cost of compliance for developing countries, enabling many of the technical assistance projects and programs. Probably in part because of the Multilateral Fund promoting the participation of developing countries, states that account for 80 percent of the consumption of CFCs have ratified the Montreal Protocol, 116 of which are developing countries.[189] The states that have ratified the Climate Change Convention account for 88 percent of the world's emissions of greenhouse gases,[190] 120 of which are developing countries.[191] Keeping in mind that the industrialized countries are still contributing most of the global emissions or consuming most CFCs, these statistics are an indication that using funding mechanisms seems to be an effective mechanism to promote participation by developing countries in environmental treaties, leading to universal participation.

Yet, in the case of the Desertification Convention, the Parties agreed not to establish a separate fund, but instead are relying on a Global Mechanism through which developed countries are to mobilize funding from *existing* sources for developing countries.[192] Whether this mechanism will be as effective an incentive as the financial mechanism used in the Montreal Protocol or the Climate Change Convention, remains to be seen.

In contrast to technical and financial assistance provisions, joint implementation as stipulated in the Clean Development Mechanism (CDM) of the Kyoto Protocol is still a controversial incentive.[193] CDM promotes technology transfers because in the effort to seek credits to use toward its emission reduction obligations, the developed countries will transfer environmentally sound technology to developing countries. However, it also entails a bureaucracy to certify the emission reductions of the different projects. Furthermore, some environmentalists claim it gives developed countries a license to pollute.[194] Yet, joint implementation can be limited in its use, and made applicable to contribute to compliance with only part of the quantified emission limitation for developed countries, the rest being done through domestic efforts, as the parties agreed to in the Kyoto Protocol.[195] In addition, joint implementation, just as emissions trading[196] is a market-based mechanism that has the potential of achieving low cost emission reductions while promoting sustainable development.

Notes

1. *See supra* text accompanying Chapter 1 note 36.

2. For a list of current OECD countries, see *supra* Chapter 1 note 27. Annexes I and II of the Climate Change Convention, however, include the OECD countries as of 1992, excluding Mexico (member as of 1994), and the Republic of Korea (1996) which joined OECD after the adoption of the Climate Change Convention. The Czech Republic (OECD member as of 1995), Slovakia (1995), Hungary (1996), and Poland are included in Annex I as countries undergoing the process of transition to a market economy.

3. *See* Climate Change Convention, *supra* Chapter 2 note 137, art. 4, ¶ 3.

4. *See infra* text accompanying and following note 55.

5. *See infra* text accompanying note 46.

6. The are, for instance, different targets among the parties of the regional agreement called the Protocol to the Convention on Long-Range Transboundary Air Pollution on Further Reduction of Sulphur Emissions. *See* Protocol to the Convention on Long-Range Transboundary Air Pollution on Further Reduction of Sulphur Emissions, June 14, 1994, annex II, 33 I.L.M. 1540.

7. *See infra* text following note 55.

8. *See* Climate Change Convention, *supra* Chapter 2 note 137, art. 4, ¶ 8.

9. *See* Torvanger, *supra* Chapter 3 note 29.

10. *See infra* text following note 17.

11. *See* Montreal Protocol, *supra* Chapter 1 note 25, art. 2.

12. *See, e.g.*, Lawrence Susskind & Connie Ozawa, *Negotiating More Effective International Environmental Agreements, in* THE INTERNATIONAL POLITICS OF THE ENVIRONMENT 156 (A. Hurrell & B. Kingsbury eds. 1992).

13. *See id.* at 157.

14. *See* United Nations, Press Release, U.N. Doc. ENV/DEV/40 (Mar. 15, 1991).

15. The proposal to create a trust fund to ensure the proper representation of developing countries was adopted by the Ad Hoc Working Group of Government Representatives to Prepare for Negotiations on a Framework Convention on Climate Change. *See Report of the Ad Hoc Working Group of Government Representatives to Prepare for Negotiations on a Framework Convention on Climate Change*, U.N. Doc. UNEP/WMO, Prep./FCCC/L.1/Report, Geneva, (Sept. 24-26, 1990).

16. *See* Montreal Protocol, *supra* Chapter 1 note 25.

17. *See* Vienna Convention, *supra* Chapter 2 note 134.

18. Montreal Protocol—London Amendments, *supra* Chapter 1 note 41, art. 5.1.

19. In fact, the Fourth Meeting of the Parties, meeting in Copenhagen in 1992, decided specifically not to establish criteria for future classification of developing countries, but instead consider individual applications by Parties for classification as developing countries as and when such applications were made. *See Report of the Fourth Meeting of the Parties to the Montreal Protocol on Substances that Deplete the Ozone Layer, Decision IV/7*, U.N. Doc. UNEP/OzL.Pro.4/15 (Nov. 25, 1992).

20. Telephone conversation with Andrew Reed, Economic Affairs Officer, Multilateral Fund Secretariat (Jan. 23, 1998).

21. *See* Hurlbut, *supra* Chapter 4 note 85, at 345.

22. *See id.*

23. Montreal Protocol—London Amendments, *supra* Chapter 1 note 41, art. 5, ¶ 5 (emphasis added).

24. A similar provision can be found in the Climate Change Convention, at ¶ 7 of Article 4, and the Convention on Biodiversity, at ¶ 4 of Article 20. *See* Melinda Chandler, *The Biodiversity Convention: Selected Issues of Interest to the International Lawyer*, 4 COLO. J. INT'L ENVTL. L.& POL'Y 173 (1993). *See also infra* text accompanying note 80..

25. *See Report of the Eighth Meeting of the Parties to the Montreal Protocol on Substances that Deplete the Ozone Layer*, U.N. Doc. UNEP/Ozl.Pro.8/12 (Dec. 19, 1996) [hereinafter Report of the Eighth Meeting].

26. Climate Change Convention, *supra* Chapter 2 note 137, art. 2.

27. *See* William K. Stevens, *Warming Could Bring Some Cold Surprises*, N.Y. TIMES, Sept. 11, 1997, at A6 (referring to Dr. Jerry Mahlman, who states that not doing enough in time can lead to regrettable consequences. In addition, Mahlman remarked: "If you get to where you don't like, there's not a lot you can do about it—you're wired for a long time." *Id.*) *See also* Reuter, *Leading Scientists Call For Global Warming Treaty*, CNN Website (visited Sept. 30, 1997) <http://www.cnn.com>.

28. *See supra* Chapter 4 note 11.

29. *See* Singer, *supra* Chapter 1 note 2. *See also Statement by Atmospheric Scientists on Greenhouse Warming*, Washington D.C., Feb. 27, 1992; Fred Singer, *Call for Emission Limits Heats Debate on Global Warming*, 2 PHYSICS TODAY 315(1997).

30. *See* Earl Lane, *Cool Toward Warming*, DENV. POST, Oct. 7, 1997, at 5A.

31. Arguably, this can be classified as an incentive that does not go to the essence of the treaties. *See* Climate Change Convention, *supra* Chapter 2 note 137.

32. *See id.* art. 12, ¶¶ 2, 5.

33. *Id.* prmbl.

34. *Id.* art. 3.

35. *See* Jean-Francois Pulvenis, *The Framework Convention on Climate Change, in* THE ENVIRONMENT AFTER RIO 92 (Lugi Campiglio et al. eds., 1994).

36. *See* Montreal Protocol – London Amendments, *supra* Chapter 1 note 41, art. 5, ¶ 3(a).

37. *See* Michael Zammit Cutajar, *Comment on Paper by Gunther Handl: The FCCC Experience, in* SUSTAINABLE DEVELOPMENT AND INTERNATIONAL LAW 47 (Winfried Lang ed., 1995).

38. *See* Kyoto Protocol, *supra* Chapter 2 note 166.

39. *See Berlin Mandate: Reviewing of the Adequacy of Article 4, Paragraph 2(a) and (b), of the Convention, Including Proposals Related to a Protocol and Decisions on Follow-up*, Conference of the Parties, 1st Sess., Decision 1/C P1., Apr. 7, 1995 [hereinafter Berlin Mandate].

40. *See* Nicholas D. Kristof, *Climate Parley to Test Japan*, DENV. POST, Oct. 5, 1997, at 5A.

41. *See* Lane, *supra* note 30.

42. Kyoto Protocol, *supra* Chapter 2 note 166. *See also* Leyla Boulton & Bethan Hutton, *Kyoto Climate Change Talks Agree Treaty at Last Minute*, FIN. TIMES, Dec. 11, 1997, at 1.

43. *See* Kyoto Protocol, *supra* Chapter 2 note 166, art. 3, ¶ 1.

44. *See id.*

45. *See id.*

46. *See supra* text accompanying note 6. (different targets among the Parties of the Protocol on Further Reduction of Sulphur Emissions).

47. *See* Joby Warrick, *White House Fosters Awareness of Global Warming but Hedges on Policy*, WASH. POST, Oct. 6, 1997, at A04. Such a clause was dropped from the final draft of the Kyoto Protocol at the last minute. *See* Boulton & Hutton, *supra* note 42, at 1. The Berlin Mandate specified that there would be no new commitments for developing countries, but that could be amended by the Conference of the Parties, the supreme body of the Climate Change Convention.

48. *See* Raymond J. Kopp et al., Weathervane Feature, *The Kyoto Protocol: Unresolved Issues* (visited Jan. 8, 1998) <http://www.weathervane.rff.org/features/feature026.html>.

49. *See* WORLD ENERGY OUTLOOK, *supra* Chapter 1 note 23.

50. Address by the President of the Republic of Argentina, *supra* Chapter 3 note 28.

51. *See* Kyoto Protocol, *supra* Chapter 2 note 166, art. 25.

52. *See* William Burns, *Global Warming the United Nations Framework Convention on Climate Change and the Future of Small Island States*, 6 Dick. J. Envtl. L. & Pol'y 147 (1997).

53. Sufficient GHG emissions by Annex I parties could be acquired if the EU were joined by Japan, Canada, Russia, and Australia, yet they would have to be joined by thirty-six additional parties, including some developing countries in order to meet the requirement of 55 ratifying countries.

54. U.S. CONST. art. II, § 2,cl. 2.

55. *See Expressing the Sense of the Senate Regarding U.N. Framework Convention on Climate Change*, S. Res. 98, 105th Cong. (July 25, 1997) (the Byrd-Hagel Resolution) (This resolution also includes the requirement that the protocol would not result in serious harm to the U.S. economy, and that the Administration give an economic analysis of the treaty's impact. *Id.*)

56. *See supra* text accompanying and following note 7.

57. *See* Montreal Protocol—London Amendments, *supra* Chapter 1 note 41, art. 10.

58. *See* Hurlbut, *supra* Chapter 4 note 85, at 355.

59. *See Nature and Extent of Projects Supported by The Mutilateral Fund, Communication from the Multilateral Fund for the Implementation of the Montreal Protocol to the World Trade Organization*, Committee on Trade and Environment, ¶ 9, WTO/CTE/W/60 (1997) [hereinafter *Nature and Extent of Projects*].

60. *Id.*

61. *See id.*

62. *See id.*

63. *See* Hilary French, *Forging a New Global Partnership*, *in* STATE OF THE WORLD 1995 at 172 (Lester R. Brown et al. eds., 1995).

64. *See infra* text following note 169.

65. *See* Henkin, *supra* Chapter 2 note 198, at 47 (stating that states normally abide by their commitments yet they balance the benefits versus the costs of non-compliance.) In the case of the Montreal Protocol there are no sanctions vis a vis a party that does not fulfill its financial commitments. However, the benefit of compliance is long term, making the Protocol more effective in fulfilling its purpose of reducing or eliminating ozone depleting substances.

66. The commitments by the Parties to pay into the Fund are a matter of interpretation of Article 10, ¶ 6 of the Montreal Protocol—some developed countries understand it as a voluntary commitment, while the developing countries see it as a compulsory obligation. E-mail from Andrew Reed, Economic Affairs Officer at the Multilateral Fund Secretariat, (Sept. 10, 1997).

67. An example of such innovative funding sources can be found in the Desertification Convention. *See infra* text accompanying note 91.

68. *See* Montreal Protocol—London Amendments, *supra* Chapter 1 note 41, art. 10, ¶ 2.

69. *See* Report of the Eighth Meeting, *supra* note 25.

70. *See id.*

71. *See* discussion *infra* Chapter 7.

72. Climate Change Convention, *supra* Chapter 2 note 137, art. 4, ¶ 3 (emphasis added).

73. *See* Daniel Bodansky, *The United Nations Framework Convention on Climate Change: A Commentary, in* GREENING INTERNATIONAL LAW 219 (1994).

74. *Id.*

75. *See id.*

76. *Id.*

77. *See* Climate Change Convention, *supra* Chapter 2 note 137, art. 11.

78. *Id.* art. 21. *See* GEF, *infra* Chapter 7.

79. *See* Biodiversity Convention, *supra* Chapter 2 note 168, art. 1.

80. *Id.* art 20, ¶ 2.

81. *See* Chandler, *supra* note 23, at 171.

82. *See* Climate Change Convention, *supra* Chapter 2 note 137, art. 11, ¶ 1.

83. *See* Biodiversity Convention, *supra* Chapter 2 note 168, art. 21, ¶ 2. *See also* Chandler, *supra* note 24, at 171.

84. *See* Biodiversity Convention, *supra* Chapter 2 note 168, art. 39 (referring to Article 21).

85. *Id.* art. 20, ¶ 4. Identical wording was used in Article 4, ¶ 7 of the Climate Change Convention, and similar wording was used in the Montreal Protocol. *See supra* text accompanying note 23.

86. *See* Chandler, *supra* note 24, at 173.

87. *See id.* at 174.

88. *See* Desertification Convention, *supra* Chapter 2 note 187, art. 2.

89. *See id.* art. 21, ¶ 4.

90. *See id.* art. 20, ¶ 2(d).

91. *See* discussion *supra* Chapter 7.

92. *See supra* text accompanying Chapter 1 note 43

93. *See* Kyoto Protocol, *supra* Chapter 2 note 166, art. 12.

94. The Clean Development Mechanism together with emissions trading and Joint Implementation (among only Annex I parties) constitute the three flexible mechanisms (Kyoto Mechanisms) of the Kyoto Protocol. *See* Kyoto Protocol *supra* Chapter 2 note 166, articles 12, 17, and 6, respectively. Only the clean development mechanism can be used by developing countries, as they have not yet committed to emission reduction targets.

95. *See infra* text accompanying note 117.

96. *See* discussion *infra* Chapter 7.

97. *See* Climate Change Convention, *supra* Chapter 2 note 137, art. 4.2(a), (b).

98. *See* Activities Implemented Jointly, U.N. Doc. FCCC/SBSTA/1997/Misc.3.

99. Kyoto Protocol, *supra* Chapter 2 note 166, art. 12. See infra text following note 114. Joint implementation among developed countries is dealt with separately in Article 6.

100. *See* Pulvenis, *supra* note 35, at 98.

101. *See* Oddmund Graham, *International Objectives with Regard to Climate Change, in* INTERNATIONAL ENVIRONMENTAL LAW 31 (Erling Selvig & Hans Christian Bugge eds., 1995).

102. *See* Kyoto Protocol, *supra* Chapter 2 note 166, art. 3.

103. Daniel Dudek & Jonathan Baert Wiener, *Joint Implementation, Transaction Costs, and Climate Change*, at 8 (last visited Apr. 4, 1999) <http://www.oecd.org/env/lists4.htm#ECO>.

104. *See* Tim Forsyth, *Technology Transfer and Climate Change Debate*, 40 ENVIRONMENT 17, 18 (1998).

105. Dudek & Wiener, *supra* note 103, at 8.

106. *See id.*

107. *See id.*

108. *See* Dudek & Wiener, *supra* note 103, at 9.

109. *See id.*

110. *See* discussion *infra* Chapter 7.

111. *See* Graham, *supra* note 101, at 31.

112. *See id.*

113. *See* Bodansky, *supra* note 73, at 492-96.

114. *See id.*

115. Kyoto Protocol, *supra* Chapter 2 note 166, art. 12.

116. *See* Kyoto Protocol, *supra* Chapter 2 note 166, art. 12.

117. *See id.* art. 12(3)(b).

118. *See* Kyoto Protocol, supra Chapter 2 note 166, art. 12(8).

119. *See* Magraw, *supra* Chapter 1 note 38, at 70.

120. *See id.*

121. *See* Benedick, *supra* Chapter 3 note 80, at 147.

122. *See* Convention on Desertification, *supra* Chapter 2 note 187, art. 18.

123. *See* UNCLOS, *supra* Chapter 2 note 11, art. 202.

124. *See* Agenda 21, *supra* Chapter 1 note 8, ¶ 34.1.

125. *Id.* ¶ 34.3.

126. *See* Nicholas Ashford & Christine Ayers, *Policy Issues for Consideration in Transferring Technology to Developing Countries*, 12 ECOLOGY L.Q. 875 (1985).

127. *See id.*

128. The developing countries must jump ahead directly from a status of under-development through to efficient, environmentally benign, technologies. *See* U.N. Doc. A/45/696/Add.1 (Nov. 8, 1990).

129. Agenda 21, *supra* Chapter 1 note 8, ¶ 34.3.

130. *Id.*

131. *See* Ashford & Ayers, *supra* note 126, at 890.

132. Climate Convention, *supra* Chapter 2 note 137, art. 2.

133. *Id.* art. 4, ¶ 5.

134. Intellectual property law consists of patent law, trade secret law, trademark law, and copyright law. With regard to technology, patent law and trade secrets are the most relevant types of intellectual property law.

135. *See* WORLD METEOROLOGICAL ORGANIZATION & UNITED NATIONS ENVIRONMENTAL PROGRAM INTERGOVERNMENTAL PANEL ON CLIMATE CHANGE, CLIMATE CHANGE: THE IPCC RESPONSE STRATEGIES (1992).

136. Michael A. Gollin, *Using Intellectual Property to Improve Environmental Protection* 4 HARV. J.L. & TECH. 215 (1992).

137. *See infra* text accompanying note 142.

138. *See* Agenda 21, *supra* Chapter 1 note 8, at 51.
139. *See infra* text accompanying note 142.
140. Montreal Protocol—London Amendments, *supra* Chapter 1 note 41, art. 10A(b).
141. *See* Climate Change Convention, *supra* Chapter 2 note 137, art. 4, ¶ 5.
142. See Katrien Vorlat, *The International Ozone Regime: Concessions and Loopholes?* 17 FLETCHER F. 151 (1993). *See also Nature and Extent of Projects, supra* note 59, ¶ 9.
143. *See id.*
144. See *Nature and Extent of Projects, supra* note 59.
145. *See* Schachter, *supra* Chapter 2 note 202, at 105.
146. *Id.*
147. *See id.* at 111.
148. *See id.*
149. *See* Agenda 21, *supra* Chapter 1 note 8, at ¶ 8.15.
150. *See* Wilson, *supra* Chapter 1 note 45, at 953.
151. *See id.* at 954.
152. *See id.*
153. *See* Agenda 21, *supra* Chapter 1 note 8, ¶ 8.19.
154. *See id.*
155. *See id.* ¶ 8.20.
156. *See id.*
157. Grad, *supra* Chapter 2 note 165.
158. *Id.*
159. *See* Wilson, *supra* Chapter 1 note 45, at 955.
160. *See* Thomas M. Frank, *The New Development: Can American Law and Legal Institutions Help Developing Countries?*, 3 WIS. L. REV. 799 (1972).
161. *See* CITES, *supra* Chapter 2 note 125.
162. *See* John Temple Lang, *Commentary: Some Implications of the Montreal Protocol to the Ozone Convention*, *in* ENVIRONMENTAL PROTECTION AND INTERNATIONAL LAW 181 (W. Lang et al. eds., 1991).
163. *See* Kiss & Shelton, *supra* Chapter 2 note 56, at 262 (positive review).
164. *See* Vorlat, *supra* note 142, at 151.
165. *See* Lang, *supra* note 162, at 183.
166. *See id.* at 184. *See* Chapter 1 note 29 (describing free-riders).
167. *See id.*
168. *See* James Cameron, *The GATT and the Environment*, *in* GREENING INTERNATIONAL LAW 102 (1994).
169. E-mail from Mr. K.M. Sarma, Executive Secretary of the Secretariat for the Vienna Convention and the Montreal Protocol (Oct. 4, 1997) (mentioning that the GATT Secretariat has attended most of the meetings of the Conference of the Parties of the Montreal Protocol, and no objections have been raised by anyone or any country). *See* Report of the General Council to the 1996 Ministerial Conference Vol. 1, Section VII, Report of the Committee on Trade and Environment, ¶ 8, U.N. Doc. WT/CTE/1 (Nov. 12, 1996).
170. *See* Montreal Protocol—London Amendments, *supra* Chapter 1 note 41, annex IV, ¶ 2.

171. *Id.* annex IV, ¶ 9.

172. *Id.* annex V.

173. *See* LYNNE JURGIELEWICZ, GLOBAL ENVIRONMENTAL CHANGE AND INTERNATIONAL LAW 170 (1996).

174. *See* Climate Change Convention, *supra* Chapter 2 note 137, art. 13; Kyoto Protocol, *supra* Chapter 2 note 166, art. 17. At the Fourth Session of the Conference of the Parties to the Framework Convention on Climate Change, in 1998, the parties agreed on the operational workings of the multilateral consultative process. It is to have a Standing Multilateral Consultative Committee (MCC) which is to consider questions regarding the implementation of the Climate Change Convention. *See* Report on the Ad Hoc Group on Article 13 on Its Sixth Session, Annex II U.N. Doc. FCCC/AG13/1998/2(1998).

175. *See* Montreal Protocol—London Amendments, *supra* Chapter 1 note 41, arts. 10, 10A.

176. *See id.* art. 5, ¶ 7.

177. *See* Kyoto Protocol, *supra* Chapter 2 note 166, art. 3. *See also supra* text following note 45.

178. *See supra* text accompanying note 49.

179. *See* Climate Change Convention *supra* Chapter 2 note 137, art. 2.

180. *See* discussion *infra* Chapter 4.

181. *See* Tenth Anniversary of Montreal Protocol, *supra* Chapter 4 note 43.

182. *See* Roland Blassnig, *Methyl Bromide Phaseout, CFC Export Licensing Only Gains at Montreal Meeting*, Chem. Reg. Rep. (BNA) (Sept. 24, 1997).

183. *See id.*

184. *See id.*

185. *See id.*

186. *See* PETER SAND, THE EFFECTIVENESS OF INTERNATIONAL ENVIRONMENTAL AGREEMENTS 11, 12 (1992).

187. *See id.*

188. *See* discussion *infra* Chapter 7.

189. *See supra* Chapter 4 note 62.

190. *See* discussion *supra* text following note 51.

191. *See* Climate Change Convention, Ratification Status as of October 1997, IUCN (visited Jan. 20,1998) <http://sedac.ciesin.org> (current information available as of Mar. 5, 1999 at <http://www.unfccc.de/>).

192. *See* Desertification Convention, *supra* Chapter 2 note 187, art. 21, ¶ 4.

193. *See* Kyoto Protocol, *supra* Chapter 2 note 166, art. 12.

194. *See* discussion *infra* Chapter 7.

195. *See* Kyoto Protocol, *supra* Chapter 2 note 166, art. 12, ¶ 3(b).

196. *See* discussion *infra* Chapter 7.

6

International Institutional Structures

To promote the participation of developing countries in international environmental agreements, international institutions are playing an ever-increasing role and new entities are being established. As mentioned in Chapter 4, they can function both as implementing agencies for treaties containing incentives for developing countries or alternately by promoting participation of developing countries in the treaties by working outside or independently of the treaties.

A need to revamp all international institutions dealing with issues relating to environment and development became apparent as the international community recognized that these two issues were interrelated. This reorganization is already underway in many of the international institutions, such as the World Bank and many other specialized agencies of the United Nations. In addition, new institutions have been established, such as the United Nations Commission on Sustainable Development (CSD).

Before the Rio Conference, there was a series of suggestions as to what kind of institutional arrangements should be established in the context of sustainable development within the framework of the U.N. system. Some of them promoted an environmental "super-authority,"[1] but most of them opted for strengthening the already existing structures. Then Agenda 21, adopted at Rio, addressed the issue in its chapter 38, "International Institutional Arrangements."[2] Here it describes the relevant entities within and outside the U.N. system—in addition to NGOs—and their functions in relation to implementing Agenda 21. However, in the five years since the blueprint for action was adopted, lack of funding has curtailed some of the developments that were supposed to have taken place, such as the upgrading of, and provision of adequate financial resources for the United Nations Environment Programme (UNEP).

The special session of the General Assembly that took place in June of 1997, reviewing the first five years of Agenda 21's implementation, also included a topic on institutional changes.[3] One important aspect of the institutional review issue, in my judgment, is that many of the relevant institutions need to modify their ongoing activities in order to be more conducive to making the multilateral environmental treaties effective in their response to global environmental threats, as these agreements will provide the parameters to make the goal of sustainable development operational. This, in turn, means facilitating effective negotiation, implementation and compliance of treaties, especially with regard to developing countries. In order to promote such effectiveness there needs to be cooperation at the international, regional, national, and local levels.

The U.N. system has the apparatus in place already, but coordination between the different entities and their functions seems to be one of the difficult issues. With the U.N. budgetary restrictions there really is very little room for overlapping projects, in the sense of unnecessary use of resources. Therefore, it is crucial that the attention of the U.N. institutions, especially the coordinating bodies, focus on the goal of promoting systematic and coherent programming within the U.N. system in pursuit of sustainable development.

Some of the international institutions dealing with environment and development will be examined below.[4] I will mainly focus on how they promote the participation of developing countries in the regulatory process to address global environmental problems. This focus has also determined the way I have classified the institutions. The following categories represent areas where they do a major portion of their work although their activities are diverse and can overlap: a) institutional structures for monitoring the implementation of international environmental instruments; and b) institutional structures providing development assistance.

Institutional Structures for Monitoring the Implementation of International Environmental Instruments

United Nations Environment Programme (UNEP)

The United Nations Environment Programme (UNEP) was established by the General Assembly in 1972 as a result of the Stockholm Conference. It was given the mandate to function as the principal body within the U.N. to address environmental issues: "The environmental conscience of the U.N."[5] This role was reiterated in Chapter 38 of Agenda 21, except it was expanded upon. Chapter 38, paragraph 23 adds that UNEP is to take into account the development aspects of environmental questions.[6]

Though UNEP was not established to address legal issues, it has played a major role in promoting the adoption of several of the more recent international environmental agreements, such as the Montreal Protocol, and especially in that capacity has had a significant impact on the development of international environmental law. UNEP is also one of the implementing agencies of the Multilateral Fund and the Global Environment Facility.

UNEP was created to monitor important changes in the environment, and promote and coordinate sound environmental practices,[7] thereby having the overall responsibility for implementing the recommendations of the Action Plan adopted by the Stockholm Conference.[8] These recommendations were arranged into three categories: 1) assessment, 2) management, and 3) support measures.[9] The Nairobi Declaration on the Role and Mandate of UNEP, adopted by UNEP's Governing Council in February of 1997, states the core elements of its mandate as follows: analysis and assessment; policy advise; promotion of cooperation; international environmental law; and the promotion of greater environmental awareness.[10]

UNEP was the first major U.N. institution to be located in a developing country, namely Kenya.[11] It is not a specialized agency, but an autonomous subsidiary organ of the General Assembly.[12] UNEP consists of a Governing Council, an Executive Director, and a Secretariat.[13] The Governing Council composed of fifty-eight members, functions as a legislative body. It reports annually to the General Assembly through the Economic and Social Council. A catalyst for environmental action, the secretariat headed by the Executive Director, functions as a coordinator for environmental action in the U.N. system. The Environmental Fund, which finances UNEP's programs, is based on funds directly from voluntary contributions from donor countries. The general U.N. budget finances only the administrative expenses of the Council and the Secretariat.[14]

Earthwatch denotes the assessment function of UNEP, which by increasing knowledge of the global environmental status, is to provide the basis for environmental management to respond to environmental threats. The functions of Earthwatch include evaluation and review, research, monitoring, and information exchange.[15] A surveillance network within UNEP, Earthwatch assesses the state of the global environment through three components: 1) the Global Environmental Monitoring System (GEMS) which monitors resources, climate, oceans, transport of pollutants, air and water quality worldwide, 2) the International Referral System for Sources of Environmental Information (INFOTERRA), a computerized 'clearing house'[16] for information exchange from over 20,000 sources in more than 100 countries, and 3) the International Register of Potentially Toxic Chemicals (IRPTC).[17] In addition, Earthwatch has two assessment components: 1) the assessment of basic human needs in relation to outer limits of the biosphere and 2) research and assessment.[18]

The environmental management component of the Action Plan includes functions "designed to facilitate comprehensive planning that takes into account the side effects of man's activities and thereby to protect and enhance the human environment for present and future generations."[19] The main areas of UNEP's activities cover—not just environmental activities—as one can see from the following: 1) environmental aspects of human settlements planning and health of peoples and the environment; 2) terrestrial ecosystems; 3) environment and development; 4) industry and environment; 5) oceans, including the regional seas program; 6) energy; 7) natural disasters; and 8) the development of environmental law. [20]

UNEP's program of action adopted by the Governing Council in 1988, the United Nations System-Wide Medium-Term Environmental Programme 1990-1995, included all of the environment-related activities of the U.N. system planned for that period.[21] Emphasizing the indissoluble relationship between environment and development, the possible effects of environmental change were to be taken into account as an aspect of planning for sustainable development in two ways.[22] The first method mentioned was the strengthening of the U.N. system's ability to take environmental factors into account throughout all development activities and assist governments in doing the same, if so requested. The second is the application of economic analysis techniques in order to reflect environmental values more appropriately in decision-making.[23]

For the biennium 1996-97 UNEP's work program stressed the relationships between environmental changes, socio-economic driving forces, and impacts on human well-being.[24] The program's main areas of activity were: sustainable production and consumption, sustainable management and use of natural resources, a better environment for human health and well-being, and globalization of the environment and the economy.[25]

UNEP has promoted several multilateral and regional environmental agreements. Having focused on three areas of environmental concern in its Montevideo Program in 1982, namely marine pollution from land-based sources, protection of the stratospheric ozone layer, and the transport, handling, and disposal of toxic and dangerous wastes, UNEP was successful in promoting the adoption of Vienna Convention and its Montreal Protocol, and the Basel Convention.[26] In addition, guidelines were adopted for land-based pollution of the seas in 1985, which eventually lead to the adoption by the Washington Conference of the Global Programme of Action for the Protection of the Marine Environment from Land-based Activities and the Washington Declaration in 1995.[27] At its 15th Session, the Governing Council established an ad hoc working group with a mandate to negotiate an umbrella convention on biodiversity.[28] This major effort eventually lead to the Biodiversity Convention,[29] which was adopted at Rio and has since come into force.

The secretariats of several conventions are administered by UNEP. These include the Vienna Convention for the Protection of the Ozone Layer and its Montreal Protocol (secretariats located in Nairobi), the Bonn Convention on Migratory Species, CITES, the Basel Convention, and the Convention on Biological Diversity.

As part of its management function UNEP also developed the regional seas program. Drafting action plans and implementing treaties, the program regulates nine different maritime regions.[30] Some of these regional seas programs are administered by UNEP and some are administered by regional bodies.[31]

Concerned with the lack of environmental law administration capacity faced by developing countries, UNEP adopted four strategies to address the problem 1) promotion of national environmental law, 2) education and research, 3) acceptance and implementation, and 4) technical cooperation.[32] In 1977 UNEP began initiatives to help developing countries formulate and implement national environmental legislation through several organizations, agencies, and individual experts.[33] In addition, UNEP's 1982-1983 medium-term objectives included identifying the difficulties governments face when they wish to become Parties to conventions or attempt to implement conventions.[34]

One of the main problems for UNEP is poor communication, which is in part due to its location.[35] Only some eighty-eight countries are represented in Nairobi. There is a lack of representation from Latin America and the Asia-Pacific area.[36]

Although UNEP is supposed to be the central organ of leadership and coordination regarding environmental issues in the U.N. system, the specialized agencies have resisted UNEP's efforts resulting in a lack of influence over the agencies' programs.[37] Likewise, with regard to govern-ments, it has no enforcement power either. Governments can refuse to give UNEP access to "confidential data" and decide not to ratify conventions.[38] UNEP depends wholly on the willingness of governments and agencies with the power and funding to take action.[39]

Lack of authority and funding, some scholars argue, has made UNEP unable to have any major influence on the policy development level of international environmental law.[40] UNEP is considered more committed to action through monitoring and assessment of environmental threats.[41]

After ten years in operation, Caldwell inferred that it appeared that the state of the environment would worsen, but that UNEP would be able to monitor "the where and why of its decline."[42] He based this on the fact that UNEP's projects that had succeeded were the ones that did not interfere with national economic or development interests or require a major refocusing of national policy and administration, in other words projects that involved monitoring, information exchange, research, and consciousness raising.[43] Governments have only undertaken substantial action in the rare cases where there has been urgent popular pressure.[44]

Now, twenty-five years after UNEP was created, the situation does not appear to have changed considerably. The environment is still deteriorating and UNEP's position has only gotten more difficult with budgetary cutbacks. Agenda 21's call for an enhanced and strengthened role for UNEP has not been heeded. In a UNEP document of 1995, there is an explanation of what happened in regard to the approach to global environmental issues after the Stockholm Conference, which may also have a bearing upon the UNEP's position.[45] After the Stockholm Conference acknowledged that a comprehensive approach was necessary, linking environment to cultural, economic, social and political factors, the environment was increasingly treated as an isolated entity that needed technical solutions.[46] Although there was a shift in the 1980's to preventive action, the emphasis is still concentrated on solving existing environmental problems.[47] UNEP gives credit to the Rio Conference for having reestablished that environment is an integral part of sustainable development and that environmental issues cannot be addressed in isolation from their economic, social, and political contexts.[48]

The Governing Council's nineteenth session, which took place in Nairobi in February of 1997, was suspended due to disagreements regarding UNEP's governance.[49] As a result of the impasse, funding for 1997 from the U.S.A., Britain, and Spain, representing 15 percent of UNEP's budget, was withheld when their proposal for improving UNEP was not adopted.[50] Later, at a special meeting of the Governing Council, held in April, a compromise was reached. A High-level Committee of Ministers and Officials in Charge of Environment was established as a subsidiary organ of the Governing Council with 36 committee members. The Committee's mandate is to make recommendations on reforms and policies to the Governing Council after considering the international environmental agenda.[51] It is too early to tell whether the subsidiary committee will dictate policy to the Governing Council or function as a shadow Governing Council.[52]

With regard to the management of UNEP, a report by the U.N. Office of Internal Oversight Services states that few of UNEP's goals are met because of mismanagement, waste, and lack of accountability and transparency.[53] Hopefully, these problems can be resolved in an efficient manner, allowing UNEP to continue its good works, especially as a promoter of international environmental agreements and as an implementing agency for several of the agreements' provisions, especially the ones aimed at assisting developing countries.

To better address policy issues in regard to UNEP's mandate to coordinate environmental activities within the U.N. system, UNEP established the Inter-Agency Environment Coordinating Group (IAEG) in 1994. This group is to act as a consultative and advisory body, not a subsidiary of the Administrative Committee on Coordination (ACC).[54] However, the relationship between IAEG, on the one hand, and the Commission on Sustainable Development (CSD) and ACC's subsidiary, the Inter-Agency Committee on Sustainable Development (IACSD), on the other hand, is not wholly clear. Clarifying UNEP's overlapping jurisdictions with ECOSOC, the United Nations Conference on Trade and Development (UNCTAD), the United Nations Industry and Development Organization (UNIDO), the United Nations Development Program (UNDP) and other agencies would be helpful for all the agencies and ECOSOC, enabling harmonization and avoiding dispersal of authority.[55]

Relevant Treaty Bodies— Conference of the Parties and Treaty Secretariats

International environmental treaties, some of which are concluded under the auspices of one or more U.N. organs, in addition to creating obligations for state parties, often establish small international organizations with their own political organs and secretariats.[56] They also include dispute resolution mechanisms,[57] such as Article 11 of the Vienna Convention for the Protection of the Ozone Layer. These treaty bodies "in effect function within the United Nations and also constitute part of the machinery for dealing with environmental matters."[58] Currently, much of the real work of governance with regard to the global environment takes place through these treaty bodies, such as monitoring treaty implementation and strengthening treaties as new scientific information becomes available.[59]

The Conference of the Parties (COP) is usually the ruling organ of the different conventions. Article 7 of the Climate Change Convention calls it the "supreme body" of the Convention.[60] The COP is the intergovernmental body that includes all the parties that ratified the convention, i.e. the nation-states. It often takes the initiative to adopt protocols to the convention.[61] The treaty secretariats are created and funded by the parties to the agreements to administer the treaties.[62] Most environmental treaties require the parties to report on their implementation of the treaty obligations to the treaty secretariat. However, there is a big gap between commitments made and implementation. On the whole, the secretariats lack the money or the power to monitor the treaties effectively and to make certain the submission of national reports is correct.[63] But lacking a supranational enforcement body, the primary enforcement mechanism, in general, consists of peer or public pressure based on the reports submitted by the parties with regard to their implementation.[64] Just as most other secretariats, CITES' secretariat, for instance, has limited funding, however, it does have substantial powers and has used them to good effect.[65] CITES secretariat can, for instance, demand information from countries that allegedly are not enforcing the measures stipulated in the treaty and request explanations from countries it believes are not fulfilling their treaty obligations.[66]

There have been suggestions to pool the resources of the secretariats by placing them in one location rather than on several different continents, as they are now.[67] This would also allow easier conveyance of scientific information, and each time a new convention was being negotiated the same techniques could be used rather than "reinventing the wheel" each time, thereby increasing the coherence of the rules.[68] Weiss questions whether such a centralized system would necessarily be more efficient, and believes greater efficiency can be induced in the present system through the use of advances in information technology.[69] Perhaps more digested information regarding procedures that are effective could to be posted on the Internet for easy access for all parties involved. We already have enough examples of centralized arrangement with large inefficient bureaucracies.

With regard to where the secretariats should be situated, there is a lot to be said for "spreading the wealth." The present system allows several nations to be hosts for these secretariats and additional nations to be hosts for the meetings of the COPs, which usually take place at locations other than the secretariats. Although this increases the transaction costs, there is prestige involved,[70] just as when countries host international conferences. Holding the COP meetings at different locations may, if well publicized, increase the public awareness of global environmental issues. Of course besides being costly, this does not improve the situation of harrowed diplomats commuting all over the world and it does not improve the access of developing countries to these negotiations, unless their trips are paid for by the U.N., as is increasingly becoming the case. However, Pulvenis questions how democratic the international society is when there is an imbalance between states with regard to the effectiveness of their representation at the conferences; a large number of developing countries have a delegation consisting of just one member, whereas developed countries usually have many times that number.[71]

The United Nations Commission for Sustainable Development, the Department of Economic and Social Affairs, and the Division for Sustainable Development[72]

The United Nations Commission for Sustainable Development (CSD) was established by the U.N. Economic and Social Council (ECOSOC) in January of 1993.[73] It has the responsibility of monitoring the implementation of Agenda 21 and other commitments and recommendations contained in the final documents of UNCED. CSD is in charge of reviewing how well national governments and institutions are protecting global natural resources and helping developing countries become full partners in the multilateral environmental agreements.

CSD functions as a subsidiary body of ECOSOC. It is made up of high-level representatives of fifty-three nations elected from U.N. member states. Each member has a three-year term and membership rotates among governments and different geographical regions. CSD meets once a year at the U.N. Headquarters. States which are not elected to CSD, organizations of the U.N. system, and accredited intergovernmental and non-govern-mental organizations can all attend the session of CSD as observers.

The Division for Sustainable Development functions as the Secretariat for the Commission and is located in New York at the new Department of Economic and Social Affairs within the U.N. Secretariat. This Department came about as the result of a merger between three departments dealing with policy formulation, analytical and normative functions, and technical cooperation activities in the economic and social fields.[74] In addition to policy analysis and coordination, the Department is to strengthen support in three major areas: sustainable development, social development and advancement of women, in addition to supporting Africa's development, the sustainable development of small island developing states and cooperation among developing countries.

The functions of CSD are to monitor the implementation of Agenda 21 throughout the U.N. system, review national reports on how states are implementing Agenda 21, review progress in the implementation of the commitments set forth in Agenda 21 by donor countries, and review and analyze information provided by NGOs.[75] The CSD can make recommendations on new arrangements needed to advance sustainable development to the General Assembly through ECOSOC.[76]

In 1993, at its first full session, CSD established two inter-sessional expert groups, one to assist with monitoring requirements and financial issues, the other to concentrate on transfer of environmentally sound technology, cooperation and capacity building.[77] Furthermore, the CSD adopted a multi-year thematic program of its work for the period 1993-1997 that would provide a framework to assess progress achieved in the implementation of Agenda 21.[78] The framework program covered nine areas, five cross-sectoral areas which were to be considered annually, and four sector areas to be considered triennially.[79] The five cross-sectoral areas included: the role of major groups; financial resources and mechanisms; critical elements of sustainability, such as changing consumption patterns and poverty; decision-making structures; and the transfer of environ-mentally sound technology. The four sectoral areas included: freshwater, human settlements, and health; toxic chemicals and hazardous wastes; biodiversity, land, forests, and desertification; and oceans, all kinds of seas, and atmosphere.[80] It is striking that CSD was only scheduled to address environmental issues every third year versus development issues every year.[81] CSD is supposed to cover both issues; one would think that meant on a fifty-fifty basis.

CSD completed a full cycle of its multi-year thematic program of work at its fourth session, in the Spring of 1996. A new multi-year program of work was recommended by the Special Session of the U.N. General Assembly (UNGASS) in June of 1997, to be adopted by CSD for the period of 1998-2002.[82] This program, in contrast to the first one, addresses both environmental and development issues on an annual basis.

For all the suggestions and discussions of the necessity of a "super-authority" to deal with global environmental and development issues, the initiative for the establishment of the CSD was as far as the negotiators got at the Rio Conference; in other words, the international community was not ready for a superstructure at this time. One writer states that CSD suffers from the same defects as UNEP: limited responsibility, financing and political support, inhibiting it from playing a coordinating role.[83] In addition, Esty states that CSD is further shackled by an unfocused mission.[84]

Perhaps CSD's greatest weakness is that it has no enforcement power. It can only coax other U.N. organs and states to take its decisions seriously.[85] French has espoused the notion that the CSD is more or less modeled on the U.N. Commission on Human Rights that also lacks formal enforcement or police powers.[86] Using the power of publicity the CSD could—just as the Commission on Human Rights does—shame countries into mending their ways in accordance with Agenda 21 and other Rio commitments.[87] However, unlike the Commission on Human Rights, the CSD would use positive reinforcement instead of reprimands.[88] This form of encouragement could be useful, but it is not happening in the case of CSD at the present time. With regard to the UNGASS meeting, CSD only requested the reports, Country Profiles,[89] and compiled the information.[90] Furthermore, since there are no legally binding treaties that fall directly under CSD, in contrast to the Human Right Commission, CSD's main function will necessarily be a central forum for reviewing progress on the implementation of Agenda 21.

Whether the CSD will actually develop such powers to shame nations to change their behavior, remains to be seen. However, requiring that governments report on their follow-up of Agenda 21, even if it is only voluntary, is at least a mechanism for urging them to implement the recommendations in the action plan. In order to have something to report on, governments need to have done something in practice.[91] Within a year of Rio, seventy governments had established national institutions (sustainable development commissions or coordinating mechanisms) responsible for integrating sustainable development concepts into domestic law and policy. By 1997, 150 countries had established such institutions.[92] In addition, local "Agenda 21 programs" were established in 1,200 cities and towns around the world. However, just before the UNGASS meeting, governments had only just agreed upon the format of their reports to the CSD on their follow-up of Agenda 21 and only some sixty-odd countries of a total of 185 member countries of the U.N. had sent their Country Profiles to CSD.

UNCED also lead to the empowerment of CSD to monitor the World Bank's activities and plans to implement Agenda 21, inviting the Bank to submit regular reports to CSD.[93] This would be one method of promoting more sustainable development practices at the Bank.[94] Yet, it remains to be seen how effectively this mandate is carried out.

CSD has also been positively viewed as a study forum or marketplace for ideas.[95] In addition, some scholars have suggested that CSD's role should be strengthened and broadened, becoming "first among equals" in U.N. functional commissions.[96] This would strengthen its coordinating role. CSD could then be at the forefront of important issues concerning sustainable development, in a sense a "conductor" for the "ensemble" of all relevant U.N. institutions, while at the same time monitoring the states' implementation of Agenda 21, giving special consideration to needs of developing countries. The jury is out on whether the CSD will prove successful in fulfilling its mandate or if it will become an inefficient U.N. bureaucracy.

The Administrative Committee on Coordination (ACC) and the Inter-Agency Committee on Sustainable Development (IACSD)

The Administrative Committee on Coordination (ACC), an inter-institutional body was established by an ECOSOC resolution in 1946 to coordinate the different U.N. organizations.[97] It consists of the Secretary General of the United Nations and the heads of the U.N. specialized agencies, in addition to the International Atomic Energy Agency.

At the same time UNEP was created in 1972, the General Assembly also established the Environment Coordination Board (ECB) under the auspices and within the framework of the ACC.[98] However, by 1977 its functions were merged with the ACC. The effectiveness of the ACC in the environmental field has been limited by several factors, among them the fact that environmental issues have been considered peripheral to many of the specialized agencies making it difficult to coordinate such issues in a forum of such high-level officials.[99] In addition, the ACC meets only twice a year which is too infrequent to resolve emerging conflicts in a constantly changing field.[100]

In 1978, a senior-level working committee called the Designated Officials for Environmental Matters (DOEM), under ACC,[101] on behalf of all U.N. organizations interested in the environment, began to deal with the planning and coordination of environmental activities within the U.N. at a more detailed level. Its second and most recent report, the System-Wide Medium-Term Environmental Programme: 1990-1995, [102] was submitted by the ACC for consideration and approval by UNEP's Governing Council.[103] However, the DOEM has not been in operation since 1992.[104] Another principal U.N. coordinating committee for environment and development issues is the Committee of International Development Institutions on the Environment (CIDIE),[105] though it is not part of the United Nations system as such.[106] It consists of UNEP, the U.N. Development Programme (UNDP), the World Bank, and eleven other intergovernmental financial institu-tions.[107] UNEP provides the secretariat of both DOEM and CIDIE.[108]

After Rio, the Inter-agency Committee on Sustainable Development (IACSD) was established. It is the newest coordinating body for sustainable development issues within the U.N. system. The Interagency is a subcommittee of the ACC and has the same composition as the ACC.

The main function of the IACSD is to reshape and coordinate the activities of U.N. agencies and programmes in line with Agenda 21. The objectives of the interagency consultations in the context of Agenda 21, Chapter 39 "International Legal Instruments," were identified in 1994 as follows:

1. to develop a coordinated approach to a framework for ensuring consistency of substantive objectives between existing and particularly new international legal instruments for sustainable development, on the one hand, and Agenda 21 and the Rio Declaration, on the other;
2. to identify activities/objectives in Agenda 21 and the Rio Declaration which are not yet but could be assisted by the creation of international or regional legal regimes;
3. to explore the potential for sharing information contained in national reports to the secretariats of existing Conventions, particularly with regard to monitoring the implementation of Agenda 21.[109]

A system of task managers has also been established by ACC to enable better coordination between U.N. entities for the implementation of Agenda 21 and for the promotion of coordinated follow-up of major U.N. conferences in the area of sustainable development.[110]

With its new subsidiary—the IACSD—and the use of task managers, perhaps the coordinating function of the ACC will prove more effective than it has been previously with regard to environment and development issues.

Institutional Structures Providing Development Assistance—Integrating Environmental Considerations into Development Projects

International environmental agreements may be moving toward more specific and detailed commitments, as opposed to general principles, yet much more capacity-building needs to be done to enable developing countries to enact and implement environmental laws on par with those of the developed countries.[111]

One of the important changes emerging, regarding institutions providing development assistance, is the need to include developing countries in the work of the institutions to a much larger extent than is presently the case. In addition, there is also a need for public participation in the decision-making process with regard to the environmental effects of certain projects, specifically, environmental impact statements.

Traditionally, developing countries were merely supposed to stand by and be grateful for the aid they received. Now, it has become clear that projects are more likely to be successful if the developing countries are involved in the policy and decision-making process, not only at the local level, but also within the international institutions that are supposed to choose and fund projects, such as the Global Environment Facility (GEF).[112]

In the following sections, I will examine the World Bank and the U.N. Development Fund, specifically its new program, Capacity 21, to see how they have succeeded in integrating environmental considerations into their development projects. To the extent they have succeeded, these institutions will have improved the developing countries' understanding of how important environmental issues are, and enabled them to participate in the regulatory process to address not only local, but also global environmental problems, thereby contributing to the practical implementation of the goal of sustainable development.

World Bank

Function and Structure. The World Bank was established in 1944, mainly to help rebuild Europe after WWII. The focus soon shifted to the developing countries, and more recently also assisting countries of the former Soviet Union and Eastern Europe.

The main function of the International Bank for Reconstruction and Development (World Bank) is the management of resource transfers to promote development.[113] The World Bank essentially has three roles to play; it's a financial, political, and at the same time, a development organization.[114] In addition, the former Bank President, Barber Conable, declared in 1991 that the Bank "must also be an environmental agency" referring to its work in the environmental field.[115] However, nowhere in its Articles of Agree-

ment is the word environment used. This is in stark contrast to the newer development banks, for instance, the European Bank for Reconstruction and Development (EBRD) which specifically lists as one of its functions "to promote, in the full range of its activities, environmentally sound and sustainable development."[116] Being the "largest single source of development lending" the World Bank exerts a major influence on economic development throughout the world.[117]. This warrants special attention because what it does, or does not do with regard to environmental issues has a bearing on what other aid agencies do. Bank involvement in a project is considered decisive as far as attracting other multilateral, bilateral, or private sources of aid or loans.[118]

The World Bank was brought into a relationship with the United Nations in 1947 through an agreement according to the United Nations Charter Articles 57 and 63, making it a specialized agency.[119]. However, the agreement also gave the Bank a greater degree of autonomy than the other specialized agencies of the U.N., especially regarding the Bank's loan and financing policy.[120] This placed the Bank in a unique position, especially as regards accountability, as will be discussed below.

The Bank's main organ, the Board of Governors, meets annually. It is composed of 180 representatives, one from each of its member states, normally the finance minister or the head of the central bank.[121] The Board of twenty-four executive directors—five of whom represent the main contributors to the Bank's capital—is mostly controlled by the industrialized countries.[122] This is due to the fact that the shareholders of the World Bank are the member governments, and their votes in the Executive Board are weighted in proportion to their contribution to the Bank's capital.[123] Bank loans are approved by the Board of Executive Directors, which also makes Bank policy.[124] Its chairman is the President of the World Bank.

The Bank's biggest priority is to reduce poverty through economic growth by focusing on policies and programs specifically benefiting poor people.[125] However, the World Bank like all banks, is in the business of granting loans or transferring money, which in some instances has superseded its goal of poverty reduction and actually degraded the environment. Many investments by the World Bank, among other major financial institutions, have promoted economic development in the developing countries by supporting the short-term exploitation of natural resources, thereby making-short-term cash flow a priority, at the expense of long-term sustainable growth.[126]

Reforms After 1987. In 1987 the Bank began restructuring its organization and established an Environment Department,[127] which is now part of the Vice Presidency for Environmentally Sustainable Development. Furthermore, as of 1989, Environmental Assessments (EAs) became mandatory for all relevant Bank-assisted projects, pursuant to Operational Directive

4.00, Annex A, which was revised in 1991 and renamed Operational Directive on Environmental Assessment (OD 4.01).[128] The borrower is responsible for producing the environ-mental assessment.[129] However, the borrower may request Bank assistance for financing EAs through a Project Preparation Facility, from the Technical Assistance Grant Program for the Environment, or from trust funds.[130]

All Bank projects go through a screening process. Projects are classified as Category A projects if they are expected to have "significant, sensitive, irreversible or diverse negative impacts" on the environment.[131] These projects require a full-scale environmental assessment. Projects deemed to have specific environmental impacts need only an "environmental analysis" and are classified as Category B projects.[132] Category C projects are those where no discernible environmental impacts are expected and therefore require no environmental assessment or analysis.[133]

The function of the environmental assessment is to ensure that the development alternatives are sustainable, taking environmental impacts into account early on in the project cycle, and considering them in con-junction with the project design.[134] By identifying ways to improve the projects environmentally, the assessments can reduce the need for project conditionality by taking appropriate measures in advance.[135] Environmental assessments can also play a major role in environmental capacity-building in the project country.[136] In addition, it provides a formal structure for coordination between agencies and for addressing the issues of affected groups and local non-governmental organizations (NGOs).[137] Furthermore, Operational Directive 4.01, paragraph 13, as interpreted by the Bank,[138] requires projects of a highly risky nature with multidimensional environ-mental concerns to have an advisory panel consisting of independent inter-national environmental experts.[139] This paragraph of the directive refers to dam and reservoir projects. Such projects have a separate environmental policy directive which specifies the selection and functions of the panel.[140]

One of the problems that have materialized in the Latin American countries is that environmental assessments or impact studies have been hurriedly adopted, often to comply with the Bank requirements, without the necessary expertise and legal framework to support the studies.[141] Few of these developing countries have adopted effective guidelines in regard to public participation as the ones in the United States, that could ensure enforcement, or penalties for omissions or errors in the studies.[142] In Mexico, the lack of complimentary legal frameworks also has lead to excessive use of environmental impact studies, in some cases the only tool to protect the environment. This in turn, has created a backlog of studies to be evaluated, annoying investors waiting for project authorization.[143] To reduce the backlog, Mexico is now developing additional environmental policy instruments, such as zoning laws and urban and sustainable development policies, that could eliminate the need for some environmental assessments.[144]

Operational Directive 4.05 covers the Bank's environmental policy on dam and reservoir projects.[145] It codifies "best practice" with regard to carrying out such projects, including careful planning to minimize or mitigate the adverse effects and a cost-benefit analysis that should include estimates of quantifiable environmental losses and necessary mitigatory measures.[146] An environmental assessment according to the Operational Directive mentioned above, is required for all dam and reservoir projects.[147] In addition, each project also requires a panel of independent environmental experts.[148]

In 1990 the Bank issued Operational Directive 4.30 on Involuntary Settlement. Due to dam construction or urban and transportation projects, such resettlement may be accompanied by deforestation, overgrazing, soil erosion, and pollution.[149] The main policy objective of the Bank is to avoid resettlement or minimize it where possible.[150] However, where resettlement is unavoidable the resettlement plan must – in addition to taking care of the displaced persons – take into account the environmental aspects.[151] Unfortunately, the Bank has not always followed its own policies and procedures as the Narmada River Sardar Sarovar Dam Project is a clear example of.

In that case, the Bank had an independent commission investigate the project which was to have brought electricity, irrigation, and drinking water to millions of people in north-western India.[152] Among other criticisms, the Morse Commission stated that with regard to the mistreatment of forcibly resettled rural poor, the Sardar Sarovar Projects were not an isolated incident.[153] In addition, it stated that the Bank preferred to listen to the Borrowers, rather than implementing its own policies.[154] This was done mainly to avoid negative flows of capital and defaults on loans.[155]

Vice President and General Counsel of the Bank Ibrahim F.I. Shihata states that a Bank-wide review of all projects involving resettlement between 1986 and 1993 shows that Bank-financed projects are responsible for a small share of the 80 to 90 million displaced persons worldwide; specifically 3% of the resettlement caused by dam construction and 1% caused by urban and transportation projects.[156] Yet he does not spell out the actual number of people; 2.5 million "development refugees"[157] is no small number of people, no matter what the context.

Operational Directive (OD) 4.02 on National Environmental Action Plans, issued in 1992, was replaced by Operational Policy Statements (OP), Bank Procedures (BP), and Good Practice Statements (GP) 4.02 on Environmental Action Plans.[158] They outline Bank policy and procedures concerning the preparation of national environmental action plans by borrowing governments, a process which began in 1988.[159] The action plans involve a comprehensive analysis of the natural resources and environmental management in each country, the objective being to develop a strategy for the short and long term to tackle emerging problems.[160] This process allows borrowing countries to focus on the environmental problems and remedies most relevant to them, in addition to prioritizing their investments and national policies affecting the environment.[161]

For other areas of the environment, the Bank is also in the process of developing new policies and procedures to replace the old directives, including directives on indigenous peoples and agricultural pest man-agement.[162] In 1993, Operational Policies were issued on water resource management (OP 4.07) and on forestry (OP 4.36) to provide guidance in these areas.[163]

Together with the European Investment Bank and UNEP, the Bank has developed a regional type environmental action plan for the Mediterranean region called the Mediterranean Environmental Technical Assistance Program.[164] The Bank serves as the executing agency for UNDP, which is providing funding, and the European Union is also involved and providing resources.[165] The focus of the program is to identify and prepare specific projects and institutional-strengthening activities, including improving environmental legislative and regulatory frameworks at regional, sub-regional, and domestic levels.[166]

The World Bank has definitely taken great strides in a relatively short time frame to improve its policies and procedures with regard to environmental issues. Yet, it will take a long time for these new regulatory schemes to show measurable effects because the life cycle of the Bank's projects usually span over several years.

Primarily Environmental Projects. The Bank has also developed free-standing or primarily environmental projects, many of which are expected to be based on the national environmental action plans.[167] These projects are primarily designed to help developing countries improve their environmental management and strengthen the institutional and legal frameworks involved in the carrying out of activities included in the action plans or other environmental protection activities.[168] There are three types of projects: the pollution management and urban environmental projects, the rural environmental projects, and the environmental institutions projects.[169]

The pollution management and urban environmental projects usually include four elements: 1) support for research on new technologies, 2) direct investment in pollution prevention and treatment facilities, 3) funding for "on-lending"[170] to businesses and agencies for improved environmental management, and 4) capacity building for environmental management which includes monitoring, training, staffing, and policy studies.[171] The rural environmental or natural resource projects include the creation or strengthening of national parks and reserves, introducing integrated pest management, integrated river basin management, investing in soil conservation, and managing forests and conserving biodiversity.[172] The national environmental institution-building projects range from establishing a policy and a legal and institutional framework to enable effective management of activities for environmental protection and the conservation of natural resources to strengthening already existing environmental agencies through staff training and technical assistance, and improving enforcement.

By 1995 the Bank's portfolio of loans for primarily environmental projects had reached $10 billion for 137 projects in 62 countries. These efforts by the Bank, if successful, will most likely promote the participation of developing countries in the regulatory process to address global—in addition to local—environmental problems.

The World Bank, in addition to its support for environmental projects or project components is also one of the largest entities to mobilize resources for the protection of the global environment. It is one of the implementing agencies of the Global Environment Facility [173] and the Multilateral Fund.[174]

Conditionality. Like all bank loans, World Bank loans also have conditions attached. In order to ensure that the measures agreed upon with the borrower are implemented, including measures to avoid or minimize environmental degradation, several legal techniques are used by the Bank. The most commonly used method is to insert specific covenants in the loan agreement, at times complemented by detailed requirements in the "project agreement" entered into with the project executing agency.[175]

In order to promote implementation, the Bank also relies on the General Conditions in the Articles of Agreement of the Bank, applying to all loans, stating that the borrower is to carry out agreed actions with due diligence, otherwise disbursements by the Bank can be suspended.[176] In the extreme case, where the project is completed but the borrower has not fulfilled her obligations, the Bank can accelerate maturity of the loan and demand immediate repayment, although this has been avoided in practice.[177]

Furthermore, the Bank also relies on its own staff supervising the projects, together with the on-going country dialogue to ensure that they are implemented consistent with loan conditionality. However, Shihata states that "much greater efforts will have to be exerted" to ensure that agreed actions are carried out, including a strengthening of the Bank's supervisory capacity in the environmental field.[178]

In the context of development lending, UNCED's attempt to balance sovereignty and global responsibility can limit sovereignty in several ways.[179] If the development project were to effect the global commons this could trigger the operation of internationally agreed standards placing conditions on how the project is carried out in the borrower's territory.[180] In the case of the Climate Change Convention, this could mean that in the future, for instance, coal-burning facilities enabled through World Bank funding, would have to be replaced with facilities using less CO_2 emitting fuels. This would interfere with the sovereign right of the borrower to determine his/her own environment and development policies.

Resistance to conditionalities to lending agreements can lead to breakdown in agreements, such as when India pulled out of the Narmada loan agreement. Yet, by using universally agreed upon environmental and development standards to play a constructive role in the Bank's relationship with its clients, such conditions could be made more politically palatable, through widespread participation and a more open and accountable decision-making process.[181]

Some Criticisms of the Bank's Activities. The Bank's supervisory capacity was very much criticized in 1993, when a Bank task force headed by Vice President Willi Wapenhans, reported that there was a decline in the quality of the Bank's portfolio of operations.[182] Many of the Borrowers were not complying with their legal covenants. In response to that report, the former Bank President, Lewis Preston, conceded that the Bank had placed too much importance on the volume of loans and not enough on the lending results or quality of projects the funding supports.[183]

It is no secret that the loan officers in the Bank have been receiving their bonuses based on how many loans they could "push out the door". However, Mr. James Wolfensohn, the new Bank President, wants to change that by rewarding staff based on project performance, rather than the number of loans approved.[184]

Despite all the Bank's efforts to improve its policies and procedures relating to environmental issues, it still seems to suffer from an implementation problem. An unavoidable question is: Why have these problems not been taken care of by now?

Part of the answer could lie in the Bank's governance structure. Perhaps a more balanced power sharing arrangement within the Bank's Executive Board, moving from weighted voting to the one-state, one-vote procedure of the U.N. would be worth considering. Sands states that having developing countries participate on an equal footing with developed countries in project decisions would allow consensus to build within the developing world as to how spending priorities are to be set globally.[185] Also supporting a more democratic voting procedure, is one interpretation of Principle 7. Viewing development assistance as a 'responsibility' developed countries bear for the pressures their societies place on the global environment in the pursuit of sustainable development, rather than generosity, would dissolve the justification for allowing donor countries to determine decision-making in the Bank.[186]

Another part of the answer to the Bank's implementation problems could lie in the conflicting interests of the Bank. Many critics say the Bank lacks political and financial accountability. In order to improve the implementation of environmental policies by the World Bank one has to understand how the accountability process within the organization deter-mines the Bank's priorities.[187] In implementing its own policies, the Bank is influenced by various actors with different policy demands, including donor governments, recipient governments, and the political and financial structures of the organizations.[188] Donor governments represented by their finance minister on the Board of Executive Directors are mostly concerned with economic issues, while recipient governments usually just want the money, especially to repay some of their debt. Part of this problem could perhaps be solved by including an environmental expert from member countries on the Board of Executive Directors.

Another problem concerning the Executive Board is that theoretically it holds management and staff accountable, but in practice the Board is quite ineffective in this context, and the autonomy of the Bank's President and administration has been growing the last few years.[189] One way to solve this problem would perhaps be to expand accountability to include all stakeholders.

In addition, Bank projects should no longer be measured mainly on the basis of whether they are financially sound and economically productive. The results of the projects also need to be measured in terms of environmental and social effects.

Wolfensohn has also pin-pointed corruption as a problem, and has stated that in developing countries and countries with economies in transition this is undermining public support of development aid.[190] He has been quoted as saying that "[c]ountries that are fundamentally corrupt should be told that unless they can deal with that, they are not getting any more money. That is part of governmental reform."[191] This is a tall order for countries which have corruption totally immersed in their culture. In many developing countries, to supplement their low salaries, government officials welcome a bribe in return for which they disregard the laws, such as pollution regulations, rather than enforcing them.

In 1994, in response to a lot of the criticisms of the Bank, it established an Inspection Panel to receive complaints by affected parties or groups and the Bank's Executive Directors with respect to the Bank's failure to carry out its own policies and procedures throughout the life-cycle of the Bank's projects.[192] The Inspection Panel, which consists of three independent members, sends the complaint (Request for inspection) to the Bank Management and requests it to provide the Panel with written evidence that it has complied with the Bank's relevant policies and procedures. Based on the complaint and the Bank Management's response, the Panel then sends its recommendations to the Executive Board.[193] If the Board determines to have the Panel proceed with an investigation, the Panel will investigate the complaint and submit a report to the Executive Directors and the Bank

President.[194] The Board, on the basis of the Panel's report and the Management's response to the Panel's findings, then decides what action is to be taken.[195] However, the scope of the complaint is limited in that it cannot include violations of "Best Practices" or "Bank Guidelines."[196] This can become a big problem because part of the reform efforts of the Bank have involved downgrading certain environment-friendly policies to "best practice" status, which means project managers are not bound by them, nor will the Inspection Panel be brought to bear on their actions.[197] The first project to be investigated by the Panel was the Arun III project, a highly debated dam project in Nepal.[198] The Bank's decision to withdraw from the project[199] was most likely influenced by the Panel's investigation.

Another reform in response to Bank criticism was the adoption of a new information policy.[200] Bank Procedures on Disclosure of Operational Information of 1993, requires that before the Bank does the project appraisal, the Environmental Assessment for Category A projects must be released locally in the borrowing country for affected groups and NGOs and submitted to the Bank.[201] After being made available locally and being received officially by the Bank, the Assessment is to be sent to the Public Information Center (PIC).[202] Hopefully, the PIC will be instrumental in increasing transparency in the Bank projects.

Transparency, developing country participation in policy-making at the Bank, in addition to local participation, and accountability of Bank staff are perhaps the most important advancements that still need to be improved upon in the Bank. Developing countries would perhaps be more willing to get involved in global environmental issues if they felt their needs were also being met at the local level.

On another level, the Bank could join the efforts toward removing subsidies that pay for activities that degrade the environment by training government officials in developing countries who negotiate concession agreements.[203] Giving the government officials financial, engineering, and environmental skills with regard to the international resource-based industries and educating them in the more intricate points of negotiation could translate into billions more in royalty payments,[204] rather than selling the concessions far under market value. Of course, here again corruption is a factor, and close ties between industry and policy makers reinforces the problem.[205] Instead of going into the bank accounts of a few industry magnates, the money could be used to subsidize environmentally beneficial technologies, such as solar panels that could, for instance, replace kerosene for energy to light the homes of rural peasants with no access to the national electricity grid.[206]

The funding for the training of government officials could be procured by adding a rubric called "special training" to the expenses involved at the appraisal stage of every project. The same technique could be used to finance the development of local capacity to participate in project design. The training of government officials could perhaps, as an alternative, be a particular Bank project, funded separately.[207]

There is no doubt the World Bank has definitely gotten a green tinge. The question remains whether this is only on paper or also in the real world. With time the newer projects following new procedures and policies hopefully will reflect a more environmentally friendly Bank. In turn, the Bank projects will function as incentives to promote sustainable develop-ment, unlike the older projects, such as the immense dam building projects, that neither took the environmental nor the social aspects into account.

United Nations Development Programme (UNDP) – Capacity 21

The United Nations Development Programme (UNDP) was created in 1965 by the U.N. General Assembly Resolution 2029 (XX) merging the Expanded Programme of Technical Assistance, managed by ECOSOC and ECOSOC's Special Fund.[208] UNDP has country offices in 134 nations, helping people to self-help in 174 countries through programs focusing on poverty elimination, environmental regeneration, advancement of women, and job creation.[209]

Governments ask for UNDP assistance to support rebuilding societies following humanitarian emergencies and war, and in facilitating sound governance and market development.[210] UNDP's main priority is eliminating poverty and building equity by helping countries build national capacity to achieve sustainable human development. Its main purpose is to assist developing countries to accelerate their economic and social development by providing technical assistance related to their national development plans and priorities. Eighty percent of its core funding goes to the least developed countries.[211]

UNDP is controlled by a 36-member board with representatives from developed and developing countries. It is an implementing agency for the Multilateral Fund of the Montreal Protocol and GEF. At the country level, UNDP is in charge of coordinating all U.N. activities.

In conjunction with the preparations for UNCED, UNDP launched a program called Capacity 21. The Capacity 21 Program is managed by the Sustainable Energy and Environment Division (SEED) of UNDP.[212] Unlike the Global Environmental Facility (GEF), to be examined below,[213] Capacity 21 concentrates on domestic environmental problems in the developing countries by financing programs that benefit mainly the 'local' environment, rather than having global environmental benefits. As most of these environmental problems are interdependent, these local efforts also con-tribute to preventing degradation of the global environment.

Capacity 21 was created to help developing countries build the capacity to formulate and implement national programs for sustainable development; developing their own Agenda 21 plans.[214] These plans are then harmonized with the National Environmental Action Plans which the World Bank sponsors.[215] Capacity 21 also promotes the integration of environmental considerations into development plans. Through the use of Environmental Management Guidelines, Capacity 21 helps countries ensure that projects do not have negative effects on the environment.[216]

Capacity 21 is a likely channel for increasing knowledge and capabilities in many areas, including technical skills needed to integrate environmentally sound technology, make sustainable development plans at the local level, and develop the environmental laws and administration needed to implement multilateral environmental treaties. Together with UNEP, UNDP's Capacity 21 can provide governments with an integrated program of environment and development law services as Agenda 21 urges, thereby promoting the participation of developing countries in international environmental agreements.[217]

An independent review of Capacity 21 was carried out in 1996. The report, on the whole, praises Capacity 21, and states that it has made excellent progress toward fulfilling its objectives.[218]

Notes

1. *See* Helsinki Declaration on the Environment, Mar. 11, 1989, 28 I.L.M. 1308 (1989).

2. *See* Agenda 21, *supra* Chapter 1 note 8, ch. 38.

3. *See* Programme for Further Implementation of Agenda 21, *supra* Chapter 2 note 190, ¶¶ 122–30.

4. *See* NGOs, *infra* Chapter 8.

5. UNEP Information and Public Affairs Branch, UNEP IN BRIEF, Nairobi, Kenya, 1992.

6. *See* Agenda 21, *supra* Chapter 1 note 8, at 38.23.

7. *See* UNITED NATIONS, THE BASIC FACTS ABOUT THE UNITED NATIONS 85 (1987).

8. *See* Mark A. Gray, *The United Nations Environment Programme: An Assessment*, 20 ENVTL. L. 292 (1990).

9. *See* Report on the Stockholm Conference, *supra* Chapter 1 note 11.

10. United Nations, Press Release, U.N. Doc. HE/948, Feb. 12, 1997 (hereinafter UNPR HE/948).

11. *See* Caldwell, *supra* Chapter 1 note 12, at 69; G.A. Res. 3004(XXVII), U.N. GAOR (Dec. 15, 1972) ("Location of the Environment Secretariat").

12. D.W. BOWETT, THE LAW OF INTERNATIONAL INSTITUTIONS 57,58 (1982).

13. Resolution on the Institutional and Financial Arrangement for International Environmental Cooperation, U.N. GAOR, adopted Dec. 15, 1972, 13 I.L.M. 234 (1974) (establishing the United Nations Environment Program, UNEP).

14. Gray, *supra* note 8, at 294.

15. *See* Report of the Stockholm Conference *supra* Chapter 1 note 11 (Action Plan).

16. *See* Caldwell, *supra* Chapter 1 note 12, at 76.

17. *See id.*

18. *See* Nanda, *supra* Chapter 2 note 147, at 89.

19. Report of the Stockholm Conference, *supra* Chapter 1 note 11 (Action Plan of the United Nations Conference on the Human Environment).

20. *See* Nanda, *supra* Chapter 2 note 147, at 90.

21. *United Nations System-Wide Medium-Term Environmental Programme 1990–1995*, U.N. Development Programme, at viii, U.N. Doc. UNEP/GCSS.I/7/Add.1 (Nairobi 1988) [hereinafter UNEP 1990-1995 Program].

22. *See id.*

23. *See id.*

24. United Nations Environment Programme, (visited Nov. 28, 1996) <http://www./unep-bri.htm> (current information available as of Mar. 5, 1999 at <http://www.unep.ch/>).

25. *See id.*

26. Kiss & Shelton, *supra* Chapter 2 note 56, at 62.

27. *Report of the Intergovernmental Conference to Adopt a Global Programme of Action for the Protection of the Marine Environment from Land-based Activities*, U.N. Environment Programme, U.N. Doc. UNEP(OCA)/LBA/IG.2/6, Washington, D.C. (Oct. 23–Nov. 3, 1995). *Global Programme of Action for the Protection of the Marine Environment from Land-based Activities*, U.N. Environment Programme, U.N. Doc. UNEP(OCA)/LBA IG.2/7.

28. *See United Nations Environment Programme: Report of the Governing Council on the Work of Its Fifteenth Session*, U.N. GOAR, 44th Sess., Supp. No. 25, at 162, U.N. Doc. A/44/25. *See also* Chandler, *supra* Chapter 5 note 24, at 142.

29. Biodiversity Convention, *supra* Chapter 2 note 168.

30. *See* Kiss & Shelton, *supra* Chapter 2 note 56, at 61.

31. Telephone interview with Jim Sniffen, UNEP Information Officer (December 4, 1996).

32. *See* Nanda, *supra* Chapter 2 note 147, at 92.

33. *See id.*

34. *See id.* at 93.

35. *See* Sniffen, *supra* note 31.

36. *See id.*

37. *See* Catherine Tinker, *Environmental Planet Management by the United Nations: An Idea Whose Time Has Not Yet Come?*, 22 N.Y.U. J. Int'l L. & Pol. 796 (1991).

38. *See* Gray, *supra* note 8, at 313.

39. *See id.*

40. *See* Nanda, *supra* Chapter 2 note 147, at 101.

41. *See* Tinker, *supra* note 37, at 796.

42. Caldwell, *supra* Chapter 1 note 12, at 89.

43. *See id.*

44. *See id.*

45. See U.N. Environment Programme, U.N. Doc. UNEP/GC.18/27 (Mar. 21, 1995).

46. *See id.*

47. *See id.*

48. *See id.* at 3.

49. *See* UNPR HE/948, *supra* note 10.

50. *See* Leyla Boulton, *United Nations: Environment Agency Funding Withheld,* FIN. TIMES, Feb. 12, 1997, at 8.

51. *See United Nations: Compromise Will Change UNEP Governance; Program Mandate Could Change Significantly,* Daily Env't Rep. (BNA), Apr. 8, 1997.

52. *See id.*

53. *See id.*

54. *See* discussion of ACC *infra* text accompanying note 97.

55. Developed from Gray, *supra* note 8, at 314.

56. *See* Paul C. Szaz, *Restructuring the International Organizational Framework, in* ENVIRONMENTAL CHANGE AND INTERNATIONAL LAW 347 (Edith Brown Weiss ed., 1992).

57. *See* Hilary French, *Reforming the United Nations to Ensure Environmentally Sustainable Development, in* PREFERRED FUTURES FOR THE UNITED NATIONS 256 (Mendlovitz ed., 1995).

58. Szaz, *supra* note 56.

59. *See* French, *supra* Chapter 3 note 79.

60. *See* Climate Change Convention, *supra* Chapter 2 note 137, art. 7.

61. *See* Vienna Convention, *supra* Chapter 2 note 134.

62. *See* S. Jacob Scherr & Jared E. Blumenfeld, *Implementing UNCED, in* GREENING INTERNATIONAL LAW 236 (Philippe Sands ed., 1994).

63. *See id.* at 25.

64. *See id.* at 23.

65. *See* French, *supra* Chapter 3 note 79, at 256.

66. *See id.*

67. *See* Geoffrey Palmer, *New Ways to Make International Environmental Law,* 86 AM. J. INT'L L. 263 (1992).

68. *Id.*

69. *See* Weiss, *supra* Chapter 1 note 24, at 699.

70. Interview with Unni Klovstad, the Permanent Mission of Norway to the United Nations (Oct. 22, 1996).

71. *See* Pulvenis, *supra* Chapter 5 note 35, at 83.

72. This section is based in part on the General Assembly Resolution, *Institutional Arrangements to Follow Up the United Nations Conference on Environment and Development*, G.A. Res. 47/191 (Dec. 22, 1992).

73. *See* ECOSOC Decision 1993/207, U.N. Economic and Social Council, (Feb. 12, 1993).

74. *See Strengthening of the United Nations System Programme Budget for the Biennium 1996-1997, Letter dated 17 March 1997 from the Secretary-General addressed to the President of the General Assembly*, U.N. Doc. A/51/529 (1997).

75. *See* Agenda 21, *supra* Chapter 1 note 8, at 38.13, 33.13, 33.21.

76. *See* KISS & SHELTON, INTERNATIONAL ENVIRONMENTAL LAW—1994 SUPPLEMENT 43 (1994); Agenda 21, *supra* Chapter 1 note 8, at 38.13(g).

77. *See* KISS & SHELTON, *supra* note 76, at 44.

78. *See* Commission on Sustainable Development, U.N. Doc. E/CN.17/1993/2 (Feb. 19, 1997).

79. *See id.*

80. *See id.*

81. *See* Kiss and Shelton, *supra* note 76, at 44.

82. *See* Programme for the Further Implementation of Agenda 21, *supra* Chapter 2 note 190, ¶ 132, annex.

83. *See* Daniel Esty, *Gatting the Greens*, 72 FOREIGN AFF. 34 (1993).

84. *See id.*

85. *See* Christopher Flavin, *The Legacy of Rio*, *in* STATE OF THE WORLD 1997 at 5 (Lester Brown et al. eds., 1997).

86. *See* French, *supra* Chapter 3 note 79, at 259.

87. *See id.*

88. *See id.*

89. The Country Profiles are meant to function as a source for decision-makers, giving them insight into what does and does not work under various cultural, social, and economic conditions. *See* Country Profiles (visited Mar. 10, 1997) <http://www.un.org/dpcsd> (current information available as of Mar. 5, 1999 at <http://www.un.org/esa/sustdev/>). Perhaps the critical question is not whether countries will submit reports, but whether they will have any real content and impact. One diplomat, questioning the usefulness of the Country Profiles, noted the that format of the reports is very schematic and does not allow for much analysis.

90. Interview with Tarcisio Alvarez-Rivero, Department of Policy Coordination and Sustainable Development (Mar. 14, 1997).

91. Idea developed from HILKKA PIETILA & JEANNE VICKERS, MAKING WOMEN MATTER 5 (1994).

92. *See Report of the Ad Hoc Open-ended Inter-Sessional Working Group of the Commission on Sustainable Development*, U.N. Commission on Sustainable Development, 5th Sess. (1997), U.N. Doc. E/CN.17/1997/13 (1997). *See*, for instance, the National Advisory Committee on Environment and Sustainable Development in Zimbabwe,

UNFCCC Secretariat, Zimbabwe: country information (visited April 3, 1999) <http://www.un/ccc/org>.

93. *Institutional Arrangements to Follow Up the United Nations Conference on Environment and Development*, U.N. Conference on Environment and Development, U.N. Doc. A/47/719, at 22 (Dec. 22, 1992).

94. *See* discussion *infra* text following note 113.

95. *See* John Herzfeld, *Environment, U.N. Meeting on Sustainable Development to Set up Look at World Progress in 1997*, Lexis 1996 DER 78 d29.

96. Flavin, *supra* note 85, at 5.

97. *See* U.N. Doc. E/62/Rev (1946).

98. Resolution on Institutional and Financial Arrangements, *supra* note 13.

99. Editors of the Harvard Law Review, TRENDS IN INTERNATIONAL ENVIRONMENTAL LAW 116 (1992).

100. *See id.*

101. *See* BIRNIE & BOYLE, *supra* Chapter 1 note 3, at 44.

102. UNEP 1990-1995 Program, *supra* note 21.

103. *See* Nanda, *supra* Chapter 2 note 147, at 94.

104. *See* Sniffen, *supra* note 31.

105. *See* BIRNIE & BOYLE, *supra* Chapter 1 note 3, at 44.

106. *See* Palmer, *supra* note 67, at 261.

107. *See* BIRNIE & BOYLE, *supra* Chapter 1 note 3, at 44. *See also* Palmer, *supra* note 67, at 261 (eight of these organizations, including the Commission of the European Communities, together adopted the Declaration of Environment Policies and Procedures Relating to Economic Development in 1980, thus forming CIDIE). *See id.*

108. *See* BIRNIE & BOYLE, *supra* Chapter 1 note 3, at 44.

109. Williams Silveira, *supra* Chapter 3 note 31, at 248.

110. *See* Programme for the Further Implementation of Agenda 21, *supra* Chapter 2 note 190, ¶ 120.

111. *See* Wilson, *supra* Chapter 1 note 45, at 966.

112. *See* discussion *infra* Chapter 7.

113. *See* Piddington, *supra* Chapter 2 note 151, at 214.

114. *See* John Horberry, *The Accountability of Development Assistance Agencies: The Case of Environmental Policy*, 12 ECOLOGY L.Q. 823 (1985).

115. Barber Conable, Speech at World Bank conference, London (1991), *reprinted in part in* Ibrahim F.I. Shihata, *The Role of the World Bank: Legal Instruments for Achieving Environmental Objectives*, *in* INTERNATIONAL ENVIRONMENTAL LAW n.116 (Erling Selvig & Hans Christian Bugge eds., 1995).

116. European Bank for Reconstruction and Development (EBRD), art. 2(1)(vii), 18 I.L.M. 1077 (1990).

117. Brundtland Commission's Report, *supra* Chapter 1 note 15, at 337.

118. *See* Philippe Sands, *Greening Bretton Woods*, *in* GREENING INTERNATIONAL LAW 73 (1994).

119. Similar agreements were made with the International Monetary Fund (IMF or "the Fund") and the International Finance Corporation (IFC or "the Corporation"), while the International Development Association (IDA) is considered to be an affiliate of the World Bank, and not really a separate specialized agency. For operational purposes, IDA is considered one with the Bank. The IFC is also an affiliate of the Bank, but it is considered to be a separate entity, distinct from the Bank. With respect to the U.N. specialized agencies, the Bank, the Fund, and the Corporation are referred to as the "financial organizations." *See* Bowett, *supra* note 12, at 65, 66, 139.

120. *See id.* This autonomy also applies to the other "financial organizations".

121. *See* Articles of Agreement of the International Bank for Reconstruction and Development, art. V, ¶ 2(a), 2 U.N.T.S. 134, *as amended* Feb. 16, 1989 [hereinafter World Bank Articles of Agreement].

122. *See* BIRNIE & BOYLE, *supra* Chapter 1 note 3, at 62.

123. *See* World Bank Articles of Agreement, *supra* note 121, art. 5, sect. 3. *See also* Horberry, *supra* note 114, at 826.

124. *Id.*

125. *See* WORLD BANK, WORLD DEVELOPMENT REPORT 1990.

126. *See* AL GORE, EARTH IN THE BALANCE 191 (1992).

127. Replacing the Office of Environmental Affairs which had been established in 1970. *See* Horberry *supra* note 114, at 849.

128. *See* Shihata, *supra* note 115, at 168.

129. *See* R.J.A. Goodland, *The World Bank's Environmental Assessment Policy*, 14 HASTINGS INT'L & COMP. L. REV. 811 (1991).

130. *See* World Bank, Operational Directive on Environmental Assessment (OD 4.01), The World Bank Operational Manual, ¶ 6 (October 3,1991) [hereinafter Operational Directive 4.01].

131. Charles E. DiLeva, *The World Bank and the Environment*, *in* INTERNATIONAL ENVIRONMENTAL LAW 289 (ALI/ABA ed., 1995). *See also* Operational Directive 4.01, *supra* note 128, ¶ 17.

132. Operational Directive 4.01, *supra* note 130, ¶ 17. *See also* Shihata, *supra* note 115, at 169.

133. *See id.*

134. *See* Goodland, *supra* note 129, at 812.

135. *See id.* at 813.

136. *See id.*

137. *See id.*

138. *See* Shihata, *supra* note 115, at 169.

139. *See* Operational Directive 4.01, *supra* note 128, ¶ 13 (the text in paragraph 13 reads "should normally engage an advisory panel", which seems to give some leeway as to whether a panel is to be engaged or not).

140. *See* World Bank, Operational Directive 4.05, Environmental Policy for Dam and Reservoir Projects. *See also* Operational Directive 4.01, *supra* note 128, ¶ 13, n.10.

141. Bureau of National Affairs, *U.N. Official Says Expanded EIS Use Without Legal Framework Posing Problems,* 19 INENV [Int'l Env't Rep. (BNA)] 552 (1996).

142. *See id.*

143. *See id.*

144. *See id.*

145. *See* Environmental Policy for Dam and Reservoir Projects, *supra* note 140, formerly Annex B of OP 4.00. *See* Shihata, *supra* note 115, at 171.

146. *See id.*

147. *See id.* at 172.

148. *See id.*

149. *See id.* at 173.

150. *See id.* at 172.

151. *See* World Bank, Operational Directive 4.30 (OD 4.30), ¶ 20.

152. *See* Sands, *supra* note 118, at 73.

153. *See, e.g.,* BRUCE RICH, THE WORLD BANK AFTER 50 YEARS: NO MORE MONEY WITHOUT TOTAL INSTITUTIONAL REFORM 7 (1993).

154. *See id.*

155. *See id.*

156. *See id.*

157. Adam Zagorin, *Damning the World Bank,* TIME, July 25, 1994, at 32.

158. World Bank, OP/BP/GP 4.02 Environmental Actions Plans.

159. *See* Shihata, *supra* note 115, at 174.

160. *See id.* at 182. *See also* World Bank, GP 4.02, ¶ 5.

161. *See* Shihata, *supra* note 115, at 175.

162. *See id. See also* World Bank, Operational Directive 4.20 on Indigenous Peoples (OD. 4.20); World Bank, OP/BP/GP 4.03 on Agricultural Pest Management.

163.*See* Shihata, *supra* note 115, at 175.

164. *See id.* at 183.

165. *See id.*

166. *See id.*

167. *See id.* at 185.

168. *See id.* at 184.

169. See WORLD BANK, MAINSTREAMING THE ENVIRONMENT—THE WORLD BANK GROUP AND THE ENVIRONMENT SINCE THE RIO EARTH SUMMIT—FISCAL 1995 at 4–7 (1995) [hereinafter WORLD BANK FISCAL 1995].

170. "On lending" is a colloquial term used by the World Bank to refer to money lent to a government which the government in turn lends to businesses.

171. *See* WORLD BANK FISCAL 1995, *supra* note 169, at 4–7.

172. *See id.*

173. *See* GEF, *infra* Chapter 7.

174. *See* discussion on the Multilateral Fund, *supra* Chapter 5.

175.Shihata, *supra* note 115, at 175.

176. *See id.* at 181.

177. *See id.*

178. *Id.* at 182.

179. *See* Sands, *supra* note 118, at 75.

180. *See id.*

181. *See id.*

182. *See* World Bank, *Effective Implementation: Key to Development Impact*, Report of the World Bank's Portfolio Management Task Force (1992) (known as the Wapenhans Report).

183. *See* Zagorin, *supra* note 157.

184. *See* Michael Holman & Patti Waldmeir, *World Bank Chief's Cry From the Heart*, FIN. TIMES, Mar. 29, 1996, at 4.

185. *See* Sands, *supra* note 118, at 78.

186. *See id.*

187. *See* Horberry, *supra* note 114, at 819.

188. *See id.*

189. *See* Bruce Rich, Statement of Bruce Rich on Behalf of Environmental Defense Fund, National Wildlife Federation, Sierra Club, and Greenpeace Before the House Committee on Banking and Financial Services Subcommittee on Domestic and International Monetary Policy Concerning the World Bank: Effectiveness and Needed Reforms 15 (March 27, 1995).

190. *See* Robert Chote, *Corruption "Undermines Aid Effort"*, FIN. TIMES, July 2, 1996, at 3.

191. *Id.*

192. *See* Rich, *supra* note 153, at 14. *See also* IBRD Resolution 93-10/IDA Resolution 93-6, ¶ 12 (adopted Sept. 22, 1993) [hereinafter Resolution]; World Bank, Bank Procedure BP 17.55 (Feb. 1997); World Bank, Inspection Panel's Operating Procedures (adopted by the Panel on Aug. 19, 1994).

193. *See* Resolution, *supra* note 189, ¶¶ 2, 17, 18, 19.

194. *See* Resolution, *supra* note 189, ¶¶ 20, 22.

195. *See* Resolution, *supra* note 189, ¶ 23.

196. Rich, *supra* note 153, at 14. *See* Resolution, *supra* note 189, ¶ 12. *See also Review of the Resolution Establishing the Inspection Panel – Clarification of Certain Aspects of the Resolution*, IBRD and IDA, Oct. 17, 1996, <http://www.worldbank.org/html/ins-panel.html> (current as of Mar. 5, 1999).

197. Deepak Gopinath, *The Greening of the World Bank*, INFRASTRUCTURE FIN., Sept. 1996, at 46, 50. To produce a more flexible system, previous procedures are being transformed into three types: 1) Operational Policy Statements (OPs) including binding substantive policy instructions 2) Bank Procedures (BPs), used in preparation of Bank operations, and 3) "Good Practice" (GP) statements, offering practical advice for Bank staff and borrowers concerning Operational Policies and Bank Procedures. *See* DiLeva, *supra* note 131, at 288.

198. *See Inspection of Arun III Hydroelectric Project Authorized*, Feb. 3, 1995, <http://www.worldbank.org/html/ins-panel.html>.

199. *See* Inspection Panel for the World Bank, Overview September 1997 Update (visited Oct. 10, 1997) <http://www.worldbank.org./html/ins-panel/overview.html>. *See* IPS, World Bank Chief to Refuse Nepali Request for Arun, Oct. 19, 1995, *available in* LEXIS, Nexis Library, WORLD, ÀLLNWS file. *See also* Daniel Bradlow, *A Test Case for the World Bank* 11 AM. U.J. INT'L L. & POL'Y 248, 280 (1996).

200. *See* Rich, *supra* note 153, at 13. *See also* World Bank, Disclosure of Operational Information BP 17.50.

201. *See* Disclosure of Operational Information BP 17.50, *supra* note 197, ¶ 12.

202. *See id.*

203. *See* David Malin Roodman, *Paying the Piper: Subsidies, Politics, and the Environment*, WORLD WATCH PAPER 133, 66 (1996).

204. *See id.*

205. *See id.*

206. *See id.* at 146.

207. The Bank could then utilize some of its experience from Venezuela, the flagship of its judicial reform program, which reflects its conviction that "sustainable economic growth depends not only on the right macroeconomic policies, but on effective institutions. . . ." *Augean Law*, ECONOMIST, Sept. 14, 1996, at 44.

208. *See* Bowett, *supra* note 12, at 64.

209. *See* U.N. Development Programme, *Overview*, <http://www.undp.org/undp/news/stepped/overview.htm> (visited Apr. 15, 1997) (current information available as of Mar. 5, 1999 at <http://www.undp.org/info/discover/overview.htm>).

210. *See id.*

211. *See id.* 212. Interview with Lisa Dokken, Environmental Specialist at UNDP's headquarters in New York (Oct. 22, 1996).

213. *See* GEF, *supra* Chapter 7. UNDP is one of the three implementing agencies of GEF.

214. *See* Dokken, *supra* note 211.

215. *See id.*

216. *See id.*

217. *See* Agenda 21, *supra* Chapter 1 note 8, ch. 8, § 19. *See also supra* Chapter 5 (on capacity-building).

218. *See* IDRIS KIKULA & NIZAR MOHAMED, INDEPENDENT REVIEW OF CAPACITY 21, 38 (1996).

7

Special Funding Mechanisms

In general, financing for the implementation of the international environmental agreements comes from the treaty parties' own resources. Yet because most developing countries are burdened with huge debts, they usually depend on external funding to help pay for environmental protection measures.

This funding has usually been in the form of Official Development Assistance(ODA). However the average ODA has been decreasing instead of increasing, falling far short of the target of 0.7 percent of the GNP as was adopted by the U.N. in the early 1980s and reaffirmed by the Brundtland Commission and UNCED.[1] On the other hand, the private capital flows have increased, yet even if they are a necessary condition for sustainable development they are not enough because many poor countries are getting very little of this funding, and in addition, sustainable development requires some types of social and environmental investments that do not attract private capital.[2] For this reason, new and additional funding mechanisms are sorely needed to promote developing countries to become parties to the environmental conventions and in turn fulfill their commitments.

Many new funding mechanisms have been suggested to implement Agenda 21, which at the same time would promote the implementation of multilateral environmental treaties at the national and international levels.[3] Several countries have begun to reduce subsidies that promote activities that degrade the environment, and have in place or have begun experimenting with emission trading programs and user fees.

At the international level, a number of innovative mechanisms have been suggested, some of which I will examine in this chapter. The Global Environment Facility (GEF) is widely considered the main financial mechanism to facilitate participation and implementation of the inter-national environmental agreements. The Multilateral Fund of the Montreal Protocol is another such funding mechanism, yet it applies only to the Montreal Protocol, as shown above.[4] Joint implementation activities, as discussed above,[5] could also qualify as special funding mechanisms. In addition, different types of debt swaps, tradable permits, and international carbon taxes will be analyzed below. All of these mechanisms serve to promote universal participation and implementation of environmental treaties.

Global Environment Facility

The Global Environment Facility (GEF) is the main financial mechanism for projects benefiting the global environment. The World Bank established GEF in 1990 at the request of industrialized country governments who saw a need for financing action in developing countries to deal with global environmental problems.[6] GEF is run jointly by the World Bank, the United Nations Environment Programme (UNEP), and the United Nations Development Programme (UNDP).[7] GEF sponsors programs to help developing countries participate in solving global environmental problems. The Facility has four mandated funding areas: preventing climate change, loss of biodiversity, depletion of the ozone layer, and protecting international waters.[8] At its inception, GEF was a pilot program with the goal of investing in projects that promote and adopt environmentally sound technologies which will produce global benefits in the four areas mentioned above.

In 1994 GEF was restructured and replenished with $2 billion.[9] The main reason the restructuring took place was because of complaints made by the developing countries that they were not having an effective say in GEF's decision-making.[10] In addition, Agenda 21, the Climate Change Convention, and the Convention on Biological Diversity, all called for a restructuring of GEF.[11] Originally, GEF was administered by the World Bank; now it has a more independent status. The World Bank has become the trustee of the GEF Trust Fund.[12] The restructured Facility has an Assembly, a Governing Council, and a Secretariat, giving it a new decision-making form.[13] In addition, participation in GEF is now open to any state member of the United Nations or any of its specialized agencies. The scope of the Facility has also been expanded as a result of the restructuring process to include land degradation. It now covers desertification and deforestation related to the four focal areas mentioned above.[14]

The Assembly consists of the representatives of all 164 states participating in GEF.[15] It meets every three years to review the general policies of the Facility, its operations, and its membership. The Council consists of thirty-two members: sixteen from the developing countries, fourteen from the developed countries, and two from central and eastern Europe and the former Soviet Union.[16] The Council's functions are, among others, to: review the operation of the Facility, ensure that GEF programs are monitored and evaluated on a regular basis and review and approve the administrative budget of GEF. The Chief Executive Officer, appointed by the Council, heads up the Secretariat and reports to the Assembly and the Council.

Decisions by the Council are taken by consensus, but if that fails any member may require a formal vote. The formal vote consists of a double weighted majority.[17] An affirmative vote represents both a 60 percent majority of the total number of participants and a 60 percent majority of the total contributions. This two-part voting system gives the recipient countries more say in matters concerning GEF's management through a "one-country, one vote," similar to that used in the U.N.[18] In addition, it also lets the donor countries keep enough control to be willing to contribute funding through the "one dollar one vote" procedure used by the World Bank.

The work of implementing GEF activities is shared by UNEP, UNDP, and the World Bank in the following manner:

- UNEP manages the Scientific and Technical Advisory Panel (STAP), an independent advisory body that provides guidance for GEF. UNEP is also the catalyst for the development of scientific and technical analysis in addition to promoting environmental management in GEF-financed activities.
- UNDP is in charge of capacity building and technical assistance activities. It is also responsible for the Small Grant Program for non-governmental organizations (NGOs) and community groups around the world.
- The World Bank, as mentioned above, is the repository for the GEF Trust Fund and runs the investment projects. It also enlists private funds in accordance with GEF objectives and national sustainable development strategies.[19]

GEF finances the incremental costs of ensuring that a project benefits the global environment. For instance, if a developing country has a project which is economically viable, such as a fossil fuel power plant, but requires supplementary funding to benefit the global environment (e.g., to switch the technology in order to use natural gas, thereby lowering emissions of carbon dioxide), then it would be eligible for GEF funding. GEF also finances innovative and demonstration projects, which have a good investment potential. In addition, GEF can finance the cost of not developing, for instance, a tropical rain forest area because of its unique biodiversity value and its value as a sink for greenhouse gases.[20] GEF would then pay the net income the country would forgo by abstaining from developing, for instance, a national park for mining purposes.[21]

At the Rio Conference, GEF was made the entity entrusted, on an interim basis, with the operation of the funding mechanism for the Framework Convention on Climate Change and the Convention on Biological Diversity.[22] One of the interesting issues regarding GEF is whether it is just another source of funding for the World Bank to tag onto its regular projects or if it really is going to make a difference for the global environment. This is important because the World Bank manages the GEF Trust Fund and in that capacity has become accountable to donors and beneficiaries through GEF Governing Council, in addition to the Conference of the Parties of the Climate Change Convention and the Convention on Biological Diversity, which are democratic entities operated under the auspices of the U.N.[23]

At present, GEF receives guidelines from the Conference of the Parties (COP) to the conventions which it is required to follow,[24] yet GEF's Council has the last word with regard to individual projects.[25] In addition, GEF does use some of the funds for projects which concern climate or biodiversity issues proposed by countries that are not members of either of the conventions.[26]

Each implementing agency is responsible for the follow-up of the projects using their own monitoring and supervision procedures. However, because the World Bank manages the investment projects, it is effectively the primary implementing agency.[27] Yet, it has to follow GEF Operational Programs to guide strategic planning in general, and task managers in the preparation of eligible projects in particular.[28] In addition, the Scientific and Technical Advisory Panel, STAP, randomly chooses projects for quality control.

Debt-For-Nature Swaps and Other Swaps

The debt-for-nature exchanges have been the most commonly used types of trades to date that have provided developing countries with funding for environmental projects and, at the same time, relieved them of part of their debt burden.

There are several models being used. One of the most common models is where a non-governmental organization (NGO) buys the debt from the creditor bank at a discount and, in return for canceling the debt, the developing country's government commits itself to using more resources on local conservation.[29] This can be done by trading the debt instrument directly for legislative protection of environmentally vulnerable lands within its territory.[30] The debt can also be transferred to a conservation organization in the debtor country, which then turns over the debt instrument to its government in exchange for local currency bonds or local currency.[31] This local group then uses the currency or bonds to finance a conservation program which it manages.[32]

The latter type of debt-for-nature swap was used in the case of Ecuador in 1987. The United States branch of the World Wide Fund for Nature (still called the World Wildlife Fund) (WWF-US), and Ecuador completed a trade where WWF-US acquired debt with a face value of $1 million at thirty-five cents on the dollar.[33] This debt instrument was then assigned to Fundacion Natura, a local conservation group, which exchanged the debt for government bonds issued in local currency, "sucres," at 100 percent of the face value.[34] The conservation activities of Fundacion Natura are to be financed by both the interest and principle of the bonds.[35]

At the outset, most of the debt-for-nature swaps were funded by private organizations after getting consent from the debtor country. Soon thereafter, the swaps were also being undertaken by the governments of developed nations modeled on the private trades.[36]

Several limitations to these trades reduce their potential for large-scale environmental protection.[37] These include the creditors' willingness to enter into such agreements and the amount of land which can be preserved in this manner.[38] Another important limitation concerns the issue that such exchanges intrude on the sovereignty of the developing countries by telling them how to use their land and manage their natural resources, creating a permanent loss of control over natural resources.[39]

Some analysts say this is not an issue because as long as developing countries enter into agreements to trade debt for nature, the swaps function as any other contract.[40] However, as long as the developing countries are in a state of despair and under enormous pressure to repay their debts, one can argue whether they have equal bargaining power. One solution is to structure the debt-for-nature swaps in such a way that the fear of loss of sovereignty is diminished.[41] This can be done by making sure that the debtor country government and local conservation groups are involved already in the initial phases. The developing countries have themselves expressed that it is in their best long-term interest to preserve the natural resource base,[42] which is important in order to attain the goal of sustainable development. Relieving some of the debt will also free up the nation's capacity for self-governance.[43]

Perhaps the most critical limitation for debt-for-nature swaps is that they are not enforceable and that debt reduction does not get to the root of the problem, because the swaps do not change the incentive for activities that lead to environmental degradation.[44]

A variation on the debt-for-nature trade, which does take the critical limitations of these swaps into account is the exchange of environmentally sound technologies for nature.[45] In return for protecting natural resources, developing countries would receive economically and environmentally sound technology from developed countries.[46]

O'Neill and Sunstein proposed the trade of technology in exchange for environmental protection in an attempt to respond to the lack of incentives to implement and distribute existing technologies to developing countries.[47]

In addition to promoting development, the swaps offer an opportunity to ensure that the development is sustainable. The exchanges enable developing countries to avoid becoming dependent on energy sources and at the same time save energy costs.[48] The savings can then be redirected toward addressing the underlying causes of environmental degradation. Rather than the short term economic relief the debt-for-nature swap offers, the technology-for-nature swap would "facilitate the recipient nation's long-term economic growth and political and economic independence."[49]

The dissemination of energy technology, O'Neill and Sunstein assert, must employ a mixture of market and non-market approaches because benefits of energy efficiency are not fully internalized through markets. In addition, due to all the unsuccessful transfers that occurred in the past, they warn that the suitability of the technology for the recipient country and local involvement must be ensured.[50]

O'Neill and Sunstein note that the exchange of energy technology for nature might occur in three different versions: 1) in the context of international agreements, 2) to be initiated by NGOs, or 3) to constitute a combination of the other two arrangements.[51] In our context, the first version is the most interesting. The second version would take place outside the realm of intergovernmental commitments. The third version would have a "nature" side of the proposal which would fulfill international obligations, whereas the technology side would fall outside of any govern-mental obligation to provide the technology, using NGOs instead.[52]

The first version, using the swap as part of intergovernmental agreements, O'Neill and Sunstein regard as a vehicle for translating the language of such international obligations into forceful commitments.[53] The proposed exchange would provide an incentive for developing countries to implement and comply with the provisions of these agreements, especially the ones concerning conservation. The trade also seems likely to provide a framework for implementing the technology provisions in the international environmental treaties. These provisions are often very vague, as was illustrated above.[54] The proposed swaps would perhaps represent a more tangible arrangement, while at the same time, pinning down the parties to more detailed rights and obligations.

At this point, however, it would probably only be a small number of industrialized countries that would be willing to enter into these agreements, since there would be no present gain for them, only long-term benefits for the global environment. In the debt-for-nature swaps, there is already a relationship between the debtor country and the creditor bank or government. The bank, if it agrees to the swap, can write off a bad loan and at least get something in return for retiring some of the debt. Yet in the case of technology-for-nature swaps, there is no prior relationship and no present gain for the developed country. However, it would be fulfilling its international commitments with regard to treaty provisions requiring the transfer of environmentally sound technology to developing countries.

O'Neill and Sunstein envision an international NGO (or a cooperative effort by developed and developing country organizations) involved as an international broker to choose the participants in the exchanges and otherwise arrange the transactions. In addition, a technology source including researchers and bilateral aid agencies could be involved on the part of the developed country. Furthermore, the developing country's involvement could include its government, an energy organization or project, in addition to a conservation organization.[55]

The proposed trade is meant to be a long-term solution to the economic and environmental problems in developing countries, but as long as the World Bank and the International Monetary Fund's proposal for debt relief is not expanded to include more than just the poorest countries,[56] I propose a hybrid between the debt-for-nature and the technology-for-nature trades. It would combine debt relief and technology. On the "debt" side, this exchange would proceed in the same way as the debt-for-nature swap, but on the "nature" side the developing countries would be responsible for investing the currency or bonds in environmentally sound technology or using the funding to develop their own endogenous technology for environmental restoration and pollution control. This hybrid exchange, the debt-for-environmentally-sound-technology swap would ensure that developing countries got the debt relief they sorely needed at the same time as they were given the capacity to deal with their environmental problems.

The debt-for-environmentally-sound-technology trade could be used to channel the transfer of environmentally sound technology to different types of industry, for instance, the mining and energy industries, where many developing countries seem to have problems coping with pollution. This could be used to facilitate compliance with the provisions of several international environmental agreements, such as the Climate Change Convention. Projects could be channeled through GEF together with expert NGO groups. This kind of swap could work in a tandem with the joint implementation mechanism mentioned above.[57]

Examples of where this type of trade could apply would be in Venezuela, Ecuador, and Brazil. I will concentrate on Venezuela, where, in 1997, the government argued that its plan to change the gold and diamond mining laws would end years of disorder in its mining sector and open the country's untamed south to development.[58] The law in effect lifts bans on gold and diamond mining in ecologically fragile areas and grants amnesty to companies that have been mining without government permission.[59]

After Rio, one would think such myopic planning was a thing of the past. Yet, relaxation of environmental regulations to promote large-scale mining is part of what the Venezuelan President at the time called the "Plan for Sustainable Development in Southern Bolivar State."[60] This is a clear example of how the concept of sustainable development can be interpreted or misinterpreted by developing countries. However, one can understand how a government, under pressure from the IMF to implement austerity measures and simultaneously grappling to find more revenue to benefit its people, three-quarters of which are living in poverty,[61] may not be thinking long-term.

Government officials argued that it is easier to regulate large-scale mining than small-scale independent mining.[62] Schemo states that "[i]n clearing the way for multinational mining companies, the country has made outlaws of thousands of small-scale miners who have been prospecting here for generations, along with newcomers who flocked here from other parts of Venezuela as the price of gold rose from $35 an ounce in the 1970s to 10 times that amount now."[63] In addition, the changes in the law are also an attempt to remove wildcat miners and "garimpeiros" or Brazilian gold panners who do not create any revenue for Venezuela.[64]

Environmentalists are predicting environmental disaster. Companies dumping mercury and disposing of cyanide in deep ponds, without a liner are allowed to continue mining.[65] Because mining with mercury takes place in an area that includes the Caroni River which supplies drinking water to 80 percent of Bolivar State, the devastating consequence of mercury has given rise to the country's highest incidence of children born with Down's syn-drome.[66] In addition, more than half the people living near the lower Caroni basin have been contaminated by mercury.[67]

A similar initiative was proposed specifically with regard to the Amazonas State in southern Venezuela. The former President proposed revoking two decrees, 269 and 2552[68] which prohibit mining and logging in the state.[69] The Upper Orinoco-Casiquiare Biosphere Reserve, the second largest protected area of tropical rainforest in the world, is located in the southern part of this state.[70] The Biosphere Reserve is home to 12,000 Yanomami Indians. Two thousand of them have already died as a result of conflicts and diseases introduced by miners, among others.[71]

It is quite obvious that the Venezuelan government of the time was not going to stop the mining, which would have been preferable from the point of view of the fragile lands within the boundaries of national parks and forest reserves where the mining is also taking place. For these lands, at least, GEF funding could be sought to compensate for the opportunity cost of halting or restricting commercial exploitation.[72] In 1996, the European Union financed an ECU 6.4 million project to develop a management plan for conservation and sustainable development of the Upper Orinoco-Casiquiare Biosphere Reserve and it feared that mining and logging would jeopardize the success of the biosphere reserve.[73]

The Venezuelan government could try to minimize the environmental problems by maintaining its present policy of conservation and community development,[74] rather than giving in to the pressures from the mining industry and escalating the present problems. Assuming mining and logging were done outside the boundaries of the national parks and biosphere reserve, the debt-for-environmentally-sound-technology trade could facilitate gold mining that caused less environmental degradation, and enabled the clean up of earlier mining sites. This would allow Venezuela to fulfill some of its commitments with regard to the international environmental agreements it has ratified, such as the Climate Change Convention and the Convention on Biological Diversity. This could be done by conserving biodiversity and enhancing its greenhouse gas sinks by preserving its national parks and the biosphere reserve.

As a condition for getting a mining concession, the government could, for instance, prohibit the use of mercury,[75] and require certain standards to be used in disposing of mining wastes, such as cyanide and tail spinnings. In addition, the distribution of responsibility between the Ministry of Environment and the Ministry of Energy and Mining for ensuring that the laws are enforced would have to be clarified, enabling them to cooperate to pursue the goal of sustainable development.[76] However, part of the problem in Venezuela, besides the pervading corruption,[77] is that it is very difficult to enforce regulations in the rain forests, due to large expanses of near impenetrable land and lack of funding for enforcement. Funding for such enforcement could, however, be made available through traditional debt-for-nature trades or from GEF.

Tradable Permits

With the adoption of the Kyoto Protocol, tradable permits are now specifically included as an implementation and funding mechanism in an environmental treaty.[78] This mechanism could therefore have been addressed above under the section examining treaty provision.[79] However, because developing countries are presently not required to reduce carbon emissions it is still only an incentive that can be used by developed countries. At the time of this writing, the Kyoto Protocol is not in effect and guidelines for emissions trading and the other two Kyoto Mechanisms are to be elaborated by the year 2000.[80] In my judgment, it is just a question of time before the developing countries will be included in some kind of emission reduction system, allowing them to take advantage of the emission trading mechanism.

In 1992, the United Nations Conference on Trade and Development (UNCTAD) suggested a system of tradable pollution permits in which a quota of tradable carbon emission entitlements (TCEEs) would be allocated to each country.[81] Industrialized countries would be allocated fewer permits than developing countries. Using an international exchange where surplus permits would be traded, developing countries would be provided with funding to speed up development. Nevertheless, it would be beneficial for developing countries to invest the money in clean technologies thereby minimizing the amount of permits needed to "cover" CO_2 emissions.[82]

In contrast to the joint implementation mechanism mentioned above,[83] which only offers bilateral trading opportunities, a tradable permit system represents multilateral opportunities for saving costs.[84] Joint implementation participants invest in specific projects, whereas under a trading system, participants buy exchangeable divisible permits, "each of which represents 'shares' in the market's abatement activity 'portfolio'."[85]

The international tradable permit system can be viewed as an offspring of the emission trading system which has been used in the United States since the enactment of the 1990 Amendments to the Clean Air Act,[86] with regard to control of acid deposition. In the U.S. emissions trading system, existing industries emitting sulfur dioxide were allocated allowances, equivalent to the amount of sulfur dioxide they were emitting.[87] The allowances are then sold by the polluter, if he is able to reduce the amount of sulphur dioxide he emits, "freeing-up" some allowances.[88] Only a certain amount of allowances are available, so each new power-producer, for instance, has to purchase allowances consistent with the amount of sulphur dioxide he would be emitting.[89] Allowances are traded on the Chicago Board of Trade.

Grad states that the process of implementing sulphur emission trades has not worked as smoothly as expected.[90] Actual implementation is not organized in a strictly market oriented manner and due to restrictions, cost savings are also impeded.[91] Grad argues that trades are most successful when they cover single pollutants from stationary sources (point sources) that are localized. He explains this as pollutants that do not travel great distances after being emitted, such as lead, thus preventing the over polluting of its own or another area.[92] This does not sound promising for greenhouse gas trades, in view of the fact that greenhouse gases are neither stationary nor localized. Furthermore, Grad states that there needs to be a credibility of regulation creating stability for the companies, a lack of overburdening restrictions, and an ease of establishing a working market in emission rights for the pollutant.

Just as in the U.S. system, the international tradable permit system would be cost effective in that it would minimize the costs of limiting carbon dioxide emissions in industrialized countries by ensuring that reductions are made first where the cost of doing so is least.[93] This is because the system gives countries an incentive to cut CO_2 emissions wherever it costs less to do so, rather than buying a permit in the market.[94] However, one might question whether this system would contribute to transferring the responsibility of protecting the environment to third world countries.[95] The industrialized countries could just expand their assimilative capacity[96] by using regions in developing countries to offset their pollution—just as with the clean development mechanism—whereas they should be changing their own production and consumption patterns. Once the assimilative capacity was reduced in developing countries, there is the possibility that we would all be worse off than we are now, since the developing countries are projected to be the major polluters in the decades to come.[97]

Yet proponents of the tradable permit system and clean development mechanism will argue that the resources made available to developing countries through the sale of permits or transfer of "credits" would enable them to develop without high emissions of greenhouse gases.[98] However, this argument is qualified with the fact that the developing countries need to have the capacity to enter the agreements voluntarily and have the capacity to evaluate their options based on adequate information.[99] As for the clean development mechanism, it means developing countries would have to incorporate into the agreement with the investor the future cost of having sold the abatement credits in the first place.[100] A system of tradable pollution permits has to be combined with policies aimed at changing consumption and production patterns and safeguards against transferring the responsibility of reducing emissions from developed to developing countries.[101]

Deciding upon the appropriate quota is a major problem for the tradable permit system.[102] The Conference of the Parties of the Climate Change Convention were finally able to agree upon emission reduction targets in Kyoto in December of 1997.[103] However, a quota system could lead industries to buy more permits abroad rather than invest in compliance mechanisms, if the price of permits were cheaper than compliance. The Kyoto Protocol addresses this issue by requiring that "[a]ny such trading shall be sup-plemental to domestic actions."[104] Whether the international marketable permit system adopted with regard to greenhouse gases is able to overcome Grad's above-mentioned misgivings remains to be seen.[105] Essential to the success of an emissions trading system is the monitoring of emissions and sequestration credits,[106] making it vital for all parties to have similar domestic legislation to implement an agreement on the trading system.[107]

International Carbon Tax

Environmental taxes are already in use in several European countries. These can be directed specifically at CO_2 emissions or greenhouse gas emissions in general. The OPEC countries and fossil fuel producing industries[108] in other countries fear the use of such taxes will give them a comparative disadvantage. Yet these taxes internalize the price of degrading the environment. In addition, they generate resources that can be used for environmental protection measures including pollution control. The taxes also change the behavior of consumers and producers toward more sustainable patterns of consumption.

Suggestions have been made to create an international tax.[109] This has been suggested as a means of ensuring significant and automatic funding of international transfers from industrialized to developing countries to support sustainable development.[110] A tax on carbon, a tax on foreign exchange transactions (the "Tobin Tax"), and a tax on international air transport have been given the most attention.[111]

In order to be politically acceptable and economically justified, studies suggest the tax would have to fulfill the following criteria: be introduced as a voluntary scheme, be legislated and collected nationally, use a large base to permit its rates to be low, be levied on activities generating global, negative externalities, most of the revenue being retained by national governments, remaining revenue being allocated to an international financial transfer mechanism, and the allocations being limited to countries participating in the scheme.[112] It seems the carbon tax would be the best candidate according to these criteria.[113]

The main drawback with such a tax scheme is that the sovereign right of taxation would be delegated away from national governments and to an international body, which states are reluctant to do.[114] Another problem with the carbon tax is that it does not guarantee the amount of reduction of carbon emissions, which depends on energy consumers and suppliers.[115] Yet, as the tax would be levied on activities that generate global negative externalities, it may be looked upon as an inevitable consequence of the globalization of the economy and rising concern about global environmental degradation.[116]

Notes

1. *See* Brundtland Commission's Report, *supra* Chapter 1 note 15, at 77. *See* Agenda 21, *supra* Chapter 1 note 8, ¶ 33.15.

2. *See* U.N. CSD, 5th Sess., ¶ 3., U.N. Doc. E/CN/1997/2/Add.23 (1997).

3. *See* Agenda 21, *supra* Chapter 1 note 8, ¶ 33.16.

4. *See* discussion *supra* Chapter 5 (in regards to financial assistance: financing implementation of the agreements).

5. *See* discussion *supra* Chapter 5 (in regards to joint implementation).

6. *See,* David Fairman, *The Global Environment Facility: Haunted by the Shadow of the Future, in* INSTITUTIONS FOR ENVIRONMETNAL AID 59 (Robert O. Keohane & Marc A. Levy eds., 1996).

7. Instrument for the Establishment of the Restructured Global Environment Facility, iii, Report of the GEF Participants Meeting Geneva, Switzerland, Mar. 14-16, 1994 [hereinafter GEF Instrument].

8. *See id.* ¶ 2.

9. This money has been committed to the GEF, but all of it has not yet been received. Telephone interview with Jarle Harstad, Senior Monitoring and Evaluation Coordinator at the GEF Secretariat (May 5, 1997).

10. *See* NANDA, *supra* Chapter 2 note 147, at 302.

11. *See* Agenda 21, *supra* Chapter 1 note 8, ¶ 33.14(iii). *See also* Climate Change Convention, *supra* Chapter 2 note 137, art. 21.3; Convention on Biological Diversity, *supra* Chapter 2 note 168, art. 39.

12. *See* Charles DiLeva, *supra* Chapter 6 note 131, at 294.

13. *See id.*

14. *See id.* at 295.

15. *See Summary Report of the First Assembly of the Global Environment Facility,* 14 SUSTAINABLE DEV. 2 (1998).

16. *See id.*

17. *See* GEF Instrument, *supra* note 7, ¶ 25(c).

18. *See* French, *supra* Chapter 3 note 79, at 260.

19. GEF Instrument, *supra* note 7, annex D, ¶ 11.

20. *See* Harstad, *supra* note 9.

21. *See id.*

22. *See* Climate Change Convention, *supra* Chapter 2 note 137, art. 21; *See also* Convention on Biological Diversity, *supra* Chapter 2 note 168, art. 39. In 1998, at Fourth Session of the Conference of the Parties to the Climate Change Convention, the Parties decided to make GEF the entity entrusted with the operation of the funding mechanism for the Climate Change Convention—no longer on an interim basis. See FCCC Conference of the Parties, 4th Sess., 'Decision 3/CP.4, FCCC/CP/1998/16/
Add.1, (1999).

23. *See* Werksman, *supra* Chapter 2 note 196, at 84.

24. *See* Climate Change Convention, *supra* Chapter 2 note 137, art.21 (The Conference of the Parties "shall decide on its [GEF's] policies, programme priorities and eligibility criteria related to this Convention.").

25. *See* Harstad, *supra* note 9.

26. *See id.*

27. *See* Andrew S. Jones, Note, *The Global Environment Facility's Failure to Promote Sustainable Forestry in Ecuador: The Case of Ecoforest 2000,* 14 VA. ENVTL. L.J. 522 (1995).

28. *See* Global Environmental Facility, *GEF Operational Programs,* (April 1997).

29. *See* Conservation International, *The Debt-for-Nature Exchange – A Tool for International Conservation,* 5 (September, 1991).

30. *See* Catherine A. O'Neill & Cass R. Sunstein, *Economics and the Environment: Trading Debt and Technology for Nature,* 17 COLUM. J. ENVTL. L. 109 (1992).

31. *See id.*

32. *See id.*

33. *See id.* at 108.

34. *See id.* at 110.

35. *See id.*

36. *See* Konrad von Moltke, *Debt-for-Nature: The Second Generation,* 14 HASTINGS INT'L & COMP. L. REV. 975 (1991).

37. *See* O'Neill & Sunstein, *supra* note 30, at 112.

38. *See id.*

39. *See id.*

40. *See id.*

41. *See id.* at 118.

42. *See id* at 113.

43. *See id.*

44. *See id.* at 121-122.

45. *See id.* at 133.

46. *See id.*

47. *See id.* at 123.

48. *See id.* at 133.

49. *Id.*

50. *See id.* at 137-138.

51. *See id.* at 139.

52. *See id.*

53. *See id.* n.182.

54. *See* discussion *supra* Chapter 5 (in regards to technical assistance including access to technology and capacity building).

55. *See* O'Neill and Sunstein, *supra* note 30, at 139.

56. The joint World Bank/IMF Heavily Indebted Poor Countries (HIPC) Initiative. *See* Jyoti Shankar Singh, *Debt Reduction for the Poorest Countries,* THE EARTH TIMES, Apr. 1-15, 1997, at 23.

57. *See* discussion *supra* Chapter 5 (in regards to joint implementation).

58. *See* Schemo, *supra* note Chapter 3 note 21, at A5.

59. *See id.*

60. *Id.* Plan for Sustainable Development in Southern Bolivar State ["Decreto de Imataca"] Presidential Decree 1.850, published in the Official Gazette of the Republic of Venezuela No. 36.215 (May 5, 1997). It is expected that the current President will revoke this controversial decree in the near future.

61. *See Perez Return to Politics*, FIN. TIMES, Mar. 25, 1997, at 4.

62. *See* Schemo, *supra* Chapter 3 note 21, at A5.

63. *Id.*

64. *Id.*

65. *See id.*

66. *See id.* 67. *See id.*

68. Presidential Decree No. 269, published in the Official Gazette of the Republic of Venezuela No. 4.106, 9. June 1989, (prohibiting all mining and suspending all current mining operations in the Amazonas State); Presidential Decree No. 2.552, published in the Official Gazette No.31.408, 19. January 1978, (prohibiting logging, deforestation, and exploitation in the Amazonas State). Both are decrees still in effect. E-mail from Andres Halvorssen, Caracas, Venezuela (May 26, 1999).

69. World Rain Forest Movement, Press Release, *Venezuela: European Parliament Adopts Resolution to Curb Logging and Mining in Amazonas*, Oct. 25, 1996, at 2 [hereinafter WRM].

70. *See* Presidential Decree No. 1.635, Official Gazette No. 34.767, 10. August, 1991. *See also* James Brooke, *Venezuela Befriends Tribe, But What's Venezuela*, N.Y. TIMES, Sept. 11, 1991, at A10.

71. *See* Michael L. Haxton, *Indigenous Peoples in Venezuela* (visited Apr. 20, 1997) <http://www.bsos.umd.edu/cidcm/mar/indvez.htm>.

72. *See* text accompanying and following note 20.

73. *See* WRM, *supra* note 62, at 2.

74. *See id.* at 3. Venezuela established its Ministry of Environment, Ministerio del Ambiente y de los Recursos Naturales Renovables (MARNR) in 1977, the first of its kind in Latin America. *See* Anita Halvorssen, *Miljovern I Venezuela* [Environmental Protection in Venezuela] (1987) (unpublished paper for the Norwegian Ministry of Environment) (on file with author). MARNR has as one of its purposes to protect the environment from irreversible damage while not delaying economic development or endangering future generations. Their Environment Act, Ley Organica de Ambiente, of 1976, art. 2 states that permits for activities that are necessary because of their economic and social benefits, are only to be issued if the permit holders guarantee the reclamation of the land. *See id.* at 7, 9. Venezuela has regulations covering air and water quality, and environmental impact studies. In 1992 it also enacted the Environmental Crime Act, which reaffirms and expands on the provisions of the Environment Act. This new act has penalties that include fines, temporary or permanent cessation of operations, imprisonment of the violator and community work. *See* Ley Penal del Ambiente, Official Gazette No. 4.358, 3. Jan. 1992. *See also MARNR Venezuela* (MARNR's website) (visited May 22, 1999) <http://www.marnr.gov.ve>.

75. There are processes that can be used in mining gold that do not include mercury or cyanide. A mine in Caribou, Colorado is an example of a small-scale mine which doesn't use mercury.

76. *See* WRM, *supra* note 69, at 2.

77. Transparency International, a research group, named Venezuela, in a survey of business executives, Latin America's most corrupt country in 1996, Schemo, *supra* note Chapter 3 note 21, at A5.

78. *See* Kyoto Protocol, supra Chapter 2 note 166, art. 17.

79. *See* discussion *supra* Chapter 5 (in regards to treaty provisions).

80. See *Buenos Aires Plan of Action, Report of the Conference of the Parties on Its Fourth Session,* United Nations Framework Convention on Climate Change, Conference of the Parties, 4th Sess., Decision 1/CP.4, U.N. Doc. FCCC/CP/1998/16/Add.1/CP.4 (1999).

81. *See* Frances Williams, *Incentives Needed for Clean Growth,* FIN. TIMES, Mar. 18, 1992, at 10. The UNCTAD report was called "A Study on a Global System of Tradable Carbon Emission Entitlements." *See* A Pilot Greenhouse Gas Trading System, UNCTAD, 1996.

82. *See* Williams, *supra* note 81.

83. *See* discussion, *supra* Chapter 5 (in regards to joint implementation).

84. *See* Dudek & Wiener, *supra* Chapter 5 note 103, at 9.

85. *Id.*

86. *See* 42 U.S.C.A. § 7651a–o (1994) (Clean Air Act Sec. 401-416).

87. An allowance is defined as an authorization to emit one ton of sulphur dioxide. *See* 42 U.S.C.A. § 7651a(3) (1994).

88. Frank P. Grad, TREATISE ON ENVIRONMENTAL LAW, ¶ 2-350.15.

89. *See id.*

90. *See id. at 2-350.16.*

91. *See id.*

92. *See id.*

93. *See* Williams, *supra* note 81.

94. *See id.*

95. *See* Michael Zammit Cutajar, *Comment on Paper by Gunther Handl: The FCCC Experience, in* SUSTAINABLE DEVELOPMENT AND INTERNATIONAL LAW 47 (Winfried Lang ed., 1995) (referring to joint implementation, which can lead to the same result as tradable permits).

96. Assimilative capacity refers to variations in geographic, ecological, and demographic conditions in different states affecting their ability to assimilate pollution and other forms of natural resource exploitation. Developing countries, on the whole have lower levels of pollution and can therefore more easily adjust to additional pollution than states that already have high levels of pollution. *See* Stewart, *supra* Chapter 3 note 161, at 2057 (describing additional elements of assimilative capacity, such as societal values, differences in wealth among nations, and their stage of economic development).

97. INTERNATIONAL ENERGY AGENCY, *supra* Chapter 1 note 23, at 49.

98. Dudek & Wiener, *supra* Chapter 5 note 103, at 11.

99. *See id.* at 47.

100. *See id.* at 46.

101. *See* Cutajar, *supra* note 95, at 47.

102. *See* JURGIELEWICZ, *supra* Chapter 5 note 173, at 141.

103. *See* Kyoto Protocol, *supra* Chapter 2 note 166, art. 3 (referring to Annex B).

104. *Id.* art. 17.

105. *See* GRAD, *supra* note 88, and accompanying text.

106. These are credits received by using forestation projects to withdraw CO_2 from the atmosphere. *See* A Pilot Greenhouse Trading System, *supra* note 81, at 10. The forestation projects are now referred to as sinks, *see* Kyoto Protocol, *supra* Chapter 2 note 166, art.3(3).

107 *See id.* at 8–9.

108. European Electricity Producers Put Forward an Alternative Approach to Carbon Tax, Origin Universal News Services Limited, May 20, 1992.

109. *See Finance for Sustainable Development: The Road Ahead,* U.N. CSD, 4th Expert Group Meeting on Financial Issues of Agenda 21, U.N. Doc. E/CN.17/1997/18, Feb. 24, 1997, at 11 [hereinafter The Road Ahead].

110. *See id.*

111. *See id.*

112. *See id.*

113. *See id.*

114. *See id.*

115. *See* JURGIELEWICZ, *supra* Chapter 5 note 173, at 141.

116. *See* The Road Ahead, *supra* note 109, at 11-12.

8

The Role of Non-Governmental Organizations (NGOs) and Other Major Groups in Promoting Universal Participation

The role of non-governmental organizations (NGOs) and other major groups in promoting the participation of developing countries in international environmental agreements is increasingly being recognized by the international community as an important one. As mentioned in Chapter 4, they can assist with the operation of the incentives within the treaties. In addition, they can also function on the outside or independent of the treaties, promoting participation of developing countries through, for instance, debt-for-nature swaps not related to any treaty, as discussed above.

"Major groups," as a concept, entered the international arena with the Rio Conference. Governments recognized the role of major groups, contributing to the UNCED process both in unprecedented numbers and diversity of cultural and economic actors, and the important role they would play at the follow-up stage,[1] including the implementation of Agenda 21 and other international instruments negotiated at Rio. In the implementation and monitoring of sustainable development activities, the "major groups" concept pertains to the participation of economic and social actors from outside the realm of governmental and intergovernmental entities. Agenda 21 identifies nine major groups as follows: 1) women, 2) children and youth, 3) indigenous people, 4) NGOs, 5) local authorities, 6) workers and trade unions, 7) business and industry, 8) scientific and technological communities, and 9) farmers.[2]

Unfortunately, Agenda 21 does not define the concept, which has lead to some confusion because several of the major groups overlap, such as women participating as individuals and through their organizations, but also through NGOs that deal with women's issues, and also as indigenous women and young women.[3]

Officially, the United Nations system only recognizes non-state actors collectively as NGOs—regardless of whether they represent women, workers or local authorities—giving them accreditation to participate in U.N. fora.[4] Among governments, U.N. agencies, and major group actors themselves, because of the lack of a clear definition, the term non-governmental organization is still used to refer to all major groups, hindering the adoption of the major groups concept with its participatory spirit.[5]

To an "outsider" the concept of major groups can seem somewhat far-fetched, as NGOs already cover a lot of the groundwork, but perhaps it does have value in that it identifies different types of non-state actors and heightens the awareness of how important it is that all of civil society participate in sustainable development decision-making. In addition, the concept of major groups allows individuals to participate as well as groups that would not qualify as NGOs. However, the scientific and technological community group and the business and industry group do not seem to fit the pattern that emerges when one looks at the other groups. All the other major groups, one can argue, have a common theme. They are all struggling for recognition and improvement of their predicament, such as basic human rights, as in the case of many indigenous peoples.

In the case of the scientific and technological community, the focus is on making their contribution to the decision-making process more open and effective.[6] This is important because the international environmental norms are greatly influenced by the scientific community, so it is important to have them participate. Yet with regard to the business and industry group, the issues are totally different. Agenda 21 focuses on making business and industry "greener" by compliance with environmental regulations, through resource efficiency, new production processes and partnerships with the greater community in which they are located, in addition to pollution control. The significance of including them as a major group will be discussed below.

In this chapter, I will concentrate on the role of the environmental NGOs in promoting the participation of developing countries in international environmental agreements, but I will also examine the role of the business and industry group in this regard, as they in many ways play a pivotal role. This special role is due to the fact that their use of natural resources and the effects of their activities on the environment, in addition to their influence on decision-making in general in developed and developing countries, play a large role in the process of international environmental lawmaking, implementation and compliance.

Definition and Legal Status of NGOs

NGOs played a role in the international arena long before the creation of the United Nations. Yet their consultative status in global governance was first formalized in the U.N. Charter, Article 71, as follows: "The Economic and Social Council may make suitable arrangements for consultations with non-governmental organizations which are concerned with matters within its competence. Such arrangements may be made with international organizations and, where appropriate, with national organizations after consultation with the Member of the United Nations concerned."[7]

NGOs are characterized as nonprofit organizations, independent of specific governmental controls.[8] They have an essential role to play in the fashioning and implementation of participatory democracy.[9] In addition, NGOs being well-established, have diverse experience, expertise, and capacity in areas which are of particular importance to the implementation and review of "environmentally sound and socially responsible sustainable development," as visualized by Agenda 21.[10] NGOs can be found at the local, national, regional, and international level.

Notwithstanding their UN consultative status, NGOs, as non-state actors and not being governmental organizations,[11] are not recognized as legal persons in traditional international law and therefore have no standing on the international plane.[12] Nevertheless, in domestic law many NGOs do have legal personality, which is a prerequisite for the granting of personality and status in international law.[13] In addition, NGOs do have standing to sue in some regional organizations, such as the European Union.[14]

As a consequence of their lack of legal personality on the international plane, NGOs, in contrast to states and international organizations, are not constrained by the rules of international law, since the rules do not apply to them. This has lead some scholars to suggest that they should have minimal standards of performance, as they acquire more real political power.[15] Tarlock posits that NGOs should be brought into established legal systems so that they can be subjected to minimum standards of responsible environmental behavior.[16] Yet, Tolbert asserts that this would be unjustified unless NGOs' rights and powers were substantially increased.[17] Perhaps their behavior will improve as the consultation process of Article 71 is increasingly used, giving them greater influence in policy making, and as NGOs are more and more brought into the realm of treaties, providing them with specific roles to play.[18] In this manner, many of their actions will be regulated by the treaties and relevant international institutions. Yet some NGOs would still prefer to remain more independent and not have a formalized role in global governance, thereby being more at liberty to criticize.[19]

NGOs have forged ahead, in spite of their lack of standing in international law, in their efforts to protect the global environment by using different techniques to gain access to international negotiations and decision-making fora. NGOs are having a growing influence on the development of international environmental law, from the first identification of an environmental problem, through the treaty-making process, and onto the implementation and compliance of treaties. As Tarlock states, "NGOs are now permanent players in the international arena, just as they are in the United States."[20]

Through the help of NGOs, several developing countries have also gotten more involved with global environmental issues, as will be illustrated below. NGOs, being subject to different limitations and not necessarily tarnished by identification with any political system, can sometimes perform functions unattainable to government organizations.[21] For instance, they are not bound to speak the party line, such as government representatives do when negotiating international agreements.[22] In addition, international NGOs are not bound by the principles of international law that prescribe non-intervention, but are free to use their influence to form domestic political agendas.[23]

As an example of how the environmental NGOs are organized in industrialized countries, I will describe the ones in the United States, as it has some of the oldest NGOs, some of them established before the turn of the century, such as the Wilderness Society, established in 1896.[24] The U.S. NGOs that are involved with global environmental issues can be divided into three groups 1) general membership organizations, such as the Sierra Club and the National Audubon Society, with broad environmental interests, but which focus mainly on domestic environmental issues; 2) international NGOs such as the World Wildlife Fund (WWF-U.S.A.) and Greenpeace that are part of a larger international network of affiliates on the regional or global level; and 3) policy think-tanks such as the Environmental Defense Fund and World Resource Institute, which have a small membership, and derive influence from scientific, technical or legal expertise.[25] As far as US environmental NGOs are concerned, they cover a broad political spectrum, from conservative to radical views, but the overall goal: a just and sustainable society—is the same for all.[26]

NGOs have also been established in developing countries as the environmental movement has burgeoned internationally, with NGOs developing alliances across national boundaries.[27] The Environmental Liaison Center International serves as such an example of an NGO, based in Nairobi, with members worldwide.[28]

At the international level, Tolbert divides the NGOs into three groups: 1) public interest NGOs, such as the World Wide Fund for Nature (WWF-International) and Greenpeace; 2) scientific NGOs, such as the International

Council on Scientific Unions (ICSU) and the Scientific Committee on Antarctic Research (SCAR); and 3) "think tank" NGOs such as the World Committee on Environment and Development (WCED) devoted to the progressive development of the law. Different ideologies are also represented at the international level, from Greenpeace at one end of the scale to the International Chamber of Commerce at the other end.

The Role of NGOs in Relation to Developing Countries' Participation in Multilateral Environmental Agreements

NGOs are having a large influence in the negotiation, implementation, and compliance process of international environmental agreements. They often initiate proposals for international cooperation to deal with environmental problems, which in turn become the basis for the negotiations of new treaties. NGOs oftentimes participate on the national delegations to treaty negotiations. In addition, they now have observer status at most international conferences, where new conventions are often adopted, as was the case at the Rio Conference, where the Climate Change Convention and the Convention on Biological Diversity were signed. This is important because in many countries NGOs help set the political agenda. Without a constituency in each country that is willing to promote treaty implementation, the agreements may not be implemented, let alone complied with.[29] NGOs are also invited as observers to some of the meetings of the Conference of the Parties (COP) of several conventions and to the semi-annual meetings of the Governing Council of GEF.[30] At UNGASS they stood side by side with government representatives, and participated in many of the related meetings.

NGOs exerted great influence in the outcome of the Amendments to the Montreal Protocol in 1990, which had a significant impact on the decision of essential developing countries to becoming parties to the Protocol. Because ozone depletion is caused by a limited number of chemicals commonly found in consumer products, NGOs were able to pressure the industry through consumer boycotts and other means, to phase out the use of CFCs.[31] By the time the Montreal Protocol was signed in 1987, new scientific evidence made it clear that the Protocol, considered a compromise, was already inadequate to even stabilize the ozone layer.[32] In addition, it had no funding mechanism to bear the cost of switching to substitutes for CFCs in the developing countries. India, China, and Brazil were not willing to sign the protocol.

Bramble and Porter note that shortly after the signing of the protocol, an international NGO, Friends of the Earth (FOE), launched a campaign to achieve a worldwide ban on CFCs in aerosol sprays and the adoption of substitutes for all uses of CFCs.[33] Each national campaign was adjusted to suit the status of its government's ozone policy. In countries such as Britain and France, where aerosols were still being used, FOE and other NGOs first called on the industry to phase out the use of CFCs, and when that did not work they resorted to consumer boycotts of CFCs.[34] In Britain, three days before a consumer boycott was to be announced, the industry declared a phase-out of CFCs.[35]

In May of 1989, a statement issued on behalf of NGOs worldwide including a call for a technology transfer fund to help developing countries eliminate their ozone-depleting chemicals, was presented at the first meeting of the Parties to the Montreal Protocol.[36] The meeting was deadlocked on the issue, but NGO observers, representing FOE in the United States and the United Kingdom, the National Resource Defense Council (NRDC), and the European Environment Bureau proposed that developed countries determine what developing countries would need to implement the protocol by doing feasibility studies.[37] A more detailed proposal in the same vein was asked for by the Norwegian government.[38] A year later, at the Second Meeting of the Parties, a compromise was reached on the funding mechanism, which brought promises from the Chinese and Indian observers' delegations to advise their governments to join the protocol.[39] NGO advocacy of a funding mechanism for assisting developing countries with technology conversion played an important role in promoting the participation of two essential developing countries, India and China. [40] Had they not joined it is quite likely that in the long term all the efforts made in regard to protecting the ozone layer would have been in vain, as the use of CFCs in these two countries with their immense populations would have surpassed the use of CFCs by all the parties to the Montreal Protocol put together.

With respect to decision-making processes and the implementation of international legal instruments, there has been an extraordinary empowerment of NGOs. NGOs perform a watchdog function with their particular interest in the regulated activity, not just regarding binding law, but also regarding "soft law" where states who fail to observe the norm are not exposed to criticism otherwise.[41] They are becoming an instrument to pressure uncooperative governments to address urgent global environmental issues.

NGOs are increasingly becoming participants in the work of intergovernmental organizations. CSD, for instance, is to receive and analyze reports from NGOs in the context of monitoring the implementation of Agenda 21.[42] Also, in the context of GEF, NGOs have their own small-grants program, administered by UNDP. In addition, a growing number of NGOs are being used by beneficiary governments to assist in the implementation of their GEF projects. NGOs also function as the managers of several programs to preserve environmentally vulnerable lands in developing countries through debt-for-nature trades, as mentioned above.[43] In the Convention to Combat Desertification, NGOs also have an important role to play. They are to function as conduits and ensure that local communities obtain the external resources they need to carry out their own programs.[44]

Other Major Groups—Business and Industry

Major groups can be found at opposite ends of the power spectrum, for instance, the "major group" entitled business and industry, is at one end, while organizations representing, for instance women or indigenous people, are at the other. Business and industry are essentially actors on the development side. They are often the 'project managers' for World Bank projects and bilateral projects.

Environmental NGOs often represent public interest groups, such as Greenpeace, the Sierra Club, and the Environmental Defense Fund. However, increasingly, associations of manufacturing groups and other business interests have also begun to appreciate the importance of integrating environment and development. Yet, their main focus is still on the interests of the corporations, which is to make profits, not necessarily to protect the environment. "Business NGOs" usually consist of big influential lobbying groups, such as the International Chamber of Commerce and the Chemical Manufacturers Association, all well represented in the seats of power through legislators "pushing" for their causes.

For business associations to represent themselves as *just* another "major group" together with farmers and indigenous people, is perhaps instrumental to maintain a device to assert real power also in this new forum.[45] Greenpeace claims, for instance, that the business and industry group called the Business Council for Sustainable Development (BCSD) participated in the Rio Conference representing itself as being on the cutting edge of corporate environmentalism, while at the same time scheming behind the scenes to minimize intergovernmental "meddling" in corporate affairs and undermining key international treaties.[46]

However, including business and industry as a "major group" can serve as a vehicle for influencing business and industry to move more in the direction of sustainable development, as they represent to a large extent, the driving force of development. In addition, they are a source of funding that can be used to promote sustainable development by, among other things, promoting the participation of developing countries in the implementation of international environmental agreements by working together in partnerships, as will be shown below.

Industry is already being urged to change its ways to more sustainable production and consumption patterns through several "business NGOs," among them are the Chemical Manufacturers Association with its Responsible Care Program and the International Chamber of Commerce with its Business Charter for Sustainable Development.[47] The World Business Council for Sustainable Development (WBCSD) distinguishes itself from other "business NGOs" in that it was created to tackle specifically the challenges the goal of sustainable development has brought to the business world. The WBCSD originated in part from the Business Council for Sustainable Development.

In 1990, Steven Schmidheiny was chosen by Maurice Strong, the Secretary General of the Rio Conference, to be the principal advisor on the business perspective of sustainable development. The following year, together with forty-eight other business leaders, Schmidheiny established the Business Council for Sustainable Development (BCSD). In conjunction with the Rio Conference, the Business Council for Sustainable Development published a report entitled "Changing Course: A Global Business Perspective on Development and the Environment," which has been widely distributed in the global business community.[48]

In 1995, the WBCSD was created through a merger between the World Industry Council for Sustainable Development (WICSD), an initiative of the International Chamber of Commerce (ICC) in Paris and the Business Council for Sustainable Development (BCSD) in Geneva.[49] The WBCSD is an association of 122 multinational companies joined by a shared commitment to the environment and to principles of economic growth and sustainable development.[50] WBCSD states that industry admits that it is now taking responsibility to undo some of its past mistakes and to ensure the quality of the future, recognizing that business has the most to offer in bringing solutions. WBCSD's goal is to "develop closer cooperation between business, government and all other organizations concerned with the environment and sustainable development."[51]

Creating partnerships between governments and business and industry, in developed and developing countries, could give developing countries access to technology and funding which may be difficult to come by at the present time, since ODA funding is decreasing. Below I will examine a possible strategy for such a partnership using the model created by the Business Council for Sustainable Development (BCSD), and adopted by its successor, the World Business Council for Sustainable Development (WBCSD).

The Business Council for Sustainable Development introduced a new concept, "technology cooperation" to replace the well-known term "technology transfer." This concept is defined as follows: "[E]ffective cooperation between business or industry parties which develop, hold, and use environmentally sound technologies, and counterparts which wish to do the same for the purposes of business development. Their ownership may be common or separate, in the public sector, or in the private sector."[52]

Technology cooperation, the BCSD asserts, has a broader set of objectives than technology transfer. The former establishes a long-term partnership in a commercial setting with a focus on developing infrastructure, wealth-generating capacities, and a country's competitiveness.

BCSD states that a large number of official development aid projects have failed because they focused on the "hardware" or the capital intensive equipment, using contractors, and did not include the know-how or "software" which was in the hands of the supplier. To solve this problem, BCSD promotes technology cooperation between two companies establishing a long-term partnership, as a way of giving the recipient and the supplier an opportunity to communicate directly. BCSD's definition of technology cooperation uses the terms "develop" and "use" of environmentally sound technology to indicate that the new partnerships are to include management and maintenance training.[53]

BCSD describes technology cooperation as the "operational enabling tool" of sustainable development. Technology cooperation is explained as being the "active lever" for business development and in turn economic development. Because technology cooperation demands international cooperation among governments and business, it is essential that the different roles are understood and respected.[54] In addition, it is important that the venture and the technology are adapted for local conditions in the host country.[55] Governments, essentially, are not to interfere in the transactions; they are only to provide the right market signals and lower the overall financial risks.[56]

One project demonstrating how technology cooperation can be implemented is the one that was managed by Northern Telecom of Canada in cooperation with the U.S. Environmental Protection Agency (EPA) and the Mexican Environment Ministry (SEDUE).[57] Northern Telecom was the first international telecommunications and electronics industry to commit itself to phase out the use of CFC solvents.[58] In 1988, it set up a successful program to phase out CFC-113 by 1992. To share its experiences in ozone layer protection, Northern Telecom was one of the founders of the Industry Cooperative for Ozone Layer Protection (ICOLP), a Washington-based association of seventeen multinational corporations, industry associations, and governments including the U.S., Japan, Mexico, and Sweden.[59]

Mexico was the first developing country to pledge to eliminate CFC solvents ten years earlier than the time mandated for developing countries by the Montreal Protocol, putting Mexico on the same timetable as developed countries.[60] In order to eliminate ozone depleting solvents from the Mexican industry, Mexico entered into a partnership with Northern Telecom and the EPA in 1991. Taking advantage of the joint efforts of government and business, SEDUE, Northern Telecom, and the EPA created a "model project" for technology cooperation. In this project the EPA assisted in creating environmental control procedures, Northern Telecom assisted in the implementation of processes and technologies, and managed a series of workshops, using ICOLP experts throughout the Mexican Maquiladora regions to introduce alternative technologies, and SEDUE facilitated investment in new technologies and provided interagency coordination.[61] Northern Telecom with funding from the World Bank, has since completed similar projects in seven other countries including Turkey, China, India, and Brazil.[62]

Technology cooperation, BCSD states, focuses on joint ventures and other types of long-term business partnerships between an enterprise in a developing country and a firm in a developed country.[63] Such technology cooperation is to be one of the main vehicles for the international transfer of technology. One version of this would be the purely commercial transaction between two equal, independent parties.[64] If in the transaction, some equity was held by the host country, then there would be four parties to the transaction: the home and host owners, and their respective governments.[65] However, BCSD recognizes that less than a third of all countries would be able to enter into such transactions on purely commercial terms. In developing countries, where neither the recipient firm nor the government could afford to enter a transaction on purely commercial terms, BCSD states that the financing of the transaction from other sources would be a political issue which "must not interfere with the direct relationship between [the] buyer and seller if the transaction is to succeed."[66] Technology transfer within multinational firms would represent the simplest form of technology cooperation.[67] Due to the formal agreement that would exist to satisfy the fiscal authorities in the participating developing country, the partnership would extend to the national governments of both home and host countries.[68]

One of the problems I see with the technology cooperation model is that it promotes business and industry to be the focus of the international transfer of technology without any checks and balances. One difference between technology cooperation and the way technology has been transferred in the past is that there is more focus on management and training, which is a shift in the right direction. In addition, there is an added dimension in the transaction: environmental considerations. However, BCSD does not suggest how one is to ensure that the technology that is transferred is actually environmentally sound. If environmentally sound technology is a relative term depending on the local circumstances as is also stated in Agenda 21, then who is to decide what is environmentally sound? Several codes of conduct have been set up by business associations and other institutions, but they are only guidelines. One way to deal with this is by ensuring that the developing countries have regulations that restrict environmentally harmful technologies.[69]

Another problem with technology cooperation is that there seems to be no change in the procedures to avoid the problems of the sixties and seventies, when foreign investments led to foreign dominance, which in some cases ended in mass expropriations in Africa and Latin America.[70] In addition, BCSD does not clarify whether it promotes non-equity forms of investments, such as technical assistance and management agreements or less-than-majority-owned joint ventures.[71] Yet, despite these misgivings, at least some of the projects have been successful, such as the ones undertaken by Northern Telecom.

At present, private capital flows are the most important source of external funding for developing countries.[72] This being the case, it would seem to be vital to get business and industry involved in pursuing the goal of sustainable development. Promoting partnerships that take into account environmental considerations as the one mentioned above are important, but developing countries need to strengthen their environmental regulations to ensure that these partnerships function in the intended manner.

Notes

1. *See Role and Contribution of Major Groups*, U.N. Commission on Sustainable Development, 5th Sess., § I, ¶ 1, U.N. Doc. E/CN.17/1977/2/Add.22 (1997).

2. *See* Agenda 21, *supra* Chapter 1 note 8, § III, chs. 23-32.

3. *See id.*

4. *See Role and Contribution of Major Groups, supra* note 1, § I, ¶ 4. The accreditation process is based on arrangements established by ECOSOC. *See id.*

5. *See id.*

6. *See* Agenda 21, *supra* Chapter 1 note 8, ¶ 31.1.

7. UNITED NATIONS CHARTER, *supra* Chapter 2 note 193, art 71. *See also* Steve Charnovitz, *Two Centuries of Participation: NGOs and International Governance*, 18 MICH. J. INT'L L. 257 (1997).

8. *See* David Tolbert, *Global Climate Change and the Role of International Non-Governmental Organizations*, *in* INTERNATIONAL LAW AND GLOBAL CLIMATE CHANGE 96, 97 (Robin Churchill & David Freestone eds., 1991).

9. *See* Agenda 21, *supra* Chapter 1 note 8, ch. 27.1.

10. *Id.* ch. 27.3.

11. Organizations with legal personality in international law are permanent associations of nation states that exercise similar powers. *See* Brownlie, *supra* Chapter 2 note 2, at 681-82. *See also* Dan Tarlock, *Environmental Law: The Role of Non-Governmental Organizations in the Development of International Environmental Law* 68 CHI.-KENT L. REV. n.18 (1992).

12. *See* Philippe Sands, *The Environment, Community and International Law*, 30 HARV. INT'L L.J. 393 (1989).

13. *See id.* at 397.

14. *See* Treaty on European Union, *supra* Chapter 2 note 146.
15. *See* Tarlock, *supra* note 11, at 75.
16. *See id.*
17. *See* Tolbert, *supra* note 8, at 95.
18. *See* Charnovitz, *supra* note 7, at 275. *See* discussion *supra* text accompanying Chapter 4 note 71.
19. *See id* at 284.
20. Tarlock, *supra* note 11, at 63.
21. *See* DANIEL BARSTOW MAGRAW, INTERNATIONAL LAW AND POLLUTION 10 (1991).
22. *See id.*
23. *See* Tarlock, *supra* note 11.
24. *See* Barbara J. Bramble & Gareth Porter, *Non-Governmental Organizations and the Making of US International Environmental Policy, in* THE INTERNATIONAL POLITICS OF THE ENVIRONMENT 316–18 (Andrew Hurrell & Benedict Kingsbury eds., 1992).
25. *See id.* at 316.
26. *See id.* at 321.
27. *See id.*
28. *See id.*
29. *See* Susskind & Ozawa, *supra* Chapter 5 note 12, at 158.
30. *See* Jones, *supra* Chapter 7 note 27, at 558.
31. *See* Bramble & Porter, supra note 24, at 336.
32. *See id.* at 337.
33. *See id.*
34. *See id.*
35. *See id.*
36. *See id.* at 339.
37. *See id.*
38. *See id.*
39. *See id.* at 340.
40. *See id.*
41. *See* Patricia Birnie, *International Environmental Law: Its Adequacy for Present and Future Needs, in* THE INTERNATIONAL POLITICS OF THE ENVIRONMENT 52 (Andrew Hurrell & Benedict Kingsbury eds., 1992).
42. *See* Commission on Sustainable Development, U.N. ECOSOC, § I.2.(f), U.N. Doc. E/CN.17/1993/2 (1993) (Organizational session of CSD).
43. *See* discussion *supra* Chapter 7 (in regards to debt-for-nature swaps and other swaps).
44. *See* Convention to Combat Desertification, *supra* Chapter 2 note 187, art. 14.
45. Grad, *supra* Chapter 2 note 165.
46. *See* CARL DEAL, THE GREENPEACE GUIDE TO ANTI-ENVIRONMENTAL ORGANIZATIONS 10 (1993).
47. *See* WILLUMS & GOLUKE, *supra* Chapter 3 note 74.
48. *See* Stephen Schmidheiny, CHANGING COURSE: A GLOBAL BUSINESS PERSPECTIVE ON DEVELOPMENT AND THE ENVIRONMENT (Bus. Council for Sustainable Dev.) (1992) [hereinafter CHANGING COURSE].
49. *See id.*

50. *See* World Business Council for Sustainable Development, *What is the WBCSD* (visited Apr. 30, 1997) <http://www.wbcsd.org>.

51. *Id.*

52. Business Council for Sustainable Development, *Report on Technology Cooperation – Technology Advisory Group Working Paper* 6 (1992) [hereinafter *Report on Technology Cooperation*].

53. *Id.* at 7.

54. *See id.*

55. *See id.*

56. *See id.*

57. *See id.* at 5.

58. *See id.*

59. *See id.*

60. *See id.*

61. *See id.*

62. *See* Northern Telecom (Nortel) (visited Jan. 26, 1998) <http://www.nortel.com/cool/environ>.

63. *See Report on Technology cooperation, supra* note 52, at 9.

64. *See id.* at 10.

65. *See id.*

66. *Id.* at 11.

67. *See id.*

68. *See id.*

69. *See* Gollin, *supra* Chapter 5 note 136, at 193.

70. *See* Charles Kennedy, *Relations Between Transnational Corporations and Governments of Host Countries: A Look to the Future*, 1 TRANSNAT'L CORPS. 67 (1992).

71. *See* Sadrel Reza, *Non-equity Forms of TNC Participation in Bangladesh* 1 TRANSNAT'L CORPS. 127 (1992).

72. *See* United Nations Commission on Sustainable Development, at 2, U.N. Doc. E/CN.17/2/Add.23 (1997).

9

Conclusion

The growing recognition that ecological and economic systems are interconnected—global interdependence—has changed the nature of international affairs. One can no longer rely on economic growth in the traditional sense to solve all the world's problems. Development and environmental issues must be integrated, as articulated in the concept of sustainable development. In this new world order, the interests and needs of developing countries can no longer be disregarded in the context of solving global environmental problems, first of all because their activities increasingly add to global environmental problems. Secondly, developing states contain most of the world's genetic library, which we all depend on. There is no longer any doubt that in order to tackle global environmental problems, developing countries need to be included in the process of finding and implementing solutions.

Global environmental problems can only be solved if all or at least most nations participate in the creation and implementation of international environmental agreements. In this manner, the concept of sustainable development is translated into specific norms. In this study, I argue that to include incentives, in effect giving developing countries differential treatment, in international environmental agreements will promote such universal participation.

My review of the development of international environmental law has shown that there is an emerging pattern with regard to the use of incentives or differential treatment for developing countries. Increasingly, international environmental agreements are including provisions specifically providing differential treatment, such as delayed compliance schedules, and technical and financial assistance for developing countries. This trend must continue and become part of the framework of international environmental law. However, on the whole, incentives should only be used for an initial period, allowing the developing countries to "catch up" with the developed countries, while simultaneously addressing environmental problems.

I have attempted to show, after an examination of the principles of equality and equity in international law, that there is room for differential treatment in what has most often been a pattern of using uniform rules or egalitarian reciprocity in treaty law. Yet this preferential or differential treatment does have strings attached, in the sense that it is only meant to promote *sustainable* development.

Analyzing the concept of sustainable development and its legal implications is a difficult task, as it has come to mean so many things to so many stakeholders. For instance, one developing country, Venezuela, considered a relaxation of its environmental regulations—allowing for increased mining in fragile lands—as a method to achieve sustainable development. Most developed countries would probably disagree with the use of this approach, because in the long term it would not lead to sustainable development. However, developing countries can argue that with most of their populations living below the poverty level, they do not have any other options. To move forward toward sustainable development, with different states having conflicting views on what that goal means, is not very helpful. Yet, I have shown that the more recent international environmental agreements are relying on sustainable development as defined by the Brundtland Commission and UNCED. As these treaties are eventually implemented, using incentives for developing countries, all states will be on the pathway that leads to sustainable development.

I have examined the conflict regarding the treatment of developing countries in the international regulatory process and have attempted to show that differential norms rather than uniform norms are more effective in promoting the participation of developing countries at an early stage in the multilateral environmental agreements. This enables all nations to strive for the same sustainable development goals as defined in the environmental treaties.

Using specific differential norms from recent treaties as examples, I have shown that the more recent use of funding mechanisms appears to make a substantial difference in promoting developing country participation in the treaties. In addition, using market mechanisms such as the clean development mechanism and emissions trading has great potential for promoting universal participation in international environmental agreements by providing incentives for the transfer of technology and financial resources to developing countries. These market mechanisms will also make conservation measures profitable for affected parties and create a profit motive for enterprises to invest, thereby motivating all stakeholders to get involved, in contrast to command and control methods that have been the most commonly used techniques in international environmental lawmaking. Yet the procedures and institutions that have to be established to make these market systems work effectively are still to be decided upon. These will determine, to a large extent, whether these market systems will be successful.

Since international institutions, in addition to NGOs, are usually the ones to urge the states to fulfill their treaty commitments, they are crucial in making the incentives for developing countries effective. UNEP, despite its many problems, still plays an important role as far as taking the initiative to address global environmental threats, and following up with programs and projects to implement the environmental treaties. I have also analyzed closely the work of the Commission for Sustainable Development as it has a major role to play in coordinating the implementation of Agenda 21, including the international environmental agreements, and concluded that it could be strengthened in its powers to make its coordinating role more effective.

The World Bank's role is becoming elusive—no longer striving for development at all costs—as I have shown. It has instituted a number of procedures to ensure that the environment is taken into account, but it is too early to say if these latest procedures, which look promising on paper, are actually effective in promoting the goal of sustainable development. In addition, I have shown how the newer and more innovative funding mechanisms are structured, such as GEF and debt-for-nature swaps, and how they can make a significant difference with respect to encouraging developing countries to protect the environment. However, GEF should be watched to make sure it operates within a democratic and transparent system of governance.

The role of NGOs in promoting universal participation is growing and, as I have shown, they are increasingly being used to assist developing countries in the implementation of environmental treaties. The introduction of other "major groups" in addition to NGOs, such as business and industry, I conclude, is a useful method to introduce divergence or balance to the process. Bringing, for instance, business and industry groups into the folds of the United Nations' sustainable development efforts has resulted in some useful partnerships. The business and industry groups can be very useful conduits for the transfer of environmentally sound technology to developing countries, enabling them to fulfill their commitments with regard to international environmental agreements. However, one has to keep in mind that these incentive mechanisms should be premised on developing countries having their own environmental frameworks to ensure that the transfers function in the intended manner.

In conclusion, differential treatment for developing countries is the most effective way to promote universal participation in the formation and implementation of international environmental agreements. These should include differential norms such as delayed compliance schedules (where appropriate) and technical and financial assistance, in addition to disincentives, such as non-compliance procedures. In order to make these incentives effective, international institutions should focus more on the goal of facilitating the participation of developing countries in international environmental agreements.

Abbreviations and Acronyms

ACC	Administrative Committee on Coordination
ASEAN	Association of Southeast Asian Nations
BCSD	Business Council for Sustainable Development
BFSP	British and Foreign State Papers
BYIL	British Yearbook of International Law
CDM	Clean Development Mechanism
CFC	Chlorofluorocarbon
CIDIE	Committee of International Development Institutions on the Environment
CITES	Convention on International Trade in Endangered Species
COP	Conference of the Parties
CSD	Commission on Sustainable Development
CTE	Committee on Trade and Environment
DOEM	Designated Officials for Environmental Matters
EA	Environmental Assessments
EBRD	European Bank for Reconstruction and Development
ECB	Environment Coordination Board
ECOSOC	UN Economic and Social Council
EPA	U.S. Environmental Protection Agency
EU	European Union
FCCC	Framework Convention on Climate Change
FOE	Friends of the Earth
GATT	General Agreement on Tariffs and Trade
GEF	Global Environment Facility
HIPC	Heavily Indebted Poor Countries
IACSD	Inter-Agency Committee on Sustainable Development
IAEA	International Atomic Energy Agency
IAEG	Inter-Agency Environment Coordinating Group
ICC	International Chamber of Commerce
ICJ	International Court of Justice
ICOLP	Industry Cooperative for Ozone Layer Protection
ICSU	International Council on Scientific Unions

IDA	International Development Association
IEA	International Energy Agency
ILC	International Law Commission
ILM	International Legal Materials
INBio	National Institute of Biodiversity
INFOTERRA	International Referral System for Sources of Environmental Information
IPCC	Intergovernmental Panel on Climate Change
IPF	Intergovernmental Panel on Forests
IRPTC	International Register of Potentially Toxic Chemicals
MARNR	Ministerio del Ambiente y de los Recursos Naturales Renovables
MARPOL	International Convention for the Prevention of Pollution by Ships
NAFTA	North American Free Trade Agreement
NGO	Non-governmental organization
NIEO	New International Economic Order
NRDC	National Resource Defense Council
ODA	Official Development Assistance
ODS	Ozone-depleting substances
PCIJ	Permanent Court of International Justice Reports
PIC	Public Information Center
SEA	Single European Act
SEDUE	Mexican Environment Ministry
SEED	Sustainable Energy and Environment Division
STAP	Scientific and Technical Advisory Panel
TCEE	Tradable carbon emission entitlement
UNCED	United Nations Conference on Environment and Development
UNCLOS	United Nations Convention on the Law of the Sea
UNCTAD	United Nations Conference on Trade and Development
UNDP	Untied Nations Development Programme
UNEP	United Nations Environment Programme
UNGASS	United Nations General Assembly Special Session
UNIDO	United Nations Industrial Development Organization
UNTS	United Nations Treaty Service
WBCSD	World Business Council for Sustainable Development
WCED	World Commission on Environment and Development (also known as the Brundtland Commission)
WTO	World Trade Organization
WWF	World Wildlife Fund/World Wide Fund for Nature

Selected Bibliography

Ashford, Nicholas & Christine Ayers. *Policy Issues for Consideration in Transferring Technology to Developing Countries*, 12 ECOLOGY L.Q. 875 (1985).

Barnes, James. *The Growing International Dimension to Environmental Issues*, 13 COLUM. J. ENVTL. L. 389 (1988).

BASIC FACTS ABOUT THE UNITED NATIONS [New York: Dept. of Public Information, United Nations] (1992).

Benedick, Richard Elliot. OZONE DIPLOMACY: NEW DIRECTIONS IN SAFEGUARDING THE PLANET [Cambridge, Mass.: Harvard University Press] (1991).

Berntsen, Thorbjorn. *Is There a Need for Changes in Consumption Patterns?*, *in* INTERNATIONAL ENVIRONMENTAL LAW 14 [Oslo: Juridisk Forlag] (Erling Selvig & Hans Christian Bugge eds., 1995).

Berthelot, Yves. *International Response to Environmental Challenges*, *in* INTERNATIONAL ENVIRONMENTAL LAW 66 [Oslo: Juridisk Forlag] (Erling Selvig & Hans Christian Bugge eds., 1995).

Birnie, Patricia W. & Alan E. Boyle. INTERNATIONAL LAW AND THE ENVIRONMENT [Oxford: Clarendon Press; New York: Oxford University Press] (1992).

Birnie, Patricia. *International Environmental Law: Its Adequacy for Present and Future Needs*, *in* THE INTERNATIONAL POLITICS OF THE ENVIRONMENT: ACTORS, INTERESTS, AND INSTITUTIONS 52 [Oxford: Claredon Press] (Andrew Hurrell & Benedict Kingsbury eds., 1992).

Bodansky, Daniel. *Symposium: Customary (and Not So Customary) International Environmental Law*, 3 IND. J. GLOBAL LEG. STUD. 106 (1995).

Bodansky, Daniel. *The United Nations Framework Convention on Climate Change: A Commentary*, *in* GREENING INTERNATIONAL LAW 219 [New York: The New Press] (Philippe Sands ed., 1994).

Bowett, D.W. THE LAW OF INTERNATIONAL INSTITUTIONS [London: Stevens] (4th ed. 1982).

Bramble, Barbara J. & Gareth Porter. *Non-Governmental Organizations and the Making of US International Environmental Policy*, *in* THE INTERNATIONAL POLITICS OF THE ENVIRONMENT 316 [Oxford: Claredon Press] (Andrew Hurrell & Benedict Kingsbury eds., 1992).

Brownlie, Ian. PRINCIPLES OF PUBLIC INTERNATIONAL LAW [Oxford, England: Clarendon Press; New York: Oxford University Press] (4th ed. 1990).

Bugge, Hans Christian. *International Environmental Law – Status and Challenges*, *in* INTERNATIONAL ENVIRONMENTAL LAW 53 (Erling Selvig & Hans Christian Bugge eds., 1995) [Oslo: Juridisk Forlag].

Burns, William. *Global Warming the United Nations Framework on Climate Change and the Future of Small Island States*, 6 DICK. J. ENVTL. L. POL'Y 147 (1997).

Cairncross, Frances. COSTING THE EARTH: THE CHALLENGE FOR GOVERNMENTS, THE OPPORTUNITIES FOR BUSINESS [Boston, Mass.: Harvard Business School Press] (1992).

Caldwell, Lynton Keith. INTERNATIONAL ENVIRONMENTAL POLICY: EMERGENCE AND DIMENSIONS [Durham: Duke University Press] (2d ed. 1990).

Carson, Rachel. SILENT SPRING [Boston: Houghton Mifflin] (1962).

Chandler, Melinda. *The Biodiversity Convention: Selected Issues of Interest to the International Lawyer*, 4 COLO. J. INT'L L. & POL'Y 173 (1993).

Charnovitz, Steve. *Two Centuries of Participation: NGOs and International Governance*, 18 MICH. J. INT'L L. 257 (1997).

Cheng Zheng-Kang. *Equity, Special Considerations, and the Third World*, 1 COLO. J. INT'L ENVTL. L. & POL'Y 66 (1990).

Cutajar, Michael Zammit. *Comment on Paper by Gunther Handl: The FCCC Experience*, *in* SUSTAINABLE DEVELOPMENT AND INTERNATIONAL LAW 47 [London, Boston: Graham and Trotman/Martinus Nijhoff] (Winfried Lang ed., 1995).

Dasgupta, Partha. *Environmental and Resource Economics in the World of the Poor*, Internet Edition, *available in* <http://www.rff.org> (visited Oct. 1997).

Deal, Carl. THE GREENPEACE GUIDE TO ANTI-ENVIRONMENTAL ORGANZATIONS [Berkeley, Calif.; Emeryville, Calif.: Odonian Press; Distribution is through Publishers Group West] (1993).

DiLeva, Charles E. *The World Bank and the Environment*, *in* INTERNATIONAL ENVIRONMENTAL LAW 289 (ALI/ABA ed., 1995).

Dowdeswell, Elizabeth. *Development of International Law*, *in* INTERNATIONAL ENVIRONMENTAL LAW 17 [Oslo: Juridisk Forlag] (Erling Selvig & Hans Christian Bugge eds., 1995)

Editors of the Harvard Law Review. TRENDS IN INTERNATIONAL ENVIRONMENTAL LAW [Chicago, Ill.: American Bar Association, Section of International Law and Practice] (1992).

Esty, Daniel. *Gatting the Greens*, 72 FOREIGN AFF. 34 (1993).

Flavin, Christopher. *The Legacy of Rio*, *in* STATE OF THE WORLD 1997 3 [New York: W.W. Norton & Company] (Lester Brown et al. eds., 1997).

Fleischer, Carl August. FOLKERETT (International Law) [Oslo: Universitetsforlaget, 5. utg.] (1984).

Frank, Thomas M. *The New Development: Can American Law and Legal Institutions Help Developing Countries?*, 3 WIS. L. REV. 799 (1972).

Freestone, David. *The Road from Rio: International Environmental Law after the Earth Summit*, 6 J. ENVTL. L. 200 (1994).

French, Hilary. *Forging a New Global Partnership*, *in* STATE OF THE WORLD 172 [New York: W.W. Norton & Company] (Lester R. Brown et al. eds., 1995).

French, Hilary. *Reforming the United Nations to Ensure Environmentally Sustainable Development*, *in* PREFERRED FUTURES FOR THE UNITED NATIONS 256 (Saul H. Mendlovitz & Burns H. Weston eds., 1995).

French, Hilary. *Learning from the Ozone Experience*, *in* STATE OF THE WORLD 1997 151 [New York: W.W. Norton & Company] (Lester Brown et al., 1997).

Gardner, Richard N. NEGOTIATING SURVIVAL: FOUR PRIORITIES AFTER RIO [New York; Council on Foreign Relations Press] (1992).

Gollin,Michael. *Using Intellectual Property to Improve Environmental Protection*, 4 HARV. J.L. & TECH. 215 (1992).

Goodland, R.J.A. The World Bank's Environmental Assessment Policy, 14 HASTINGS INT'L & COMP. L. REV. 811 (1991).

Gore, Albert. EARTH IN THE BALANCE: ECOLOGY AND THE HUMAN SPIRIT [Boston: Houghton Mifflin] (1992).

Grad, Frank P. TREATISE ON ENVIRONMENTAL LAW [New York, N.Y.: M. Bender] (1973).

Graham, Oddmund. *International Objectives with Regard to Climate Change, in* INTERNATIONAL ENVIRONMENTAL LAW 31 [Oslo: Juridisk Forlag] (Erling Selvig & Hans Christian Bugge eds., 1995).

Gray, Mark Allan. *The United Nations Environment Programme: An Assessment*, 20 ENVTL. L. 291 (1990).

Guruswamy, Lakshman D. et al. INTERNATIONAL ENVIRONMENTAL LAW AND WORLD ORDER [St. Paul, Minn.: West Pub. Co.] (1994).

Handl, Gunther. *Controlling Implementation of and Compliance with International Environmental Commitments: The Rocky Road from Rio*, 5 COLO. J. INT'L ENVTL. L. & POL'Y 305 (1994).

Handl, Gunther. *Environmental Security and Global Change: The Challenge to International Law*, 1 YB. INT'L. ENVTL. L. 29 (1990).

Henkin, Louis et al. INTERNATIONAL LAW: CASES AND MATERIALS [St. Paul, Minn.: West Pub. Co.] (2d ed. 1987).

Henkin, Louis. HOW NATIONS BEHAVE [New York, Published for the Council on Foreign Relations by Columbia University Press] (2d 1979).

Hodas, David. *The "Rio" Environmental Treaties Colloquium: The Climate Change Convention and Evolving Legal Models of Sustainable Development*, 13 PACE ENVTL. L. REV. 96 (1995).

Hohmann, Harald. PRECAUTIONARY LEGAL DUTIES AND PRINCIPLES OF MODERN INTERNATIONAL ENVIRONMENTAL LAW [London, Boston: Graham & Trotman/Martinus Nijhoff; Norwell, MA: Kluwer Academic Publishers Group] (1994).

Horberry, John. *The Accountability of Development Assistance Agencies: The Case of Environmental Policy*, 12 ECOLOGY L.Q. 823 (1985).

Hourcle, Laurent. *Book Review, Mortgaging the Earth: The World Bank, Environmental Impoverishment, and the Crisis of Development, Bruce Rich*, 28 GEO. WASH. J. INT'L L. & ECON. 751 (1995).

Hurlbut, D. *Beyond the Montreal Protocol: Impact on Nonparty States and Lessons for Future Environmental Regimes*, 4 COLO. J. INT'L ENVTL. L. & POL'Y 353 (1993).

INTERNATIONAL LAW AND POLLUTION [Philadelphia: University of Philadelphia Press] (Daniel Barstow Magraw ed., 1991).

Jones, Andrew S. *Note: The Global Environment Facility's Failure to Promote Sustainable Forestry in Ecuador: The Case of Ecoforest 2000*, 14 VA. ENVTL. L.J. 522 (1995).

Jurgielewicz, Lynne M. GLOBAL ENVIRONMENTAL CHANGE AND INTERNATIONAL LAW: PROSPECTS FOR PROGRESS IN THE LEGAL ORDER [Lanham, MD: University Press of America] (1996).

Kaku, Michio. VISIONS: HOW SCIENCE WILL REVOLUTIONIZE THE 21ST CENTURY [New York: Anchor Books] (1997).

Kennedy, Charles. *Relations Between Transnational Corporations and Governments of Host Countries: A Look to the Future,* 1 TRANSNAT'L CORP. 67 (1992).

Kiss, Alexandre & Dinah Shelton. INTERNATIONAL ENVIRONMENTAL LAW [Ardsley-on-Hudson, N.Y.: Transnational Publishers; London, Eng.: Graham & Trotman] (1991).

Lane, Earl. *Cool toward warming,* DENVER POST, Oct. 7, 1997, at 5A.

Lang, J.T. *Commentary: Some Implications of the Montreal Protocol to the Ozone Convention, in* ENVIRONMENTAL PROTECTION AND INTERNATIONAL LAW 179 [London, Boston: Graham and Trotman/Martinus Nijhoff] (Winfried. Lang et al. eds., 1991).

Leonard, H. Jeffrey & David Morell, *Emergence of Environmental Concern in Developing Countries: A Political Perspective,* 17 STAN. J. INT'L L. 281 (1981).

Ling, Bing. *Developing Countries and Ozone Layer Protection,* 6 TUL. ENVTL. L.J. 91 (1992).

Magraw, Daniel. *Legal Treatment of Developing Countries: Differential, Contextual, and Absolute Norms,* 1 COLO. J. INT'L ENVTL. L. & POL'Y 70 (1990).

Mann, Howard. *Comment on the Paper by Philippe Sands, in* SUSTAINABLE DEVELOPMENT AND INTERNATIONAL LAW 72 [London, Boston: Graham and Trotman/Martinus Nijhoff] (Winfried Lang ed., 1995).

Meadows, Donella et al. LIMITS TO GROWTH: A REPORT FOR THE CLUB OF ROME'S PROJECT ON THE PREDICAMENT OF MANKIND [New York, Universe Books] (1972).

Moltke, Konrad von. *Debt-for-Nature: The Second Generation,* 14 HASTINGS INT'L & COMP. L. REV. 975 (1991).

Nanda, Ved. INTERNATIONAL ENVIRONMENTAL LAW AND POLICY [Irvington-on-Hudson, N.Y.: Transnational Publishers] (1995).

Ntambirweki, John. *The Developing Countries in the Evolution of an International Environmental Law,* 14 HASTINGS INT'L & COMP. L. REV. 924 (1991).

O'Neill, Catherine A. & Cass R. Sunstein. *Economics and the Environment: Trading Debt and Technology for Nature,* 17 COLUM. J. ENVTL. L. 109 (1992).

ON GROWTH (Willem L. Oltmans ed., 1974).

OUR COMMON FUTURE/WORLD COMMISSION ON ENVIRONMENT AND DEVELOPMENT [Oxford; New York: Oxford University Press] (1987).

Pallemaerts, Marc. *The Future of Environmental Regulation: International Environmental Law in the Age of Sustainable Development: A Critical Assessment of the UNCED Process,* 15 J.L.& COM. 652 (1996).

Pallemaerts, Marc. *International Environmental Law from Stockholm to Rio: Back to the Future?, in* GREENING INTERNATIONAL LAW 16 [New York: The New Press] (Phillipe Sands ed., 1994).

Palmer, Geoffrey. *New Ways to Make International Environmental Law,* 86 AM. J. INT'L L. 263 (1992).

Piddington, Kenneth. *The Role of the World Bank, in* THE INTERNATIONAL POLITICS OF THE ENVIRONMENT 225 [Oxford: Claredon Press] (Andrew Hurrell & Benedict Kingsbury eds., 1992).

Pietila, Hilkka & Jeanne Vickers. MAKING WOMEN MATTER [London; Atlantic Highlands, N.J.: Zed Books] (1994).

Porras, Ileana, *the Rio Declaration: A New Basis for International Cooperation, in* GREENING INTERNATIONAL LAW 27 [New York: The New Press] (Philippe Sands ed., 1994).

Pulvenis, Jean-Francois. *The Framework Convention on Climate Change, in* THE ENVIRONMENT AFTER RIO: INTERNATIONAL LAW AND ECONOMICS 92 [London, Boston: Graham and Trotman/Martinus Nijhoff] (Lugi Campiglio et al. eds., 1994).

Rawls, John. A THEORY OF JUSTICE [Cambridge, Mass.: Belknap Press of Harvard University Press] (1971).

Reza, Sadrel. *Non-equity forms of TNC participation in Bangladesh* 1 TRANSNAT'L CORP. 127 (1992).

Rich, Bruce. MORTGAGING THE EARTH, THE WORLD BANK, ENVIRONMENTAL IMPOVERISHMENT, AND THE CRISIS OF DEVELOPMENT [Boston: Beacon Press] (1994).

Roodman, David Malin. *Paying the Piper: Subsidies, Politics, and the Environment, in* WORLD WATCH PAPER 133 (1996).

Ross, Alf. A TEXTBOOK OF INTERNATIONAL LAW: GENERAL PART [London; New York: Longmans, Green] (1947).

Sachariev, Kamen. *Promoting Compliance with International Environmental Legal Standards: Reflections on Monitoring and Reporting Mechanisms,* 3 Y.B. INT'L ENVTL. L. 32 (1992).

Sand, Peter H.. *Trusts for the Earth: New International Financial Mechanisms for Sustainable Development, in* SUSTAINABLE DEVELOPMENT AND INTERNATIONAL LAW 183 [London, Boston: Graham and Trotman/Martinus Nijhoff] (Winfried Lang ed., 1995).

Sand, Peter H. LESSONS LEARNED IN GLOBAL ENVIRONMENTAL GOVERNANCE [Washington, D.C.: World Resources Institute] (1990).

Sands, Philippe. *International Law in the Field of Sustainable Development: Emerging Legal Principles, in* SUSTAINABLE DEVELOPMENT AND INTERNATIONAL LAW 63 [London, Boston: Graham and Trotman/Martinus Nijhoff] (Winfried Lang ed., 1995).

Sands, Philippe. *International Law in the Field of Sustainable Development,* BRIT. Y.B. INT'L L. 324 [London: H. Frowde; Oxford University Press] (1994).

Sands, Phillipe. *Introduction, in* GREENING INTERNATIONAL LAW xv [New York: The New Press] (Phillipe Sands ed., 1994).

Sands, Philippe. *The Environment, Community and International Law,* 30 HARV. INT'L L.J. 393 (1989).

Sands, Philippe. *Greening Bretton Woods, in* GREENING INTERNATIONAL LAW 73 [New York: The New Press] (Phillipe Sands ed., 1994).

Schachter, Oscar. INTERNATIONAL LAW IN THEORY AND PRACTICE [Dordrecht, The Netherlands; Boston: M. Nijhoff Publishers; Norwell, MA.: Sold and distributed in the U.S.A. and Canada by Kluwer Academic Publishers] (1991).

Schachter, Oscar. *The Emergence of International Environmental Law,* 44 J. INT'L AFF. 457 (1991).

Scherr, S. Jacob & Jared E. Blumenfeld. *Implementing UNCED, in* GREENING INTERNATIONAL LAW 236 [New York: The New Press] (Philippe Sands ed., 1994).
Schmidheiny, Stephen. CHANGING COURSE: A GLOBAL BUSINESS PERSPECTIVE ON DEVELOPMENT AND THE ENVIRONMENT [Cambridge, Mass.: MIT Press] (1992).
Schneider, Jan. WORLD PUBLIC ORDER OF THE ENVIRONMENT: TOWARDS AN INTERNATIONAL ECOLOGICAL LAW AND ORGANIZATION [Toronto, Buffalo: University of Toronto Press] (1979).
Schoenbaum, Thomas J. *Free International Trade and Protection of the Environment: Irreconcilable Conflict?*, 86 AM. J. INT'L L. 713 (1992).
Shihata, Ibrahim F.I. *The Role of the World Bank: Legal Instruments for Achieving Environmental Objectives, in* INTERNATIONAL ENVIRONMENTAL LAW [Oslo: Juridisk Forlag] (Erling Selvig, Hans Christian Bugge eds., 1995).
Stewart, Richard B. *Environmental Regulation and International Competitiveness*, 102 YALE L.J. 2052 (1993).
Susskind, Lawrence & Connie Ozawa, *Negotiating More Effective International Environmental Agreements, in* THE INTERNATIONAL POLITICS OF THE ENVIRONMENT 156 [Oxford: Claredon Press] (Andrew Hurrell & Benedict Kingsbury eds., 1992).
Szasz, Paul C. *International Norm-making, in* ENVIRONMENTAL CHANGE AND INTERNATIONAL LAW: NEW CHALLENGES AND DIMENSIONS 41 [Tokyo: United Nations University Press] (Edith Brown Weiss ed., 1992).
Szasz, Paul C. *Restructuring the International Organizational Framework, in* ENVIRONMENTAL CHANGE AND INTERNATIONAL LAW: NEW CHALLENGES AND DIMENSIONS 340 [Tokyo: United Nations University Press] (Edith Brown Weiss ed., 1992).
Szell, Patrick. *Ozone Layer and Climate Change, in* ENVIRONMENTAL PROTECTION AND INTERNATIONAL LAW 167 [London, Boston: Graham and Trotman/Martinus Nijhoff] (W. Lang et al. eds., 1991).
Tarlock, A. Dan. *Environmental Law: The Role of Non-Governmental Organizations in the Development of International Environmental Law*, 61 CHI-KENT. L. REV. (1992).
THE EARTH SUMMIT: THE UNITED NATIONS CONFERENCE ON ENVIRONMENT AND DEVELOPMENT (UNCED) [London, Boston: Graham and Trotman/Martinus Nijhoff] (Stanley Johnson ed., 1993).
THE EFFECTIVENESS OF INTERNATIONAL ENVIRONMENTAL AGREEMENTS: A SURVEY OF EXISTING LEGAL INSTRUMENTS [Cambridge, Eng.: Grotius] (Peter H. Sand ed., 1992).
Tinker, Catherine. *Environmental Planet Management by the United Nations: An Idea Whose Time Has Not Yet Come?*, 22 N.Y.U. J. INT'L L. & POL. 796 (1991).
Tolbert, David. *Global Climate Change and the Role of International Non-Governmental Organizations, in* INTERNATIONAL LAW AND GLOBAL CLIMATE CHANGE 96 [London, Boston: Graham and Trotman/Martinus Nijhoff] (Robin Churchill & David Freestone eds., 1991).
Vorlat, Katrien. *The International Ozone Regime: Concessions and Loopholes?*, 17 FLETCHER F. 151 (1993).

Weiss, Edith Brown. *Environmental Equity: The Imperative for the Twenty-First Century, in* SUSTAINABLE DEVELOPMENT AND INTERNATIONAL LAW 18 [London, Boston: Graham and Trotman/Martinus Nijhoff] (Winfried Lang ed., 1995).

Weiss, E. Brown. IN FAIRNESS TO FUTURE GENERATIONS: INTERNATIONAL LAW, COMMON PATRIMONY, AND INTERGENERATIONAL EQUITY [Tokyo, Japan: United Nations University; Dobbs Ferry, N.Y.: Transnational Publishers] (1989).

Weiss, Edith Brown. *International Environmental Law: Contemporary Issues and the Emergence of a New World Order,* 81 GEO. L.J. 706 (1993).

Werksman, Jacob D. *Greening Bretton Woods, in* GREENING INTERNATIONAL LAW 76 [New York: The New Press] (Philippe Sands ed., 1994).

Williams Silveira, Mary Pat. *Essay: International Legal Instruments and Sustainable Development: Principles, Requirements, and Restructuring,* 31 WILLAMETTE L. REV. 239 (1995).

Williams Silveira, Mary Pat with Barbara Ruis, *International Law for Sustainable Development: An Attempt at Definition,* 2 NAFTA, LAW AND BUSINESS REVIEW OF THE AMERICAS 13 (1996).

Willums, Jan Olaf & Ulrich Goluke. FROM IDEAS TO ACTION—BUSINESS AND SUSTAINABLE DEVELOPMENT—THE ICC REPORT ON THE GREENING OF ENTERPRISE [Oslo: Ad Notam Gyldendal] (1992).

Wilson, William. *Environmental Law as Development Assistance,* 22 ENVTL. L. 954 (1992).

Index

For Product Safety Concerns and Information please contact our EU representative GPSR@taylorandfrancis.com Taylor & Francis Verlag GmbH, Kaufingerstraße 24, 80331 München, Germany

Printed and bound by CPI Group (UK) Ltd, Croydon, CR0 4YY
14/09/2026
02216256-0006